Cunegonde's Kidnapping

THE LEWIS WALPOLE SERIES IN
EIGHTEENTH-CENTURY CULTURE AND HISTORY

The Lewis Walpole Series, published by Yale University Press with the aid of the Annie Burr Lewis Fund, is dedicated to the culture and history of the long eighteenth century (from the Glorious Revolution to the accession of Queen Victoria). It welcomes work in a variety of fields, including literature and history, the visual arts, political philosophy, music, legal history, and the history of science. In addition to original scholarly work, the series publishes new editions and translations of writing from the period, as well as reprints of major books that are currently unavailable. Though the majority of books in the series will probably concentrate on Great Britain and the Continent, the range of our geographical interests is as wide as Horace Walpole's.

CUNEGONDE'S KIDNAPPING

A Story of Religious
Conflict in the Age of Enlightenment

Benjamin J. Kaplan

Yale UNIVERSITY PRESS
New Haven & London

Published with assistance from the Annie Burr Lewis Fund
and the Louis Stern Memorial Fund.

Yale University Press books may be purchased in quantity for educational, business,
or promotional use. For information, please e-mail sales.press@yale.edu (US office) or
sales@yaleup.co.uk (UK office).

Set in Janson Roman type by IDS Infotech Ltd.,
Chandigarh, India.
Printed in the United States of America.

Library of Congress Control Number: 2014942535
ISBN 978-0-300-18736-6

A catalogue record for this book is available from the British Library.

This paper meets the requirements of ANSI/NISO Z39.48–1992 (Permanence of
Paper).

10 9 8 7 6 5 4 3 2 1

For Katy, with all my heart

CONTENTS

Contents

ILLUSTRATIONS

ACKNOWLEDGMENTS

Never have I enjoyed my work as a historian so much as when researching and writing this book. The pleasure it has given me to immerse myself in such a dramatic and vivid story makes me especially grateful to everyone who has lent me assistance. I want to thank first the Leverhulme Trust and the John Simon Guggenheim Memorial Foundation for research fellowships that supported the project. My thanks go similarly to University College London for research leave and other support. The staffs of the archives where I conducted my research were extremely helpful and accommodating, in particular Dr. Stefan Flesch and Mr. Ulrich Dühr of the Landeskirchliches Archiv Düsseldorf, Frau Margarethe Dietzel of the Stadtarchiv Aachen, and Mevrouw drs. L. Wiggers of the Regionaal Historisch Centrum Limburg. Mr. Thomas Richter, who is conducting doctoral research on the Aachen Protestant congregations, generously shared with me his knowledge and collected sources. Monsieur Jean Marie Fastré of the Abbaye du Val-Dieu, Belgium, went to extraordinary lengths to help me obtain an image for an illustration. I was kindly shown the interior of the Vaals Reformed church and the baptismal basin made in 1762 by Em. ds. C. J. Hollemans. My doctoral student Jaap Geraerts conducted research for me in the Regionaal Archief Tilburg. I learned a great deal from the feedback of audiences who heard me present papers that drew on the research for this book. For such feedback I wish to thank colleagues and students at UCL, Columbia, Yale, Cambridge, and Amsterdam Universities; at the Low Countries Seminar of the Institute for Historical Research; the Sixteenth Century Studies Conference; the Reading Early Modern Studies Conference; and a symposium on mixed marriage held at the Deutsches Historisches Institut in Rome. I have appreciated the skill and professionalism of my editor at Yale University Press, Jennifer Banks; her assistant, Heather Gold; cartographer Bill Nelson; and my agent, Valerie Borchardt. I wish to acknowledge also the useful comments and suggestions made by the anonymous scholars who read my manuscript for the Press. Finally, my wife, Katy, performed the invaluable service of reading a draft of the entire manuscript and helping me improve its narrative qualities.

A portion of the Introduction was previously published as part of an article, "Religious Encounters in the Borderlands of Early Modern Europe: The Case of Vaals," in *Dutch Crossing* 37 (2013): 4–19 (online at www.maneypublishing.com/journals/dtc). Similarly, a portion of chapter 1 was previously published as part of an essay, " 'For They Will Turn Away Thy Sons': The Practice and Perils of Mixed Marriage in the Dutch Golden Age," in *Piety and Family in Early Modern Europe: Essays in Honour of Steven Ozment*, edited by Benjamin J. Kaplan and Marc R. Forster (Aldershot, UK: Ashgate, 2005), 115–33, copyright © 2005. My thanks go to Maney Publishing and Ashgate Publishing for permission to reprint these items.

CAST OF MAIN CHARACTERS

Family

Sara Maria Erffens	Wife of Hendrick Mommers
Hendrick Mommers	Husband of Sara, journeyman cloth shearer
Cunegonde (Cunigunda) Mommers	Sister of Hendrick
Mathias Erffens	Father of Sara, master cloth shearer

Clergy

Johannes Wilhelmus Bosten (Father Bosten)	Pastor (parish priest) of the Catholic parish of Vaals
Frans Hendrick Bosten	Curate (assistant priest) of the Catholic parish of Vaals
Quirinus Finck	Curate of the (Catholic) parish of St. Adalbert, Aachen

Petrus Rademacker	Father Bosten's predecessor
Johannes Pferdmenges	Calvinist minister for Burtscheid

Villagers

Anna Olivier	Midwife
Martinus Buntgens	Sexton of the Catholic parish of Vaals
Andries Buntgens	Father of Martinus, courier
Conrad Wolff	Blacksmith

Rioters

Sebastian Gimmenich	Farmhand at Melaten, later farmer of the Grosse Neuenhof
Johannes Grommet	Farmhand
Hendrick Lotmans	Servant of Conrad Wolff
Pieter Koetgens	Farmhand (innocent)

Officials

Abraham van den Heuvel	Lieutenant governor (lieutenant drossaard) of the Land of 's-Hertogenrade; dies August 1762
Willem Frederik de Jacobi de Cadier	Successor of Van den Heuvel as lieutenant governor
Count Charles Bentinck, Lord of Nijenhuis	Governor (hoog drossaard) of the Land of 's-Hertogenrade
Johan Frans à Brassard	Burgomaster of Vaals
Isaac Daniel Fellinger	Secretary of the Vaals district court; dies June 1764
Peter Strauch	Burgomaster of Aachen

Lawyers

Stephan Arnold Schmalhausen	Solicitor for Father Bosten; deacon of the Vaals Reformed congregation
H. J. Wilkin	Barrister for Father Bosten
Johann Wilhelm Hasenclever	Solicitor for the lieutenant governor; succeeds Fellinger as court secretary
J. J. Levericksvelt	Barrister for the lieutenant governor

Other

Johann Arnold von Clermont	Textile manufacturer

1. Vaals and its environs. Detail from an eighteenth-century map of the Lands of Overmaas.

Kerkrade
OOSTENRYKS
'S HERTOGEN
RADE
Vroenrade
Kloosterrade
HERTOGEN
RADTE
Heiden
Scheid
't Slot
Horbach
Richterich
Mons
Salvator
St
Wurselen
AKEN
Haren
Borchet
abt
Catkhoven
Frankeburg
Bornscheit
Cense de Bruai
Schondorp
Im Vorst
Hepschett
Einelens
Brandenburg
Walem
Hebschit

Cunegonde's Kidnapping

Introduction

Every historian dreams of discovering buried treasure—of finding, in the archives and libraries where we sift through mountains of paper, unknown documents that bring the past to life and change our understanding of it. For us, these are like nuggets of gleaming gold, entrancing our eyes with visions of bygone worlds. Usually we have to make do with source materials that others have mined before us, extracting new value from them by posing new questions and applying new methods. But one evening in the summer of 2008, I had the good fortune to strike it rich. Of all places, it was in the Dutch National Archive in The Hague, whose collections have probably been pored over and sifted more carefully by generations of scholars than those of any other archive in the Netherlands. Nowadays, of course, its inventories are searchable electronically. It was thanks to this technological advance that I was able to search hundreds of its collections, even rather unlikely ones, for cases of child kidnappings.

At the time, I was conducting research into the history of interfaith—or, to use a more common term, religiously "mixed"—

1

marriages. This is not a much studied topic, even among scholars interested in the history of religious toleration and conflict. Until fairly recently, historians showed great interest in the ideal of tolerance articulated by famous writers such as Locke and Voltaire. They also investigated the laws and policies by which rulers granted certain freedoms to religious dissenters. They did not, though, study how ordinary people of different faiths interacted and related to one another in daily life. That was partly due to an exclusive focus, now long outdated, on great men and great events. It was also because they did not conceive of toleration primarily in behavioral terms. Only in recent years have historians turned their attention to what I would call the practice of toleration: the arrangements and accommodations that enable people of different faiths to live with one another peacefully. How exactly these work, how they break down, and why religious toleration prevails at some times and places but not others are questions of great relevance to our world today.

Of all the forms toleration can take, mixed marriage has always seemed to me the most intimate and possibly also the most demanding. In premodern Europe, to marry someone of another faith was to bind yourself to that person in a sacred and presumably permanent union. It was to allow fundamental differences of belief, practice, and values to penetrate one's home and private life. How could husbands and wives leave each other to practice their faith peacefully if they believed that it meant consigning their beloved spouse to burn in hell? If they believed that other faiths were evil, how could they get into bed with the enemy in the first place? Churches prescribed rules on matters ranging from diet and sex to rhythms of work and rest—think, for example, of the abstinence required of Catholics during Lent: Whose rules would prevail within a mixed household? In a patriarchal world, did men impose their religious views on their wives? And most fraught of all, how would mixed couples raise their children? These were, on one level, highly personal questions, yet a host of outside parties felt intense concern about them: extended family members, clergy, government officials, even ordinary members of a couple's community. All these groups claimed, under certain circumstances, a right to intervene to ensure that a couple's children were raised in the "true" faith.

In premodern Europe, the marriage of a Christian to a Jew or Muslim was illegal and invalid unless one party converted. "Mixed marriage" therefore meant the marriage of Christians who belonged to different churches. This wasn't a possibility in most parts of Europe until the sixteenth century, when the Protestant Reformation had the unintended, cataclysmic effect of splitting western Christendom into rival churches: Catholic, Lutheran, Reformed (Calvinist), Anabaptist, and so on.[1] By the end of the century, these rivals had defined themselves in opposition to one another and were teaching their followers that, to be pious Christians and loyal adherents of the one "true" church, they had to hate its enemies, who were also God's enemies. It is no wonder that a series of bloody religious wars ravaged the Continent. Yet the picture was far from uniformly dark. From the British Isles to the plains of Lithuania, tens of thousands of communities, large and small, always remained religiously mixed, and in them, people of different faiths usually found some modus vivendi that, for longer or shorter periods, kept the peace. In the case of most of these communities, relations among the different Christian groups have never been studied in detail. Nevertheless, it seems probable that in most of them, at least a few men and women of different faiths were joined in wedlock.

Above all, the United Provinces of the Netherlands, or Dutch Republic for short, gained a reputation in the seventeenth century as home to many mixed couples. Officially this haven of toleration was a Calvinist polity, and all government officials in it were required to support the Dutch Reformed Church. Behind a thin facade of religious unity, though, the Republic was in fact the most religiously diverse, pluralistic land in Europe. Foreigners who visited Amsterdam and other cities marveled at how peacefully, by and large, the followers of many different faiths managed to live alongside one another, worshiping God in their own way. According to many observers, mixed marriages played a big role in fostering this toleration. In 1602, for example, a pamphleteer remarked that "Heromnes," the Dutch everyman, "would not stand for the burning of heretics. For what if one man saw his niece, another his uncle, a third his son, [and] yes, some their wives, flesh of their flesh, who are dearer to them than their own souls, suffer unto death? . . . What do you think, sirs, would it succeed? What joy would there be, do you think?"[2] The answers to these rhetorical questions were of course no, none: bonds of kinship and affection uniting people of different faiths made the very prospect of persecution painful. Generalizing, some historians and social scientists have suggested that, whether the groups in question are religious, racial, or otherwise defined, intermarriage increases mutual acceptance and promotes good relations. Many regard rates of intermarriage as a measure of the toleration prevailing among groups.

Yet in the course of my research, I was finding—not surprisingly—that not all mixed marriages in the Dutch Republic were harmonious. Not all of them were even peaceful: occasionally, for example, one spouse (usually the man) resorted to violence or intimidation to coerce his partner to convert. What intrigued me most, though, were the cases I encountered of child kidnappings. Although these cases varied, the most common perpetrators of the kidnappings were members of the child's own family. In one typical scenario, one of the child's parents had died, a common occurrence in that era. Then some relative of the deceased might spring into action to prevent the surviving spouse from imposing his or her religion on the child. With time, I concluded that most child kidnappings in that era resulted from struggles to determine the religious upbringing of children, most often the children of mixed couples. And so I began to look systematically in the inventories of archives for cases of such kidnappings. That is how I came upon an extraordinary dossier.

It was in the collection of the secretariat of the Dutch *stadholders*— not a place where one would think to look for documentary sources on mixed marriage, for the stadholders were political and military, not religious, leaders. Moreover, the dossier had been misfiled: some archivist had labeled it as coming from 's-Hertogenbosch, a city in Brabant, instead of 's-Hertogenrade, a small territory in the far southeast of the Republic, in the modern-day province of Limburg. And it was massive: comprising some 163 documents, the dossier ran to over 1,500 manuscript pages.[3] Dating from the 1760s, it recorded not just any kidnapping but an attempted baby-snatching. Someone had burst into a Reformed church in the middle of a baptism, grabbed the baby as it was being held by its godmother over the baptismal basin (Calvinists used small, portable basins rather than fonts), and tried to run off with it. That person had been a young Catholic woman named Cunegonde, who had wanted to bring the child to be baptized instead by a Catholic priest. Who was this woman? What fervor, misunderstanding, or madness had moved her to attempt such a rash act? Cunegonde had not made it to the doors of the church with the baby but had immediately been arrested. The story, though, hardly ended there. Two nights later, Cunegonde had herself been "kidnapped"—at least, that was the word used by Dutch authorities when a throng of armed Catholics freed her from arrest and whisked her away, rescuing her from impending punishment. In the face of this double outrage, local officials had launched a series of prosecutions. The massive dossier I found consisted of trial documents. The juiciest of them were records of interrogations: in these, participants in the events, many of them illiterate, reconstructed the different scenes of the drama, recounting their words and actions in minute detail. To my initial puzzlement, though, the documents derived, not from the trial of Cunegonde or her liberators, but from that of the local Catholic pastor, a man named Johannes Wilhelmus Bosten. Like a shadowy éminence grise, it seemed, he had been fingered by Dutch authorities as the mastermind behind events.

Thrilled by my find, I began telling Dutch friends that I was investigating an episode of religious conflict down in Limburg, in a little village named Vaals. To my surprise, they all seemed to know the place, and even to have visited it, typically on a school outing or family holiday. Vaals, it turned out, is famous among the Dutch on account of the so-called Drielandenpunt, or "Three Countries Point," that rises on its edge (figs. 2, 3). At an elevation of 322.5 meters (less than a thousand feet), the Drielandenpunt has the dubious distinction of being the highest point in the Netherlands, a famously flat, water-logged country. It is also the point where the borders of the Netherlands, Belgium, and Germany meet—hence its name. From 1839 to 1919, it was even, uniquely, a four countries point, since there existed then a tiny sliver of an artificial country named Moresnet whose border met there as well. Poised atop a hill called the Vaalserberg, in a rolling landscape where pastures and tilled fields, villages and little woods pleasantly alternate (though there is industry and a major city also nearby), since the 1920s the Drielandenpunt has been promoted commercially as a place worth visiting. Blighted with all the trappings of mass tourism, it has been equipped with an informative monument, lookout tower, maze, gift shop, café, snack bar, and of course a large parking lot. Today, the Drielandenpunt attracts more than a million visitors per year. I soon joined them.

Modern-day Vaals owes much of its identity to its location at the intersection of three states. Since 1976 it has formed a center point

2. Modern map of the Netherlands, showing Vaals located at the far southeastern tip of the country.

3. The Three Countries Point today. A pillar marks where the Dutch, German, and Belgian borders intersect. The circle surrounding the pillar uses bricks of different colors to indicate the territories of the three countries. A thin slice of the circle to the right indicates the former location of Morsnet.

of the Maas-Rhine Euroregion, an association established to promote cooperation among the adjacent parts of Germany, Belgium, and the Netherlands in areas such as education and economic development. The further European integration has proceeded, the more the entire town has become a site of tourism and commemoration. In 1994, a former customs guardhouse on the Dutch-German border was converted into a tiny, one-room museum called the Klèng Wach (which in the local dialect means "small guardhouse") (fig. 4). In it, memories of national divisions are cast as the historical recollection of a thankfully bygone era. A statue of *Rencontre* (encounter) on the town's main thoroughfare is one of several recent monuments

4. The Klèng Wach. A former customs guardhouse on the Dutch-German border, now a tiny museum devoted to the history of the border. The building directly behind it is on the former site of the Catholic rectory where Father Johannes Wilhelmus Bosten lived. The row of pillars to the right extends across what used to be the main road between Vaals and Aachen; a movable barrier formerly stood in their place.

erected to symbolize the union or friendly meeting of nations in today's Europe.[4]

In the early modern era, Vaals was likewise a place of intersection and encounter. What is now the Dutch-German border divided Vaals from the territory of Aachen, an Imperial Free City in the Holy Roman Empire. Something resembling the Dutch-Belgian border divided Vaals from the Duchy of Limburg, which formed part of the Southern Netherlands, ruled by the Spanish, later

Austrian, Habsburgs. Vaals itself belonged to 's-Hertogenrade, one of the three Lands of Overmaas (so called because, viewed from Brussels, they lay on the far, eastern side of the river Maas). These lands were partitioned in the seventeenth century between the Dutch and the Habsburgs. In fact, together with the adjacent villages of Vijlen and Holset, Vaals formed a little enclave of territory belonging to the Dutch Republic, separated from the other Dutch-held Lands of Overmaas by the German County of Wittem. Such anomalies—patches of land belonging to a state but separated from the rest of its territories—scarcely exist anymore. The most important difference from today, though, is that in the early modern era, the borders dividing Vaals from its neighbors were religious as well as political. For whereas the Dutch Republic was officially Calvinist, Aachen, Limburg, and Wittem were all staunchly Catholic. Surrounded by Catholic states, Vaals was an outpost, not only of the Republic, but of "the true Reformed religion." That made it a site of intensive engagement—and as we shall see, conflict—between Protestants and Catholics.

The deeper I delved into my documents, the more clearly I saw that the location of Vaals was crucial to understanding the story of "Cunegonde's kidnapping." Cunegonde Mommers was a German Catholic from the parish of Würselen, in the territory of Aachen. Her brother Hendrick had married a Dutch Calvinist from Vaals named Sara Maria Erffens and had settled with her in her native village. The baby Cunegonde tried to snatch was their newborn son, who was being baptized in his mother's church. The fellow Catholics who freed Cunegonde from her detention lived less than an hour's walk from Vaals but across the border on Aachen soil, which is where they transported Cunegonde, beyond the reach of Dutch authorities—or so they hoped.

The story opened my eyes to a startling fact, that people of different faiths did not live "together" only in religiously mixed communities. Previously, like other scholars, I had usually thought of toleration in terms of people cohabiting the same towns and villages, neighborhoods and streets. But consider a person residing on or near a border between a Calvinist and a Catholic state, or between any two states with different official religions. There were hundreds of such borders in early modern Europe. They were especially dense in the German lands of central Europe, where political authority was fragmented into a huge number of principalities, cantons, cities, and other sovereign units. Some of these were tiny, while others had highly irregular shapes, with enclaves and exclaves that intertwined them inextricably with their neighbors. Even if their own communities were religiously homogeneous, people living in such places would still have encountered people of another faith regularly through cross-border contacts and travel. This was especially true in an age when borders were seldom policed and were not even defined always in precise geographic terms. Inevitably people who lived in adjacent or nearby communities would meet, do business, socialize, perhaps even marry one another. In this way, I realized, many more Europeans than is commonly recognized experienced religious diversity. They too had to wrestle with all the dilemmas it posed in an age when religion powerfully shaped the identity of individuals and communities.

Not that Vaals was ever a purely Calvinist community, or its neighbors purely Catholic. To the contrary, the case of Vaals shows how incredibly complex and fertile the religious mixing in a borderland could be. Despite belonging to a Calvinist polity, most of the inhabitants of Vaals were in fact Catholics, who formed the largest religious minority in the Dutch Republic. For their part, all the neighboring Catholic states had smaller, Protestant minorities. Thus, in an ironic twist, most of the Protestants who attended church in Vaals did not reside there. Instead, they traveled to Vaals on Sundays from their homes in the city of Aachen, from Eupen in the Duchy of Limburg, and from Burtscheid, a village just south of Aachen ruled by a Catholic abbess. To hundreds of Protestants in neighboring territories, forbidden to worship where they lived, Vaals offered a sanctuary, and the Protestant churches in Vaals were actually built for their use. Thus in this modest village, which as late as 1750 had no more than a dozen houses at its nucleus, there rose no fewer than four Protestant churches. One was Dutch Reformed (Calvinist), but services in it were conducted, for the sake of the visitors, mostly in German. The other three were Walloon (French-speaking Calvinist), Lutheran, and Mennonite. Meanwhile, Catholics in Vaals had use of the village's old parish church. That was a privilege of which Catholics outside Overmaas, elsewhere in the Republic, could only dream. Why did they enjoy it? Because of the character of the region as a borderland. In a host of ways, the political borders that crisscrossed it offered protection and support to religious minorities of all stripes. Ultimately I concluded that the story of Cunegonde's kidnapping was as much about borders as it was about mixed marriage. It revealed how ordinary people as well as authorities employed and took advantage of political borders to pursue religious goals. And it demonstrated that, contrary to appearances, those borders were not just constricting; they offered possibilities and forms of freedom that would not have existed without them.

Having found this trove of documents in The Hague, I set out, as would any good scholar, in search of sources that would contextualize and help explain the extraordinary story they told. And did I find them! Many sources lay in Maastricht, the capital of Dutch Limburg and site of the provincial archive; many more in Aachen and Düsseldorf. From them I learned that the two kidnappings of 1762 were by no means isolated events. To the contrary, they brought to a climax more than two decades of sporadic religious violence in the region of Vaals. Twice in that interval, Dutch authorities had had to dispatch troops to Vaals to protect their core-ligionists. Far from ending the episode, moreover, the prosecution of Cunegonde, her liberators, and the Catholic pastor had only inflamed passions. Catholics had responded with a wave of violent attacks. In reprisal, Dutch authorities had closed all the Catholic churches in 's-Hertogenrade. By the time it ended, the episode had taken on the proportions of a minor international incident. Almost by accident, I had stumbled on an unknown religious war—not a declared, official war between states, but an unofficial, popular one pitting Catholics and Protestants in the region against one another.

The most startling fact, though, was that this war had been fought in the middle of the eighteenth century. If it had taken place in the sixteenth or seventeenth century, at least a partial explanation would have lain ready to hand, for those centuries, especially the period from roughly 1550 to 1650, are conventionally labeled Europe's Age of Religious Wars. Religious strife was so common and wide-spread during them that, in the minds of many historians, it constituted the norm rather than the exception. The violence in Vaals, by contrast, took place during the so-called Age of Enlightenment, a period when Enlightenment thought is believed to have placed a defining stamp on European culture. Indeed, the violence peaked during the very decade that features in many history textbooks as the apogee of the High Enlightenment. Cunegonde attempted her baby-snatching in 1762, and the prosecutions that ensued took five years. In that interval, some of the most profound, influential works of Enlightenment thought rolled from Europe's printing press-es: Rousseau's *Émile* and *The Social Contract*, Voltaire's *Treatise on Tolerance* and *Philosophical Dictionary*, Beccaria's *On Crimes and Punishments*, Lessing's *Laocoon*, and the final text-volumes of Diderot and d'Alembert's monumental *Encyclopedia*. Of all the ideas articulated in these works, none was more central to the value system of the Enlightenment philosophes than the ideal of religious tolerance. The most renowned of all philosophes, Voltaire (whose satirical novella *Candide* featured a fictional character named Cunegonde), waged a feverish campaign for tolerance in precisely the same years.

Unlike most thinkers of earlier centuries, the philosophes did not conceive of tolerance as merely a concession to regrettable realities. They hailed it as a moral virtue, an expression of true Christianity, and one of the foundations of civil society. Eager to dispel what they called the darkness of ignorance and superstition with the light of reason, they defined tolerance as the expression par excellence of reason in religious matters. While some Enlightenment thinkers were hostile to organized religion, most wished to propagate what they considered to be more reasonable forms of religious belief and practice. Either way, the philosophes detested nothing more than fanaticism and its many expressions: bigotry, intolerance, persecution, strife, dogmatism, censorship. Deploying every old argument for tolerance they knew, they fashioned new ones as well. They recast religious freedom as one aspect of a broader freedom of thought and expression—a freedom for every individual to believe and, as Voltaire put it, "to think only what his reason . . . may dictate."[5] This freedom, claimed the philosophes, was a universal right which all humans held by nature.

The timing of religious conflict in Vaals raises obvious questions about the influence of Enlightenment ideas in eighteenth-century European society. Sweeping claims have often been made about the scope of that influence. Since the nineteenth century, many historians have credited the Enlightenment for transforming "the European mind" or some other such unitary entity. In recent decades, most scholars have qualified their claims by identifying, if only loosely, the groups about whom they are writing: "educated Europeans," "the literate sectors of European society," "polite culture."[6] They usually go on, though, to ignore the rest of society—and to obscure by their silence how much of society they are ignoring. By one recent estimate, only 5–7 percent of Dutch households participated in "educated culture" and "the national cultural network."[7] Yet the Dutch Republic had one of the highest literacy rates in Europe. Historians concede that, numerically speaking, rural folk participated in this culture far less than urbanites, and Catholics far less than Protestants. What then should we expect in a place like Vaals or in the other rural, Catholic communities where millions of Europeans lived? Many philosophes held a dark view of their plebeian contemporaries. They saw peasants in particular as inhabiting a world very different from their own, a world of primitive customs, irrational superstitions, bestial appetites, and blind faith.[8] Of course, we must not adopt the philosophes' prejudice and disdain. Nor should we oversimplify by drawing a neat division between an enlightened, elite culture and an unenlightened, popular one. Still, the religious conflict in Vaals offers a window onto the behavior and mentalities of massive social groups whom cultural historians all too often ignore.

The timing of our story also raises questions about how the history of toleration is usually written. According to most scholars, the past five hundred or so years of western history have witnessed a gradual, evolutionary "rise of toleration." The most decisive step in this evolution, it is said, took place in the eighteenth century, when, thanks to the Enlightenment, violent religious conflict in Europe became a thing of the past. Discredited as the product of a primitive mindset, religious enmities ended. Europeans embraced toleration as a positive good and a mark of the higher level of civilization they had achieved. From there, toleration increased further in the nineteenth and twentieth centuries, culminating in our modern commitment to religious freedom as a fundamental human right. Thus conceived, the promotion of tolerance by the Enlightenment philosophes is no isolated story; it forms a critical component of a grand narrative about the progress of western civilization.[9]

As I pointed out in a previous book, though, that narrative is problematic, both factually and conceptually.[10] The 1760s would not have marked a high point in the campaign for tolerance if persecution had already ceased by then. Voltaire's *Treatise*, for example, was prompted by the execution in Toulouse of a French Calvinist named Jean Calas for purportedly killing his son rather than allowing him to convert to Catholicism. As Voltaire showed, the accusation was patently false. That same year, French judges wrongly condemned to death the Protestant family of Elisabeth Sirven for similarly murdering a would-be convert to Catholicism, and a French Calvinist minister was hanged for carrying out his pastoral duties.[11] It is not difficult to compile a long list of religious persecutions and conflicts in eighteenth-century Europe. Such is the attachment, though, of scholars and nonscholars alike to our modern narrative of progress that such episodes have been dismissed as anachronisms or exceptions to the rule. How many exceptions, one might ask, are needed to call the grand narrative itself into question? One might ask also whether Enlightenment influence promoted toleration as unequivocally as claimed. As we shall see, members of the Dutch ruling elite had new, "enlightened" reasons in the eighteenth century to endorse old Protestant prejudices against Catholicism.

Another part of the grand narrative relates the rise of toleration not to Enlightenment ideas but to social and economic forces. Social scientists especially have propagated the view that the spread of capitalism—one thinks of globalization in our own, contemporary context—promotes rational, economic thinking at the expense of religion and knits people together in a network of mutual interest. Again, though, many facts belie the theory, including our episode in Vaals. The 1760s saw the dawn of the Industrial Revolution. From my sources I learned that the region of Vaals was one of the earliest sites of this profound transformation. Economically it was no backwater. Merchants and manufacturers in its flourishing textile and metals industries purchased raw materials from Scandinavia and Spain, recruited skilled labor from Poland and southern Germany, and sold their products to Russia and the Levant. Workers in these industries—like Hendrick Mommers, a journeyman cloth shearer—were mobile, and increasingly found themselves reduced to the status of a proletariat. Forces for economic and social modernization were powerfully at work in Vaals, and far from assuaging old religious conflicts, they exacerbated them.

What follows, then, is a true story. It belongs to the genre of microhistory: it does not revolve around any famous figures or events, but thanks to a wealth of exceptional sources, it has a profusion of vivid detail. Scenes are sketched, conversations recounted, precisely as they are given in the original documents.[12] Of course, not all these documents agree with one another: in case a historian wasn't aware of the problem already, legal sources deriving from a trial invariably contain at least two versions of events, the prosecution's and that of the defense. In fact, the dilemma goes deeper, since some witnesses—not least, Cunegonde herself—were inconsistent, varying their accounts when they testified for a second or third time. My rule of thumb, in a case in which so much was contested, has been to recount things as matters of fact if the account of them given by a source was never contested, if they are attested by multiple sources that do not differ substantially, or if the evidence for them is overwhelming. The rest I leave to you to judge. Above all, I leave you to make up your own mind about the indictment on which the pastor, Father Bosten, stood trial. Did he order Cunegonde to go into the Reformed church, get the baby, and bring it to him for baptism? After she was arrested, did he arrange the expedition that freed her?

In the final analysis, the value of a microhistory is twofold. It can bring to life a precious fragment of a lost past, restoring voices to the illiterate and agency to obscure individuals. It can also change our understanding of the past by calling attention to phenomena previously unknown or ignored. One story can always be dismissed by sceptics as exceptional; by itself it cannot overthrow an accepted narrative. But it can raise questions about it, and suggest other possibilities.

CHAPTER ONE

Between Them Sleeps the Devil

In the chill hours before dawn on Tuesday, 13 April 1762, Sara Maria Erffens gave birth to a baby boy. Though a woman of true grit, she must have felt an edge of terror in the face of her perilous ordeal: the previous time she had borne a child, she had barely survived, been bedridden for three and a half months, and the infant had never seen its first birthday. It was a common story in eighteenth-century Europe, where, despite improving conditions, infant mortality rates remained high and many mothers died in childbirth. At least Sara had the reassurance of an experienced midwife. At seventy-six, Anna Olivier was a right old crone, illiterate and hard of hearing, but she was a skilled healer relied on by men as well as women in the Dutch village of Vaals. This time things turned out better for both mother and child. When the moment of supreme danger had passed, Sara's husband, Hendrick Mommers, entered the room. Anna asked the couple, "How shall the child be baptized?"[1]

"None of your business," replied Sara sharply. "That's a matter for my husband; I have spoken with him, and he shall tell you."

"But I must know, since if the child is going to be baptized Roman Catholic, I'm supposed to make [the sign of] a cross over it."

"None of your business," repeated Sara. "Your job is to help bring the child into the world, clean and take care of it, and then take it [to church] to be baptized. Then I'll give you your money and you can go."

Anna did as told and busied herself. Approaching the bed where his wife lay, Hendrick asked more tentatively, "How do you want it done?" Sara answered sternly, "You know what we agreed." Hendrick made no reply, but as he escorted Anna out of the room and down the stairs of the house where the poor couple lodged, she heard him exclaim, "The devil take me before I let the child be baptized Calvinist!"

Scandalized by Hendrick's imprecation, Anna left the house and walked to the local Catholic church to hear early morning mass. On the way, she pondered Hendrick's and Sara's words. Sara apparently believed that she and her husband had agreed that their child would be baptized in her own Reformed church. But then why didn't she just say so—why had she left it to Hendrick to instruct Anna at a later time where she should bring the infant for baptism? Hendrick hadn't contradicted his wife to her face. Yet only three days earlier, he had assured the local Catholic pastor that the couple had agreed to baptize and raise their children in the Catholic faith. And now, out of his wife's earshot, he was swearing in the most offensive language that she would not get her way.

How was this baby, born to a Calvinist mother and a Catholic father, supposed to be baptized? Ambiguity and contradiction swirled around the issue. Like the winds of a tornado, they would soon blow away the tenuous religious peace of Vaals and its surrounding region. To understand how this vortex was generated, we need first to consider the attitudes and difficulties surrounding religiously mixed marriage in early modern Europe.

There is a saying in Dutch, *Twee geloven op één kussen, daar slaapt de duivel tussen:* two faiths in one bed (literally, on one pillow), between them sleeps the devil. It means that if a husband and wife are of different faiths, they will have an unhappy marriage. The saying itself is modern, but the warning it expresses was a commonplace going back at least as far as the sixteenth century. The sundering of western Christendom in that tumultuous age gave the issue of mixed marriage an unprecedented urgency, for across large parts of Europe, people for the first time adhered to rival Christian faiths. All the major churches that emerged from this epochal change vehemently condemned mixed marriage, calling it "improper," "offensive," and a "sin against God." All the major churches tried to dissuade their followers from marrying people of other faiths and disciplined those who failed to heed their admonitions, excluding them from the rite of communion and demanding that they show repentance. The Catholic Church, which counted marriage among its seven sacraments, considered mixed marriage a form of sacrilege. As late as 1741, Pope Benedict XIV denounced those who, "driven shamefully mad by an insane love, do not abhor in their souls . . . these detestable unions, which Holy Mother Church has always damned and forbidden." Even in the Dutch Republic, where mixed marriage was relatively common, only one group, the Waterlander Mennonites, did not combat it.²

In part, the churches opposed mixed marriage out of a concern for matrimony, which all deemed a sacred, divinely ordained institution. How, they asked, could pious Christians live in peace with spouses whose most fundamental beliefs differed from their own? How could they not combat falsehood and evil when it infected their home? Religious differences, they warned, would destroy marital harmony and undermine the bonds of affection that should join husband and wife. By the same token, they would lead wives to disobey their husbands and children their parents, threatening the God-given patriarchal order of society.

In part, the churches' opposition to mixed marriage also expressed a wider cultural prejudice—a sense that there was something unnatural and unsavory about mixing and mixedness per se. In early modern France, mixed marriages were sometimes called "motley," like the outfits worn by court jesters and other fools. More commonly, they were called "unequal," the same term used for matches between rich and poor, young and old. One might draw a parallel, though it is not exact, to the revulsion and fear some people felt in the nineteenth and twentieth centuries for what they called "miscegenation." To early modern church leaders, religious hybridity seemed as monstrous as did racial hybridity to modern racists. In their view, truth and falsehood, good and evil had as little in common with one another as did black and white; a person was either a member of Christ or a minion of the devil. But religiously mixed households created a murky gray zone; they blurred and obfuscated the clear, sharp boundaries that the churches strove to establish between themselves. At least a whiff of uncertainty hung over the orthodoxy and loyalty of all members of such households.

Above all, the churches opposed mixed marriage out of fear that through it they would lose members. Inevitably, they recognized, people in mixed marriages would be exposed to "error." Some would be perverted by it, lost to the church, and damned. Worse still, the children of such marriages would, as one Catholic author put it, "suck in heresy with [mother's] milk."[3] They, and with them the family's future generations, were in danger of being lost as well. This was the ultimate, and oldest, argument against marrying nonbelievers: "For they will turn away thy sons from following me, that they may serve other Gods" (Deut. 7:4). So strong were these fears in Rome that for three centuries, the papal curia refused to approve dispensations for mixed marriage except in extraordinary circumstances. Only in 1858 did the curia issue a general instruction that dispensations could be granted under certain conditions:

mixed couples had to promise that the Protestant would allow the Catholic spouse to practice their faith unhindered, that the Catholic would do their utmost to convert the Protestant spouse, and that all the couple's children would be raised "in the sanctity of the Catholic religion." Previously, the cardinals in Rome doubted—with good reason—whether such promises were enforceable and so preferred not to approve mixed marriages under any condition. In the absence of a general rule, Catholic bishops and synods were left to establish their own guidelines as to when priests might join mixed couples in matrimony. The result was variation and a good deal of confusion. In practice, Rome's mute hard line gave scope for others—clergy, secular rulers, and sometimes ordinary laypeople—to exercise their own judgment.[4]

In a mirror image of Catholic fears, Europe's Protestant churches likewise regarded mixed marriage as a spiritual and institutional threat. Their concern did not diminish for a long time; to the contrary, at least in the Dutch Republic, it may even have increased in the late seventeenth and early eighteenth centuries. Simultaneously, though, the concern narrowed, coming to focus almost exclusively on Protestant-Catholic unions. This important, twofold change has not been noticed by many historians, nor does it match the kind of change most expect to have occurred in an age that saw the dawn of the Enlightenment. Whereas previously the Dutch Reformed churches had taken a stand against all mixed marriages, now they began to move in the direction of approving marriages to other sorts of Protestants. The change reflected a growing ecumenical appreciation for the scope and depth of the beliefs and values which the Reformed shared with other Protestants. But it also reflected a new sense of solidarity against common enemies, foremost among which remained the Roman Catholic Church.

In 1708, the first book by a Dutch Protestant directed specifically against mixed marriage was published in Amsterdam. It was entitled *Weighty Reasons Not to Enter into the State of Matrimony with Papists [Roomsgesind]. Presented as a Christian Instruction for All Protestants, Particularly Reformed, Lutherans, and Mennonites.* The book's author claimed that the Catholic Church had launched a devious plot, seeking "to storm God's church . . . with wives, and to entice our simple members through marriage to abandon our community and embrace their errors and idolatries."[5] Other Protestants feared more the coercion, even violence, which Catholic husbands might direct against their wives. Never, claimed a group of Dutch ministers in 1716, had these threats been greater. With some reason, though not enough to justify their exaggerated claims, they and their colleagues were convinced that the Reformed churches were losing members to the Catholic foe, and in a prolonged campaign, they petitioned the various governing bodies of the Republic to take countermeasures.

The highest of these bodies was the Dutch States General, whose members will play a critical role in our story, especially at its end. The States General was an assembly of delegates representing the seven provinces of the Netherlands that had ended up, in the late sixteenth century, breaking away from their Habsburg rulers and forming a new country. Each province had one vote in the assembly, and the most important decisions required, at least in theory, unanimous consent. That was because, from the birth of the Republic to its demise in the 1790s, each province was considered a sovereign entity. Ruled by its own provincial States, every province was legally equal to every other one, and even Holland, by far the richest and most populous, enjoyed no constitutional superiority. In practice Holland wielded enormous clout, especially since it bankrolled over half the Republic's budget. It didn't hurt either that the seat of Holland's provincial government, the Binnenhof in The Hague, was also the seat of national government. Known as Their High and Mighty Lordships, the States General were charged with conducting the common business of the Republic, like waging war, and in this task they had the assistance of the Council of State, which functioned largely as their executive arm. In domestic affairs, though, the scope of common business was quite restricted, since the various provincial States, above all the States of Holland, jealously guarded their autonomy. They, not the States General, issued laws, set taxes, and appointed officials for their provinces. The only domestic territories over which the States General exercised direct sovereignty were the so-called Generality Lands. These were territories situated along the southern and eastern borders of the Republic that the Dutch had conquered by force of arms, mostly from the Habsburgs during the Eighty Years' War (1568–1648). They included States-Flanders, States-Brabant, States-Upper-Gelderland, and States-Lands of Overmaas, where Vaals was located (fig. 5).[6]

Calvinist ministers from Overmaas, joined by colleagues from other Generality Lands, played a leading role in the campaign to convince the Dutch "regents"— the nobles and city magistrates who, through the various States, ruled the Republic—to combat mixed marriages. Their special engagement with the issue was no accident. Because the Generality Lands had remained under Catholic rulers longer than any of the seven provinces, these conquered territories had a unique religious profile: despite their belonging to an officially Calvinist state, across most of them Catholics always constituted the overwhelming majority of the population. This meant that local Calvinists found slim pickings when seeking suitable marriage partners among their coreligionists. Almost inevitably, some married Catholics. The large Catholic population also created a milieu in which, in some respects, Catholic social and cultural norms predominated, counterbalancing somewhat the Calvinist monopoly on political power. From the worried perspective of a Calvinist minister, this milieu made it dangerously

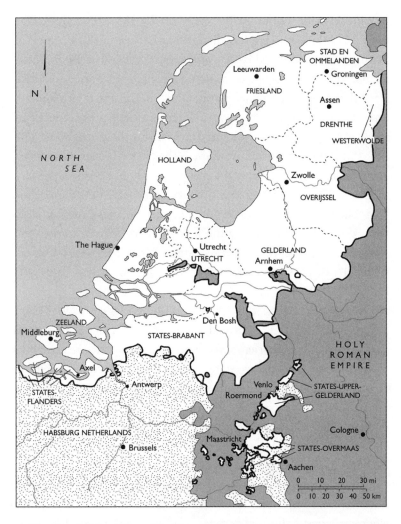

5. The Dutch Republic and its Generality Lands, States-Flanders, States-Brabant, States-Upper-Gelderland, and States-Overmaas, where Vaals was located.

likely that Calvinists who married Catholics would feel pressure to assimilate, to accommodate their spouse's preferences (for example, concerning how their children were raised), or even to convert.

The regents proved receptive to the ministers' pleas. Not as receptive as the ministers would have liked: they never obtained the laws they requested forbidding outright all marriages between Calvinists and Catholics (a measure that some Catholic prelates, too, hoped would pass). Such a prohibition was implemented in the 1730s, but only for military officers and some government officials. Starting in the late seventeenth century, though, the regents did place unprecedented restrictions on mixed couples. At the urging of ministers, they issued a series of placards, or edicts, requiring Catholics to promise not to hinder their partners from exercising their faith or from raising their children in it. Such placards were enacted in four of the Republic's seven provinces. The two most powerful governing bodies of the Republic took a different tack. In 1750, the States General issued for the Generality Lands a particularly important placard. Under its terms, no Calvinist male under the age of twenty-five or Calvinist female under twenty (the age of majority for the two sexes) could marry a Catholic. Promises of marriage between a Calvinist and a Catholic had no legal force, so that before the wedding itself either party could change his or her mind. And to encourage couples to reconsider, the marriage banns—the public announcements of a couple's intent to marry—could be proclaimed only at six-week rather than one-week intervals. This extended to twelve the number of weeks that had to pass from the date a couple registered to marry, either with a minister or magistrate, to their wedding day. In 1755, the States of Holland issued a placard that included the same provisions plus a few more. To the disappointment of ministers, though, neither the States General nor the States of Holland restricted the freedom of mixed couples to decide how to raise their children. This, counseled some jurists, would violate the "natural freedom" of parents, who "by all rights hold complete power and authority" over their children.[7]

Consequently, in the Generality Lands, as in Holland, the law allowed parents to choose. In practice, mixed couples decided the issue in varied ways. In some cases, "patria potestas"—the patriarchal authority of the father—prevailed, and children were raised in their father's faith. In other cases—not as many, but still a significant proportion, at least in Holland, where we have good data—all the children were raised in their mother's religion. Some couples alternated, baptizing and raising their first child in one parent's faith, their second in the other parent's, and so on, continuing back and forth with subsequent progeny. In still other families, the sons "followed" the father, the daughters the mother: that is, boys were raised in their father's faith, girls in their mother's. This division by gender was, according to some contemporaries, the most common practice among mixed couples. Attested in other lands as well, it may have been the same across Europe as a whole. In the Duchy of Jülich, one of the German territories that neighbored the Lands of Overmaas, the practice was even prescribed by law.

Why was this practice adopted so widely? Without contemporary explanations, we can only hypothesize. Clearly, it encouraged sons to identify with their fathers, daughters with their mothers, and to take on their parent's religious identity as they would their gender identity and, commonly, their social roles. A second reason seems at least as important: when followed by many families, the practice froze into place the demographic balance between faiths. True, children could in theory choose their own faith when they reached the "age of discretion," commonly set at twelve or fourteen. Yet as everyone knew, most adults remained loyal to the faith in which they were reared. Thus unless an equal number of children, in the aggregate, were raised in each faith, a couple of generations could suffice to produce a massive shift in the number of adherents each church could claim. Such a shift would have challenged the stability of religiously mixed communities. Churches with dwindling memberships would likely have felt threatened, whereas those with expanding ones might have tried to assert their new strength. The practice described above removed both threat and temptation. Whatever current relations were between the faiths, it tended to perpetuate them. Whether by law, custom, or prenuptial contract, it was lay society that embraced this practice; no church ever officially sanctioned it. Informally, though, the churches went along with it. Driven by fear, they opted for the safety of the status quo over the prospect of potential gain.

The story of Hendrick and Sara offers a stark example of how these attitudes and difficulties played out in individuals' lives. From it we can see how the fate of a mixed couple's children depended not only on the strength of a husband and wife's religious commitments but also on the circumstances of their marriage, the character of their relationship, and the pressures to which they were subjected.[8]

Hendrick Mommers was a poor man. He grew up in a hamlet named Driesch, in the parish of Würselen, in the rural territory—the so-called Reich—of the German city of Aachen. Like everyone else in his small community, he was raised a Roman Catholic. Hendrick was the third of nine children born to his mother, Maria, and his father, like him named Hendrick, who worked in a brass foundry in Stolberg, a small town in nearby Jülich. Our Hendrick trained in the other great industry of the region, textiles, and became a journeyman cloth shearer, part of an army of laborers who had few prospects of rising in their trade. Though he lived in Aachen, he worked just outside the city in the village of Burtscheid, a booming textile center (fig. 6). It was there probably that he met the Calvinist girl Sara. A native of Vaals, Sara had moved in 1755 to

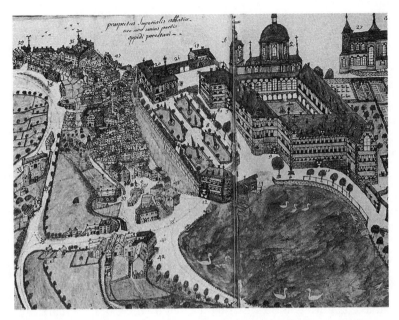

6. Burtscheid. Aquarelle drawn in 1754, showing the Burtscheid Abbey in the center and to the left a group of houses where industry was concentrated.

Burtscheid with her stepmother and her father, Mathias, a master cloth shearer; perhaps Hendrick even worked at some point for Mathias. At any rate, Sara, whose maternal grandfather had been burgomaster of Vaals, came from a higher socioeconomic stratum than Hendrick. He was about thirty-one, she twenty-three years old when they met.[9] Was it love? Probably, at least on Sara's part, for she had no material incentive to take up with a man who relied on her for financial support, and his Catholic faith made the match highly problematic. What is certain is that the couple had sex, Sara got pregnant, and in June 1760, still unmarried, she bore a son, whom she named after her father. This was Sara's first experience of childbirth, the one that almost killed her and left her soon mourning a dead infant. During her illness, a penniless Hendrick left Sara, presumably in the care of her family, while he went off to fend for himself. At this difficult time, Sara suffered further when the leaders of her Calvinist congregation censured her for fornication.

None of these tribulations deterred Sara from continuing her relationship with Hendrick, and in the summer of 1761 she again became pregnant by him. Around the same time, the couple resolved to marry. They had become in some respects a suitable match for each other: given Hendrick's poverty, no one would have regarded him as a catch, but then, given her prior pregnancy and the public stigma she bore for it, Sara herself would now have been considered "damaged goods" on the marriage market. Reflecting this balance, it was agreed between the lovers that neither would impose their faith on the other (in other circumstances, Catholic men sometimes used extramarital pregnancies as leverage, refusing to marry their Protestant lovers unless the women converted). Likewise, the couple agreed that any boys they had would be raised in Hendrick's faith, any girls in Sara's.

The problem was, the couple could not find anyone who would join them in matrimony on these terms. Hendrick and Sara first approached the curate of the Catholic parish where they lived, that of St. Adalbert in Aachen. This curate, whose name appropriately was Quirinus Finck, played a dirty trick on them—in the name, of course, of saving souls. At first, he appeared to go along with their wishes. He registered the couple and issued the banns for their marriage first one week, then the next. The third week, though, he refused to issue the banns for the final time. Hendrick and Sara went to ask why. He answered that he would not proceed further unless the couple promised by a written contract to baptize and raise all their future children in the Catholic faith. The couple returned home to ponder their options, and this is where the ambiguities and contradictions of their story begin. As recounted by Hendrick and Sara several years later, testifying jointly, Hendrick at this point proposed a deception: they would accede to the curate's demand and sign the contract. Privately, though, Hendrick would give Sara a written statement promising the opposite of the contract, that all their children would in fact be baptized and raised Calvinist.[10] When requested by the magistrates before whom they were testifying, Sara produced Hendrick's statement. It read as follows: "I, Hendrick Mommers, promise Sara Maria Erffens by this contract that she may raise the children with whom God blesses us in the faith in which she was born. [And] although we have been put in a position of having publicly to break [this promise], I will not break it with her but will keep it as long as God grants me life. And if we should have to suffer for it greatly here, I promise you with heart and mouth that I shall go with you to a place where you enjoy greater freedom."[11] Hendrick and Sara returned to Father Finck, who drew up a detailed contract by which the couple repudiated their original agreement to divide the children by gender, which according to Finck "no Catholic authority, spiritual or temporal, would endorse"—a fine statement of ecclesiastic principle but a falsehood with regard to Catholic princes such as the dukes of Jülich. Sara had to swear that, even as her children grew older, she would encourage them to attend mass on Sundays and feast days, take communion at Easter, and observe the prescribed fasts.[12] On 18 July 1761, in the presence of the curate and two witnesses, Hendrick and Sara signed the contract.

A few days later, the couple were startled to discover that Father Finck was still unwilling to marry them. As we have seen, the Catholic Church had no consistent, universal standard for approving mixed marriages. The same was true locally in Aachen, which belonged—as did Vaals—to the Catholic diocese of Liège. Church authorities there had issued at least two different rules back in the seventeenth century, and neither of them permitted a priest to officiate at the wedding of a mixed couple without the approval of the vicar general. The more severe of the two rules forbade any wedding unless the Protestant partner abjured his or her faith. But Hendrick and Sara could not be expected to know this, and in practice neither rule was strictly adhered to anyway.[13] Finck used this ambiguity, and the couple's ignorance and vulnerability, to extract as many concessions from them as he could. Having coerced Hendrick and Sara into promising to baptize and raise their children Catholic, he now demanded that Sara convert to Catholicism. This she absolutely refused to do. Like her parents and grandparents before her, Sara was a committed Calvinist: as a teenager she had made a public profession of faith, submitted to church discipline, and been accepted as a full member of her congregation. She did not just attend sermons, as some of her coreligionists did, but also took communion—or at least she had done so until the leaders of her congregation had barred her as punishment for having had sex with Hendrick. Rather than convert, she preferred to remain a marked sinner among her fellow Calvinists. "Well then," declared an angry Hendrick to the curate, if you won't marry us, "the contract we signed before you is void," and the couple departed.[14]

So Hendrick and Sara did what lawyers today call forum shopping: they went in search of an authority prepared to marry them on more amenable terms. They next approached the head of Sara's Calvinist congregation in Burtscheid, Minister Johannes Pferdmenges. Like his colleague in Aachen, Gerhard von Hemessen, and his colleague in Eupen, Abraham Schmitz, Pferdmenges lived among his congregation, providing pastoral care to them in their homes. Also like his colleagues, he could neither preach nor administer the sacraments on Catholic territory, where he and his congregation survived "under the cross" of persecution. He could conduct regular services only across the Dutch border in Vaals, where the three foreign congregations shared use of the Reformed church building and worshiped together with the Calvinists of Vaals. On 29 August, Hendrick and Sara appeared before Pferdmenges, an elder, and a deacon. Because the wedding would take place in Vaals, the three church officers followed Dutch law in their dealings with the couple. That law did not impose on the officers the duty (or give them the right) to exact any promises from the couple. It did, though, require them to determine, even if the man and woman were not minors, whether the couple's parents consented to the marriage. Sara's father, Mathias, himself a former elder, sent word that he approved of the marriage, "but on condition that Hendrick Mommers would keep the promise made to him and his daughter"—namely, that the couple's children would all be raised "in the true Reformed religion."[15]

What followed was an extraordinary exchange. As recounted later by Pferdmenges and the deacon (the elder had in the meantime passed away), "Hendrick Mommers assented to this commitment completely freely, promising solemnly that all the children God gave them would be raised in the Reformed religion. And although it was remonstrated to him more than once that he would do better to give up this person, who adhered to the Reformed religion, since according to the rules of the Roman Catholic religion he could not keep his promise, he nevertheless insisted on it, [saying that he] wanted to, and would, keep his promise faithfully, [and that] his conscience was none of our concern."[16]

According to their account, then, the church officers tried to dissuade Hendrick from making a promise that he could not in good conscience keep. Like their Catholic counterparts, they opposed mixed marriage, and they seem to have preferred a pious Christian of any stripe to a faithless, disobedient one. So, in an ironic twist, these Calvinists found themselves admonishing Hendrick to behave as a good Catholic, obey the rules of his church (as they understood them), and abandon the match. In a revealing response, Hendrick made light of their admonition; it appears that he himself did not worry a great deal about his conscience. He was right not to concern himself regarding the validity per se of the marriage: since 1741, the Catholic Church had officially recognized as valid weddings performed by Dutch ministers for mixed couples, as well as for Protestant ones. In the eyes of the Church, though, such weddings remained illicit, and a promise by a Catholic to have his children raised Protestant was utterly unconscionable.

As required by Dutch law, Pferdmenges issued the banns for Hendrick and Sara over the following twelve weeks, and on 22 November, the couple were married in the Reformed church of Vaals.

Hendrick mentioned none of these complications when, on 10 April 1762, he first met the Catholic pastor of Vaals, Johannes Wilhelmus Bosten. Hendrick and Sara had moved only recently to Vaals, where they lodged in a house on the Groene Driesch. It was the day before Easter, and Bosten had dispatched his sexton, Martinus Buntgens, to summon his new parishioner. Bosten explained later that he had wished to "instruct" Hendrick regarding communion, which was to be administered in church the next day, and to admonish him of his duty to receive the sacrament. Hendrick came that evening to Bosten's home, the parish rectory, where Bosten's brother later found the two men sitting on a brazier to keep warm. "How shall it be with the children born from your marriage?" asked Bosten.[17] Hendrick informed Bosten of the written contract he and his wife had signed in Aachen before the curate of St. Adalbert and promised that, in accord with it, all the children "will follow me, the Roman Catholic father." Asked pointedly whether he had made any subsequent contract, Hendrick denied doing so, before either Minister Pferdmenges or anyone else. To the contrary, he had warned his wife that if the minister pressed him on the issue of children, he, Hendrick, "would rather get up and leave [her] unmarried" than agree to a Calvinist baptism. In fact, the essence of the Calvinist church officers' account is verified by a note made at the time in the Burtscheid marriage register. Yet Hendrick told Bosten that Pferdmenges had never even raised the issue.

The uncertainty and confusion that arose three days later when Sara gave birth to a baby boy is thus scarcely surprising. Hendrick and Sara had made four different agreements concerning the religious upbringing of their children. In the first, they had agreed to follow a widespread custom, raising any boys they had in Hendrick's faith and any girls in Sara's. According to this agreement, the newborn should have been baptized Catholic. In the second, made at the insistence of Father Finck, they had promised to raise all their children Catholic. In the third, made privately between Hendrick and Sara, they had resolved the opposite. And in the fourth, made when they registered to be married by Pferdmenges, they had again pledged to baptize and raise their children Calvinist. Nobody knew all of this except Hendrick and Sara themselves.

The couple deserves some pity—after all, the leaders of their respective churches, joined by Sara's father, Mathias, put Hendrick and Sara under intense, conflicting pressures. If Finck planned in advance his stepwise escalation of demands, the couple may even be considered victims of entrapment. Hendrick and Sara coped partly by telling people what they wanted to hear, making the promises demanded of them. But they never yielded completely: Sara refused to convert, the couple went forum shopping, and Hendrick rebuffed repeated urgings not to marry Sara. Actually, the couple could have satisfied both sides of the religious divide by abandoning the match, but on this point they showed a stubborn determination. By the time they resolved to marry, their relationship had already survived censure, illness, poverty, and the death of a child. Hendrick and Sara did not flinch from braving further obstacles together. Clearly, they felt a powerful commitment to each other.

That said, Hendrick was manifestly a vacillating, lying braggart whose shoulders must bear much of the blame for the tragedy that ensued. Just a few weeks later he would repeat to the Catholic pastor of Burtscheid the boastful falsehood by which he misled Bosten. The blasphemous oath that Anna Olivier—and others in the house—heard Hendrick swear suggests likewise more mouth than courage. For her part, Sara too was guilty of deception in signing Finck's contract. She had a family of somewhat higher status and wealth than did the indigent Hendrick, and in Vaals he was living on her turf; these factors tilted the balance of power in the relationship in her favor. Yet Sara also showed an inner steel her husband lacked. Hendrick may not have been a pious man, but he did prefer his children to be baptized and raised Catholic. He did not dare, though, stand up to his wife and her family. In a sense, then, the reason the religious fate of Hendrick and Sara's baby remained so unclear was that the spouses had never resolved the issue between themselves.

CHAPTER TWO

Baptism Is Baptism

From a theological perspective, it scarcely mattered how Hendrick and Sara's baby was baptized—whether by a minister or priest, in a Calvinist church or a Catholic one. Catholic and Calvinist church leaders had long ago recognized each other's baptismal rites as valid. As early as 1439, Pope Eugene IV had acknowledged the grace-giving efficacy of any baptism, more or less, that used water and invoked the Trinity, so long as the sacrament was performed with the correct intent. In the sixteenth century, when the breakup of western Christendom gave the issue great urgency, the Catholic Council of Trent had reaffirmed this position. Both Catholic and mainstream Protestant leaders were leery of anything that resembled rebaptism, a practice they associated with Anabaptist radicals. Rome therefore discouraged the inclination of priests in some parts of Europe, including the Habsburg Netherlands, to perform conditional baptisms (in which a priest would intone, "If you are baptized, I do not baptize you, but if you have not yet been baptized, I baptize you") if they had any doubt of the validity of a person's prior baptism. Conditional baptisms were not approved or practiced after the 1620s in the provinces of the Dutch Republic, nor were they in the diocese of Liège, where our story takes place. To be sure, the Catholic rite included elements, most notably the exorcism of demons, which many Protestant ones omitted. If a Protestant converted to Catholicism, these elements might be performed in a supplemental ceremony. This was not the general custom, though, in the Liège diocese, precisely for the reason, as a pastoral handbook explained, "lest the uneducated common folk think that we deem their [the Protestants'] baptism invalid, and that it is necessary to baptize them again for a second time."[1]

But of course baptism was not just a spiritual transaction. It was also a rite of initiation by which a person was inducted into a religious community. With its performance, a person entered into a relationship not just with Christ but with a group of fellow Christians. As the matter was generally understood in the eighteenth century, baptism by a priest made a person Catholic; baptism by a Calvinist minister made them Calvinist (though not, in the Dutch Republic, a full church member, which required the kind of informed, voluntary commitment Sara Erffens made as a teenager). Through baptism, churches claimed newborn infants as belonging to them. The relationship was conceived as anything but transient. How a child was baptized was how it presumably would be raised; an explicit commitment to that effect was part of the Calvinist rite. True, there was always the possibility of subsequent conversion. But in parts of Germany, at least, popular belief held that baptism created an indissoluble pact, a *Taufbund*, by which one belonged to a church irrevocably. Conversion, according to this belief, was impossible; violating the Taufbund was a sin, and the right thing was for everyone to seek salvation in the religion of their parents. Clergy felt compelled to preach against these views.[2]

For mixed couples, the baptism of a child in one church or another signified which of its parents it would "follow" religiously. It forged a bond, opening up a whole area of intimacy and sharing, with one parent, while distancing the child from its other parent. By the same token, it aligned the child more closely with one of its two sets of extended kin. For nonrelatives as well, baptism marked a child as belonging to their own religious community or to a rival one. Even if one did not believe that a child's salvation was at issue, the social stakes were high. In the eighteenth century, most Protestants came to acknowledge that salvation could be attained in any one of the principal Protestant churches. Nevertheless, conflicts between them over the baptism of mixed couples' children still occurred. For example, a dispute arose in Vaals in 1752 when the Lutheran minister there, Zacharias Ennighman, violated the prenuptial contract of a mixed couple. The husband, a Lutheran, was a prominent cloth manufacturer, while his Calvinist wife was stepdaughter of a local magistrate. In accord with their contract, the couple's first child had been baptized in the Vaals Reformed church and the second in the Lutheran; to continue the pattern of alternation, the third should have been baptized in the Reformed church. After Ennighman—probably at the parents' request—baptized the child as a Lutheran, the wife's stepfather brought a complaint against him in the district court, and the local consistory, which governed the Vaals Reformed church, mobilized its superior body, the regional classis, which in turn lobbied the top law enforcement officer of 's-Hertogenrade, the lieutenant governor. A matter of regret between people "who call each other brothers," the dispute was eventually settled by mediation, and the "brotherly love and good harmony . . . between the two [Reformed and Lutheran] congregations" was restored.[3]

Such goodwill was utterly lacking between Protestants and Catholics in Vaals. Whether a child there was baptized in a Catholic church or a Protestant one (whether Reformed or Lutheran) placed it on one side or another of a simmering, undeclared religious war. So it is no wonder that, when Sara Erffens gave birth on the Tuesday after Easter, 1762, powerful forces began immediately to mobilize. On one side stood Sara's family—the Erffens clan, headed by her father, Mathias.[4] Born around 1705, Mathias was a proper patriarch. At twenty-four he had married the daughter of a former burgomaster of Vaals, a Walloon immigrant who had moved to the village from Liège. She had borne him at least four children, including Sara. After she died, Mathias had remarried and, in his late forties, started a second family. His second wife, Anna Gertrud Spaemans, continued to produce offspring for him even as the children by his first marriage had children of their own. A stalwart Calvinist, Mathias served as elder of the Vaals Reformed congregation before moving in 1755 to Burtscheid. Both of his wives and many, if not all, of his children were full members of the Reformed Church. As a master cloth shearer, Mathias seems to have been neither rich nor poor. By the measured way he spoke, though, and the way others spoke of him, one can tell that he was a figure of some dignity and stature.

On the other side, Hendrick's immediate family was less prosperous and slightly more distant. His parents lived in Würselen, on the far side of Aachen, to the east of the city, as did some of his siblings. Hendrick had only more distant relatives in the immediate vicinity of Vaals. There was the blacksmith Conrad Wolff, who lived just a ten-minute walk from Vaals on the main road to Aachen. He was captain of the militia of his rural quarter, the so-called Vaalserquartier of the territory of Aachen. Crucially, there was also Martinus Buntgens, the sexton of the Vaals Catholic church, and Martinus's father, Andries. How precisely they were related to Hendrick Mommers is unclear, but their claim of kinship—to him and to his newborn child—was never challenged. As sexton,

Buntgens was charged with maintaining the church building, whose keys he kept. Among other duties, he guarded the church's liturgical objects, prepared them for use, and assisted in the celebration of mass. He also functioned as general factotum for the pastor, conveying messages and summoning people. Sometimes his sixty-five-year-old father stood in for him. A courier by profession, Andries Buntgens stood out among the rural folk of the area for wearing a powdered wig. Like his son, Andries was a busybody who seemed to know every Catholic in the parish. The two men were ready witnesses at Catholic weddings, and both had numerous godchildren.

The most powerful figures to mobilize on the Catholic side, though, were the pastor of Vaals, Johannes Wilhelmus Bosten, and his younger brother Frans Hendrick. Both in their forties, the two men came from the nearby village of Mechelen, in the County of Wittem. How their father had made a living is unclear, but in any event he had died prematurely (possibly in a fight), leaving their mother somehow to manage with nine children ranging in ages from two to nineteen. Johannes Wilhelmus was the eldest. Thanks to an uncle in the church, who provided the required funds, he was ordained just a couple of years later. In 1741 he was appointed pastor of Vaals, a respectable but modest position with a benefice that was small even by the standards of rural parishes.[5] But Father Bosten—for so shall we often refer to Johannes Wilhelmus—seems to have been contented. (Calling priests "Father" is a modern usage; contemporaries addressed Bosten rather as "Sir" or "Lord Pastor"—*Heer* or *Heer Pastoor*, or the German equivalent—a title that expressed rank rather than pastoral role.) He proved a diligent and effective pastor who trod with skill the fine line an early modern clergyman had to walk between respect and popularity. In 1751 he managed to persuade the canons of the Aachen Minster, who received most of the tithes from his parish, to pay for his church to be enlarged and entirely rebuilt.[6] Father Bosten lived in an old rectory with a barn, a stable, an enclosed yard, and a meadow behind it on which he kept some animals. Frans Hendrick, also a priest, held the subordinate position of curate. That meant above all that he assisted the pastor in performing the required masses on the four altars of the parish church, which was dedicated to the Apostle Paul. He also ran the local Catholic school. Perhaps he resented his meager living (none of the altars of the church were endowed), or perhaps he chafed at serving under his brother, who was five years older. Whatever the reason, Frans Hendrick had a nasty streak to him, and a sharp tongue. Still, until 1762, both men seem to have gotten along well enough with their Calvinist neighbors. Father Bosten even considered the village burgomaster, Johan Frans à Brassard, who lived next door to him, a personal friend. That was about to change.

It was still early morning when midwife Anna Olivier left the house where Hendrick and Sara lodged and walked to the Vaals Catholic church. There Frans Hendrick performed the first mass of the day. The curate knew all about Hendrick and Sara—at least, he knew as much as his brother, for the evening before Easter he had found Father Bosten together with Hendrick in the rectory. On that occasion, the pastor had repeated to his brother what Hendrick had told him about the upbringing of the couple's children, and Hendrick had confirmed it all. Clearly Hendrick had also told the priests, if they did not know already, about his wife's pregnancy. That Tuesday morning, the curate knew that Sara had already gone into labor. So when he had the chance to speak with Anna after mass, he asked, "Is it a boy or a girl?"[7]

"A boy," replied Anna.

"Why haven't you brought it?"

"They won't tell me," but "if I understand the wife correctly, it's going to be baptized Reformed."

"I don't believe it. Mommers came to us and said that we would baptize it." He continued, "You have to speak to Mommers and tell him that he must bring his child here for baptism." Anna returned to the house on the Groene Driesch and conveyed the curate's message.

"Today's shopping day," objected Hendrick. "There's no time for a baptism. Go to the pastor and tell him on my behalf, I'm going in search of godfathers and godmothers." Anna immediately suggested a couple of possibilities: the sexton Buntgens and the tenant of a nearby farmstead, both of them Hendrick's kin. But Hendrick was dismissive: "I don't want them; I'm going to look for others."

In the meantime, someone, probably the curate, told Bosten about the infant's birth. Without delay, the pastor dispatched Martinus Buntgens to summon Hendrick to him. Agnes Korr, mistress of the house where Hendrick and Sara lodged, was at home when Buntgens arrived. Standing on the wagon road in front of her house, the sexton asked whether Hendrick was at home. Answering yes, she called up to Hendrick, who came down from the couple's room and went out to speak with Buntgens. Hendrick then went off somewhere—Agnes did not know where. When he returned a short while later, she overheard intermittent clips of an exchange between Hendrick and his mother-in-law, Anna Gertrud Spaemans, who had come presumably to see and help Sara with the newborn. "What business do you have with the pastor?" asked Anna sharply. From the kitchen below, Agnes heard Hendrick's mother-in-law excoriate him: "You have no business with the pastor!" Sara's family was not about to let Hendrick have his baby baptized Catholic.

Hendrick later denied heeding the pastor's summons. He admitted, though, to speaking to Bosten that morning, supposedly in a chance encounter. The two men met on a field above the pastor's meadow, where according to Hendrick, the pastor imperiously commanded him: "What you agreed with your wife is all null, you must bring me the child, by force, you must take it away from your wife." "Pastor," Hendrick supposedly replied, "the child shall be baptized, it's strong enough, but I shall not take it away from my wife, lest by the commotion she again get sick for fourteen weeks, as happened formerly, and poverty forced me to leave her." This was a reference to the illness Sara had suffered after giving birth the previous time. Predictably, the pastor gave a very different account of the conversation. According to him, Hendrick promised, without any pressure, to bring him the newborn for baptism that afternoon.

Early that evening, Bosten again dispatched Buntgens to Hendrick. Again we have conflicting accounts of the ensuing conversation. According to Hendrick, Buntgens said to him, "Mommers, by order of the pastor you will have your child baptized, and that immediately, by force, this very evening you must bring it, what you agreed is null." Bosten, by contrast, claimed to have instructed Buntgens merely to ask Hendrick why he hadn't sent the child to him that afternoon, as agreed in the morning, and to tell Hendrick that he must bring the child that same evening, as the pastor was ready and waiting to baptize it.

What are we to make of this conflicting testimony? It matters because Bosten was subsequently accused of having used force—not himself directly, but through the instrument of Cunegonde—to try to prevent Hendrick and Sara's baby from being baptized Calvinist. In the course of Bosten's trial, the prosecution cited Hendrick's testimony repeatedly to establish that the accusation was consistent with Bosten's other behavior—that the pastor had a record of inciting others to violence to achieve his goal. It is impossible to corroborate either man's account of their conversation in the morning, since no one else was present. For the evening, though, we have testimony also from Buntgens, who told the judges that he had spoken to Hendrick as follows: "The Pastor has sent me to you again to ask why you have not brought the child for baptism, as you agreed this morning with the Pastor, and [to say that] if you will not come [yourself] to the Pastor, you are to send the child [with someone else] to be baptized, as the [Pastor] says, that he cannot do otherwise than hold you to [your agreement], as it is his duty to see to it that children of Catholic fathers are baptized Catholic." Under questioning, Buntgens denied having used the phrase "by force." He admitted, though, that he did tell Hendrick "that such a contract, by which the children are to be raised in the mother's religion, was null and void and against the rules, and he was not obliged to fulfil it." The sexton claimed to have said this to Hendrick at the pastor's specific instruction.

Although Buntgens was no disinterested witness, it is noteworthy that his account of the evening conversation agrees as much with Hendrick's as it does with Bosten's. Speaking on the pastor's behalf, the sexton did apparently command Hendrick to bring the child to him for baptism. Buntgens did also tell Hendrick that any agreement to have the baby baptized Calvinist was invalid and should not be honored. Hendrick repeated himself considerably in his accounts of the morning and evening conversations, which suggests that he was eliding the two into one. Perhaps, though, he was conveying accurately the gist of the pastor's message, if not in the morning, then at least that evening.

According to Buntgens, Hendrick answered him as follows: "Tell the pastor not to worry, I have made another contract, by virtue of which the children must all go with me, for after all, among the Reformed the father must bring the child for baptism. That I cannot do, [and] after that I'll bring it to the pastor. I would have brought the child to the pastor already, if not for fear that it would affect my wife, who's just given birth, and make her sick, and who would then give me financial support? Plus, various of the

Reformed have been to my home, saying, let the child be baptized in our church, and the Reformed have promised me new clothes and also some furniture. But I shall not do it, and I shall bring the child [to you] for baptism."

Buntgens returned to the rectory and reported "that Hendrick Mommers feared that his wife, who opposed it, might be affected and get sick if he brought the child, and that he was surrounded by his wife's Reformed relatives—he was the only Catholic among them—and that the relatives had also promised him new clothes [and] furniture, [and] that he at present was very poor and so could not do as he wished. Nevertheless, he would bring the child for baptism this evening, when his wife's relatives were gone, or at least would come speak to the pastor early the next morning." This part of Buntgens's account would later be confirmed by the Catholic pastor of Burtscheid, Norbertus Wirtz, who a couple of weeks later summoned Hendrick during a work break to hear his version of events. According to Wirtz, Hendrick told him, too, of pressure from Sara's relatives and offers from them of badly needed goods—bribes, in effect, to let his son be baptized in the Reformed church.

Later that evening, Bosten paid the sexton's father, Andries, a visit. Andries was already in bed when an agitated Bosten knocked on his door.

"Master Andries," said the pastor, "what should I do? I fear that the child [of Hendrick Mommers] will be snatched from me [*ontvoerd*] and baptized in the Reformed church."[8] Mommers, explained the pastor, "was clearly being stopped by one of his wife's Reformed relatives, for he, of his own accord, had promised to send the child to [me] for baptism and not in the Reformed church."

Initially, Andries did not know what advice to give the pastor. He remarked, though, that, being kin to Mommers, he would not like to see his child baptized in the Reformed church. The nub of the problem seemed clear to the two men: at the moment, Mommers dared not do as he wished, "as he was presently alone in his house among the Reformed relatives of his wife." After some consideration, one of the two—neither could subsequently recall which—proposed a solution: they could summon Hendrick's father or another member of his family to come speak with him. This would counterbalance the pressure of his in-laws and impel Hendrick, they hoped, to do "out of respect for his parents or close relatives" as he ought. Whoever proposed the plan, the other warmly embraced it, and Andries offered to go himself the next day to fetch Hendrick's father or some other member of his family if Hendrick failed to bring his baby to the pastor.

What neither Bosten nor Andries nor the midwife, Anna Olivier, knew was that Mathias Erffens had already made arrangements for his grandchild to be baptized in the Vaals Reformed church.

The next morning, Wednesday, 14 April, Anna Olivier was on her way to mass when she saw Hendrick in the road. She asked him what she should tell the pastor regarding the baptism. "I'll go speak to the pastor myself," he answered.[9]

Bosten performed mass that morning, assisted by Andries Buntgens. At the end of the celebration, the pastor retired into the sacristy, where Anna found him together with his brother the curate and Andries. "Do you have the child?" Bosten asked her.[10]

"No, [Mommers] has gone to your house, and if he's not there, then he's gone to the Reformed minister."

"Let him go," Bosten replied. "Baptism is baptism, he can raise the child as he pleases." He continued, "It's one and the same to me, I'm just sorry that I've been had by him."

At this point, Andries repeated the offer he had made to Bosten the previous night: "Sir, shall I fetch him?" (meaning Hendrick's father).

"Yes, I would appreciate that, Master Andries," he replied. "Go bring one of his parents here to speak to their son," and, he continued, "then they can see what he wants to do."

Andries asked Anna where Hendrick's father lived and what his name was. "In Würselen," she replied. She didn't know the name of the house where he resided, but she knew that his name was Hendrick, like his son's.

Bosten then turned to the midwife. Ultimately, it was she who would carry the child to one church or the other. "Anna, take your time, until the relatives from Würselen are here and we hear what the man [Hendrick] wants," he said. "You'll be summoned, [but] you don't know where Hendrick Mommers has gone today, and I don't know either." The curate urged her likewise to make herself scarce until Andries had returned with one of Hendrick's relatives.

But Anna balked: "Sir, if they call for me, I must go."

"Must you then do it so readily?" asked the pastor.

"Yes," she replied, "if I didn't go, they could expel me from the district."

Anna's fear may have been exaggerated, but if she did as the pastor requested, she certainly risked the authorities' revoking her license to practice as midwife. For many years, this pious Catholic who attended mass daily had brought children for baptism to the appropriate church, depending on their parents' faith. Interestingly, it was an aspect of her duties the midwife felt comfortable with. Once long ago Bosten had asked her, "Do you feel no compunction about bringing children to the Reformed church for baptism?"[11] "Why shouldn't I do it?" she had answered defiantly. "I hear no evil there. You [meaning the pastor] say everything in Latin, but in the Reformed church I hear the baptism in German." Anne understood that, in Catholic teaching, Calvinist baptisms were valid, and she appreciated being able to understand the words of the rite. Her unlettered ecumenism, however, put her at odds with those who were less tolerant. The curate Frans Hendrick, for one, tried to shame her. "Anne carries on two shoulders," he once remarked, meaning that Anna was a coward who did whatever was asked of her. "A decent man wouldn't speak that way to me," she retorted.

Andries set off immediately for Würselen. He had no time to lose, for the trip took a good two hours on foot. Once there, he quickly located the house he was seeking, but Hendrick's father was absent: it being a workday, Hendrick senior was laboring in Stolberg. Hendrick's mother had died some years earlier. The only people Andries found at the parental home were a sister-in-law of Hendrick's and, crucially, his twenty-three-year-old sister Cunegonde. Both women, along with one of Cunegonde's brothers, probably lived with the ageing widower. In Cunegonde's case, the arrangement was not a matter of choice, for not only was she unmarried, but she also suffered from some kind of mental disability. What kind is not entirely clear, though we will hear much about it as our story progresses. The villagers of Würselen called Cunegonde a simpleton; today, we would probably say that she had an intellectual or cognitive disability. In some respects, though, she was highly capable, and Andries clearly didn't realize immediately the scope of her problem. Cunegonde and her sister-in-law offered Andries refreshment, serving him bread with butter and cheese, and a glass of beer to wash it down. Andries told them of the birth of Hendrick's child, of their brother's promise to bring the infant for baptism in the Catholic church, of his failure to come at the agreed time, and of the danger that the infant might be baptized in the Reformed church.[12] On the pastor's behalf, he enjoined them, "if they cared at all about the child, they should come quickly to prevent an [unfortunate] outcome."

The two women replied that they cared greatly about the child, and Cunegonde told Andries that her brother had promised she would be the child's godmother. At this point, either Cunegonde offered to go with Andries to Vaals, or Andries demanded that she go with him. He may even have invoked Father Bosten's authority in doing so: in later testimony, Cunegonde would claim that Andries said to her, "The pastor of Vaals . . . sends word that you must come to Vaals to stand as godmother at the baptism of your brother Hendrick's child." If true, Andries was taking liberties with his commission, for it seems almost certain that Father Bosten didn't even know Hendrick had a sister.

Like a character in a fairytale, Cunegonde then dressed for the trip, putting on a red pinafore and red riding hood. The sister-in-law, meanwhile, stepped out of the house briefly and spoke with some people. When she returned, she voiced a concern—tragically well founded, as it turned out—that Cunegone might not be up to the task at hand:

"They say it would be better if I went with him. I fear you will mishandle the affair."

"No, I'm going with him," replied Cunegonde. "My brother promised me that I would be the child's godmother, and I'm going to do it."

"Then see to it that you handle the affair well. If you don't, I'll kill you when you return."

The two travelers arrived back in Vaals around four o'clock in the afternoon, and Andries took Cunegonde straight to the rectory. Leaving her to wait at the gate, Andries went in to find Bosten. Quicker than you could recite three "Our Fathers" (as Bosten later put it), the two men emerged, and Andries introduced the pastor to Cunegonde.

"Who is this?" asked Bosten.[13]

"This is the sister of Hendrick Mommers, who, if the child is baptized by you, is supposed to be godmother."

Now addressing Cunegonde, the pastor said, "Your brother came to me just a little while ago and said that he would send me his child for baptism in a half-hour." Bosten ordered Andries to show Cunegonde the way, by a shortcut through his own meadow, to the house on the Groene Driesch; there she would find her brother and be able to speak with him. Only a few minutes after the two set off, though, Bosten received startling news from an acquaintance, a bricklayer named De Theun who had come to drink a beer with him: "Pastor, a lot of Reformed people have gone to the Reformed church with a Reformed child. It's already so long ago that the child will already have been baptized." All the flummoxed pastor could reply was, "That must be Hendrick Mommers' child." And indeed it was.

The previous day, Mathias Erffens had approached Pferdmenges with the request that the minister baptize his newborn grandson. As Pferdmenges later recounted: "On the thirteenth of April of this current year, Mathias Erffens came to me in the morning and informed me that his daughter, the wife of Henricus Mommers, had given birth to a son, and that Henricus Mommers, the father of the child, had come to him and asked him as father-in-law to make arrangements for the child to be baptized by a Reformed preacher—the sooner the better, as the [Catholic] pastor of Vaals would not leave him in peace and wished to baptize the child."[14] Mathias would always claim to have acted at Hendrick's request, and Hendrick himself gave inconsistent testimony on this point. In any event, Hendrick certainly never informed Bosten of a decision to baptize his child in the Reformed church. To the contrary, that Wednesday afternoon, just before his sister arrived in Vaals, Hendrick had again promised to send the child to Bosten for baptism, and indeed had pledged to do so imminently. If Norbertus Wirtz is to be believed, Hendrick was drunk. Bolstered by some liquid courage, he had gone to Bosten and said to him: "Look everyone, there's the preacher (pointing), but I did not call for the preacher to baptize the child. I shall see what happens. They say that, as father, I must be present at the baptism, and without me they won't baptize it. But the devil take me if I'm going to go there. I've expressly had something stronger to drink today, and I'm going to have it out with those people. I'm going to protest what they're doing, and bring the child to you, my pastor, for baptism immediately."[15] Perhaps, then, the course of events that afternoon took Hendrick, too, by surprise. Contrary to his belief, it was not strictly required, only conventional, among the Reformed for fathers (and never mothers, who remained in confinement after birth) to attend the baptism of their children.

By the time the bricklayer informed Bosten of what was happening, the infant had been in the Reformed church a considerable time. Anna Olivier had delayed the proceedings as long as she could— so long that Pferdmenges had sent someone to inquire what was holding things up. The midwife, it seemed, could not be found. Eventually, though, with the minister and others waiting impatiently inside the church, she had brought them Hendrick and Sara's baby.

Running out into his meadow, Bosten called to Andries and Cunegonde, telling them to return. When they did, he again addressed Cunegonde. What he said to her at that moment is critical, for on it would turn much of the prosecution's case in the pastor's trial. Both the prosecution and defense would return repeatedly to this brief exchange, so not only do we have conflicting accounts of it from the two sides, but the individuals involved gave different versions of their accounts during their multiple testimonies. By his own account, Bosten said the following, or something very similar, to Cunegonde: "It's too late. The child, I've been told, has already been baptized in the Reformed church." He continued, "There's no point in your going to your brother's house, for he

53

must be at the baptism of his child. . . . If you want to speak to your brother, you must go to the churchyard. There you'll find [him], and see what has happened." During the trial, Cunegonde gave a starkly different account. According to her, Bosten commanded her: "The child is already in the beggars' [that is, the Reformed] church to be baptized. Young lady, you must go get it out of there. Then bring it to me, and we'll take it to the Catholic church to baptize it." "Sir," replied Cunegonde, "I've never been here before in my life. I don't know where the church is." By way of reply, Bosten turned to Andries Buntgens: "Master Andries, go with her to the churchyard."[16]

From his house next door, Johan Frans à Brassard watched as the elderly Andries conducted Cunegonde (though he did not know her name at the time) the short distance up the road from Bosten's rectory to the Vaals churchyard (fig. 7). He then saw Cunegonde walk straight to the door of the Reformed church, while Andries headed in the direction of the Catholic church.

Cunegonde found a small group of people in the Reformed church when she entered it.[17] There was Minister Pferdmenges; midwife Anna Olivier; elder Peter Schmits; deacon Stephan Schmalhausen and his father, Henricus, a local magistrate; Mathias Erffens, who was to be the child's godfather; Johanna Renotte, the sister of his deceased first wife, who was to be its godmother; the baby itself; and perhaps a few others. They were gathered at the northern end of the church, some sitting, others standing around a table upon which sat a small portable basin, the kind Calvinists used for baptisms in preference to a permanent font (figs. 8, 9). By coincidence, the Calvinists who worshiped in Vaals had decided only a few months earlier to purchase a fine new basin made of gilded silver. They were probably still using the old one, though, that April day. When Cunegonde burst in, Johanna was holding the infant above the basin and Pferdmenges was sprinkling its head with water, or

7. From Father Bosten's rectory to the Vaals churchyard. This eighteenth-century drawing shows the view from the Vaals-Aachen border toward the center of Vaals. In the left foreground is the Catholic rectory, and behind it is the Walloon church. Running from center foreground to background is the main road from Aachen to Vaals. It ends at the Vaals churchyard, where a couple of coaches (presumably belonging to Protestant churchgoers) are parked. In the center background are the medieval church tower and some of the attached church buildings.

had just done so: it was the climactic moment of the ritual. Startled eyes turned immediately to the intruder, who headed straight for the infant. Rising from his seat, Stephan Schmalhausen tried to hold Cunegonde back. "Where do you think you're going, woman, where?" he asked. Cunegonde gave no answer, but shoved the

8. Interior of the Vaals Reformed church. View toward the north showing where Hendrick and Sara's baby would have been baptized, at a table below the pulpit. On the left, a *herenbank* for church officers; on the right, one of the entrances to the church.

deacon in the chest so hard he almost fell backward onto the floor. She rushed to the table and grabbed the baby with both hands. As Johanna held fast to the baby's legs, the two women—the Calvinist godmother and the would-be Catholic godmother—began a dangerous tug-of-war. At that point, one of the men seized Cunegonde by the arms and broke her grip on the baby.

An astonished Pferdmenges addressed Cunegonde: "I pray you, for God's sake, leave the church. Think where you are, what you are doing, and what you have already done. Leave us in peace to administer the holy sacrament." Cunegonde just stood silently.

9. Baptismal basin purchased in 1762 by the congregations that worshiped together in the Vaals Reformed church. Reformed Protestants used a basin of this sort in preference to a font. Made in 1736 of gilded silver, the basin is inscribed "Tauff = Becken zum dienst der sich in der reformirten Kirche zu Vaels versammelnden Gemeinen 1762" (Baptismal basin for use by the congregations that meet in the Reformed church in Vaals, 1762). It now belongs to the Nederlandse Hervormde Gemeente of Gulpen-Vaals.

Anna Olivier then spoke up: "I asked Mommers, the child's father, in which church the child should be brought for baptism, and received as answer: in the Reformed church."

"If the father," asked Pferdmenges, "arranged for me to be asked to baptize the child, and you brought it to me at the father's order, then why such a commotion?"

"I don't know," answered Anna. "Baptism is baptism, it can be administered by you or by us." She turned to Cunegonde:

"Ach, you wretched woman! What have you done on this soil, where the Reformed are masters?"

Cunegonde still said not a word. Then, after a moment's pause, she lunged furiously again for the baby. This time she was driven back from the table. Henricus Schmalhausen sent a messenger to fetch armed guards. Then he closed the door of the church and, in the name of the law, declared the young woman under arrest. As she realized her situation and the certainty of punishment, Cunegonde began to weep.

CHAPTER THREE

On This Soil

About a hundred and twenty yards from the Vaals Reformed church, on the old road toward Aachen, stands a weathered, grayish blue stone (fig. 10). In size and shape it resembles a miniature grave marker. Though worn, an eagle, the heraldic symbol of Aachen, can still be made out chiseled on its face. Placed on this spot by the city's magistrates in the sixteenth century, the stone once marked the boundary of Aachen's territory, the point where the city's sovereign authority ended and the Lands of Overmaas began. Cunegonde Mommers passed it with Andries Buntgens on her way from Würselen to Vaals. When she did, she left her homeland and set foot on foreign soil, where people of a different, hostile faith ruled.

Unlike Catholic Aachen, the Dutch Republic was a Calvinist polity. However varied the beliefs were of its citizens and however much toleration they enjoyed, Calvinism was the Republic's official creed and the (Calvinist) Reformed Church its official church. This remained true in the eighteenth century, despite the growing willingness of Dutch authorities to grant other churches

10. Boundary stone along the road between Vaals and Aachen, marking the border between the Reich of Aachen and the Land of 's-Hertogenrade. The stone is inscribed with an eagle, Aachen's coat of arms.

special privileges on an ad hoc basis. Alone of all clergy, Reformed ministers received salaries from government and served as chaplains to state institutions. Only they shared with magistrates the authority to join couples in matrimony. Only Reformed deacons received public funds to succor the poor. Only Reformed schoolmasters could teach in public schools. The law did not require anyone to belong to the Reformed Church or attend its services. But it did exclude Catholics and other Protestants from most government offices, and it required everyone to defer to the Church's official status as the institutional embodiment of the "true" Christian faith. Catholics in Overmaas and other Generality Lands were pointedly warned not to "disturb, hinder, abuse, or treat insolently by word or deed" the Reformed ministers in the performance of their duties or "the good people of the [true] religion" in their worship.[1]

Cunegonde broke this law flagrantly and violently. In disrupting the administration of a Reformed sacrament, she committed what amounted to sacrilege. In trying to run off with Hendrick and Sara's baby, she was also guilty of attempted kidnapping. For so outrageous an act, the magistrates of Vaals would inevitably insist on punishing her severely. Did she not grasp this? Did she really imagine she could wrest the baby from a whole group of people and run off with it without being caught? How, after a moment for reflection, could she have lunged for little Mathias Hendrick (for so the baby was named) a second time, when the impossibility of success should by then have been crystal clear? Perhaps she acted on impulse, gripped by religious fervor and her own passions. Perhaps, as she claimed, she was obeying a command. Either way, Cunegonde's reckless, futile behavior demonstrated more than a normal degree of folly. It raised questions about her capacity to assess a situation and even her sanity. These questions would be explored in the criminal investigation that followed and would be debated at length in Father Bosten's trial.

There is an additional factor, though, that helps explain Cunegonde's behavior: if she had committed the same act anywhere in the Reich of Aachen, she would never have been prosecuted. It would have been the Reformed minister, Pferdmenges, who was guilty of a crime in performing a baptism, and Cunegonde would probably have been treated as a heroine for attempting to rescue Hendrick and Sara's child from him. Just a short distance away, on the other side of the border, the law was completely different. By her own account, Cunegonde had never crossed that border before; in all likelihood she had never been anywhere in the Republic. This does not mean Cunegonde was ignorant—that she did not know Vaals belonged to the Dutch or that her actions were illegal there. In a moment of high tension, though, it may have caused the poor, disabled young woman considerable confusion that in this strange place, all the rules of engagement between Catholics and Protestants were different from those she knew. Her past experience of a mighty Catholic establishment and a beleaguered Protestant minority may have given her a sense of power and impunity that, under the circumstances, was wholly misplaced.

If so, it was a sense she shared with many of her countrymen and -women. For as unique as it was, Cunegonde's attempted baby-snatching fit a pattern: it involved a Catholic from the territory of Aachen committing an act of violence against Protestant worship and worshipers in Vaals. Thanks to its location, Vaals was the place where the fervor of intolerant Catholic populations collided with the presence of a Protestant state. Surrounded as it was by Aachen to the east, the Habsburg Duchy of Limburg to the south, and the County of Wittem to the north and west, Vaals formed an outpost not just of the Republic but of Protestantism. It symbolized a religion hated and feared by Catholics in neighboring territories, above all by the famously devout, notoriously turbulent people of Aachen. Location gave Vaals a unique religious identity and role. In the process, it made the village a focal point for Protestant-Catholic conflict.

The borders dividing Vaals from its neighbors cast a long shadow. Their influence extended to a distance of about four hours' travel from the village, encompassing a region that included the Lands of Overmaas, Aachen and its Reich, and parts of Limburg, Liège, and Jülich. Within this broad zone, the proximity of political borders affected not just religious but also economic, social, and cultural life, whose threads were of course tightly interwoven. The entire zone thus had the character of a borderland.[2] Incredibly intricate and in some respects quite unlike modern ones, the borders dividing the Dutch Republic from its Catholic neighbors offer a key to understanding many aspects of our story.

Ostensibly, the border between Vaals and Aachen's Reich was clear enough. Back in the late Middle Ages, the magistrates of Aachen had built a wall around their territory. It consisted of an earthen embankment topped by a thick hedge of bushes and trees, with a ditch running parallel just outside it. It had little value as a defensive fortification, but it kept casual intruders out and gave the magistrates some control over their perimeter. Along each of the roads radiating outward from the city was an opening in the wall, where entrance and egress was controlled by a movable barrier. Such a barrier stood on the road to Vaals, which, from Aachen's perspective, was the main road westward toward Maastricht and the rest of the Republic. Every year in May, the burgomasters of Aachen led a troop of soldiers and officials in an inspection tour around the circumference of their territory. The annual Landritt had a practical purpose, to ensure that wall and barriers were properly maintained, but it was also a symbolic act of possession, asserting power over a defined space.[3] All of this demonstrated a precocious sense of territoriality—a sense, developed by most European rulers only in the seventeenth and eighteenth centuries, that a state corresponded to a clearly delineated geographic area.

The reality was far more complex. In the first place, Aachen's embankment wall did not run along the very edge of the territory the city claimed. Rather, it ran inside the edge. To define the limits of their jurisdiction, city magistrates placed boundary stones like the one that still stands along the old road between Aachen and Vaals. It was positioned some sixteen feet beyond the barrier. More than a hundred such stones were dotted around the territory of Aachen, beyond the wall, but they were not positioned so as to establish anything resembling a line. Nor was their meaning always agreed: neighbors sometimes claimed land between the stones and the wall as belonging to them, and Aachen sometimes claimed land beyond the stones. Thus in 1663 a dispute erupted between Aachen and the Republic over the precise location of the border in Vaals. Citing ancient charters and oral tradition, the city claimed that its "jurisdiction and territorial superiority" extended to some fifty houses in the village and, crucially, to the Vaals parish church. The Dutch based their counterclaims on the fact that the rulers of Overmaas, not Aachen, had always exercised civil and criminal jurisdiction over people and houses in the contested area, right up to the embankment and the barrier. To fortify their argument, they had a surveyor draw a "figurative map" (fig. 11) that showed the embankment, the barrier, and the adjacent boundary stone, which Aachen itself had placed there. Aachen's magistrates had to concede the point. Henceforth, the stone would mark an undisputed point where the Vaalserquartier of the Reich ended and the Dutch district of Vaals (which included the villages of Holset and Vijlen) began.[4]

The Dutch Republic never marked the limits of its territory as did Aachen. True, by the mid-eighteenth century, it had placed a number of stones or posts in the Lands of Overmaas, mostly along roads, where they informed incoming travelers that they were coming under the Republic's authority and laws. Such markers remained exceptional, though, and none of the roads into Vaals seem

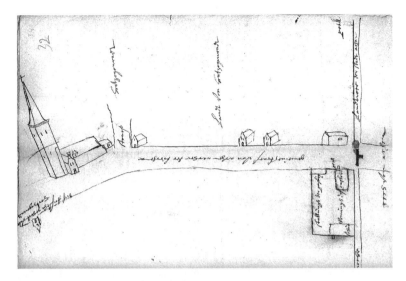

11. "Figurative map" drawn in 1663 during a dispute over the location of the border. From left to right, it shows the Vaals parish church of St. Paul, the road leading from Vaals to Aachen with a few houses along it, the Catholic rectory (with the boundary stone shown in fig. 10 in front of it), and the movable barrier that blocked the road, with Aachen's defensive embankment running parallel to the barrier in both directions.

to have had them. Segments of the border around Vaals ran along waterways, namely the Senserbach and the river Geul (fig. 12). But despite the representational clarity of the maps that the Dutch were so good at making, much of the border had no precise geographic coordinates on the ground. Indeed, some parts of it were inherently ambiguous, as where the border between Vaals and Limburg ran through thick woods. Aachen placed a boundary marker near the spot that we today call the Three Countries Point, but that was because a road ran into its territory there. The spot doesn't seem to have had any special significance, and it certainly didn't attract visitors.[5]

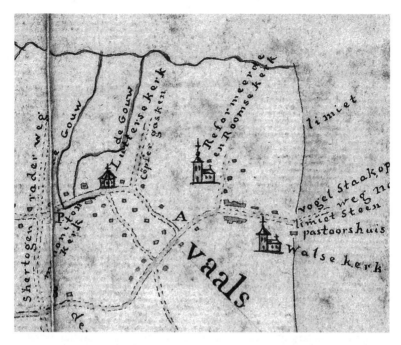

12. Anatomy of a village. Map from 1766 showing the center of Vaals, including its five churches, the Catholic rectory, and the border with Aachen. Small squares mark the location of houses.

That is because territory was not fetishized then as it was later, in the modern era. Indeed, until sometime in the eighteenth century, territory was not the primary means of defining the extent of a state. As the terms of the dispute between the Republic and Aachen reveal, two such modes coexisted in tension with each other. One defined a state spatially as extending over a certain territory; the other defined it in terms of "jurisdiction," that is, as a group of communities over which its rulers held certain powers and prerogatives. Whatever was "dependent" on a community or "attached" to it—for example, a hamlet associated with a village—

fell under the same jurisdiction, regardless of location. Neither the communities nor their dependencies had to be physically contiguous. On the contrary, in an extreme case like Dutch Overmaas, they could be "scattered like peppercorns across the map."[6]

It was in 1632 that the Dutch first managed, by military conquest, to seize from the Habsburgs some parts of the Lands of Overmaas, along with the strategic fortress city of Maastricht. In 1648, by the famous Peace of Westphalia, the two parties agreed to partition Overmaas, and in 1661 they finally signed a Partition Treaty. In their negotiations, the Dutch favored the territorial principle: they proposed taking the Land of Valkenburg and leaving the Lands of Dalhem and 's-Hertogenrade to the Habsburgs. This plan would have provided the Dutch with a sizable, cohesive territory adjacent to Maastricht—a hinterland whose fertile soil could feed the city's burghers and garrison. The devoutly Catholic Philip IV, however, insisted on partitioning each of the three Lands, community by community. This enabled him to retain under his sovereignty, and thus to protect, several monastic institutions and the manors of many Catholic nobles. Typical for the age, the 1661 treaty specified the extent of Dutch and Habsburg rule by enumerating, one by one, the districts, parishes, seigneuries, villages, and other units that fell under the jurisdiction of each party. From 's-Hertogenrade, for example, the Dutch got the district of Vaals, which formed a detached enclave, plus two other districts, which allowed the Republic to control the trade route between Maastricht and Aachen; the Habsburgs got a set of districts that included the Augustinian abbey of Kloosterrade. The Dutch got four separate chunks of Dalhem, the Habsburgs two. Scattered among these peppercorns were also entities, like the County of Wittem, that belonged to neither the Dutch nor the Habsburgs. The Lands of Overmaas were already fragmented in the Middle Ages, but the Dutch and the Habsburgs went a big step further, breaking them up into bite-size pieces (fig. 13).[7]

13. Fragmented territories. Eighteenth-century map showing the portions of the Lands of Overmaas held by the Habsburgs and the Dutch (the map has been altered so that the Dutch portions are shaded). The map also shows the surrounding territories: the Duchy of Limburg to the south, the Bishopric of Liège to the west and southwest, Aachen to the east, and the Duchy of Jülich to the east and northeast. The County of Wittem and other autonomous territories of the Holy Roman Empire are interspersed.

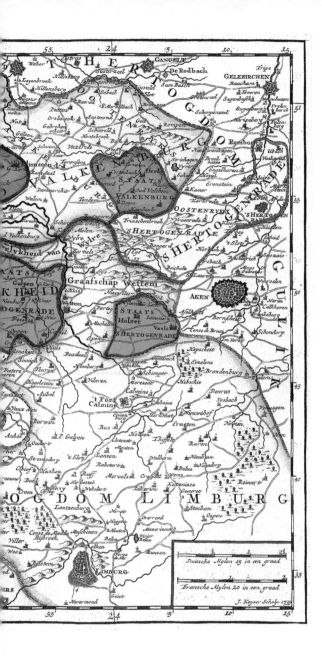

This morselization was an extreme version of a common state of affairs in the early modern era, especially in the lands of central Europe. A heritage of feudalism, the principle of jurisdiction gave birth to a vast number of tiny states as well as to larger ones with irregular shapes and scattered parts. Aachen, for example, with its diminutive Reich, was one of more than fifty imperial cities in the Holy Roman Empire that constituted a sovereign polity, recognizing no lord above it other than a distant emperor. The dukes of Jülich, the regional heavyweights in that part of the empire, found Aachen's autonomy extremely irksome and did what they could to undermine it.[8] In turn, Aachen had to suffer Burtscheid, an autonomous town just a fifteen-minute walk from the city gates. Burtscheid fell under the sovereign rule of the Cistercian abbey that rose on a hill at its center and enjoyed the same "imperial free" status as did the city.

Fragmentation and small size greatly reduced the power of many early modern states. The morselization of the Lands of Overmaas had similar, far-reaching consequences. So severely did it undermine the effective power of both Dutch and Habsburg authorities that the region became notorious for disorder and lawlessness. Vagabonds, gypsies, military deserters, criminals: with foreign soil never more than half an hour away, they needed to evade law enforcement officers for only a short distance to escape their clutches. This problem reached epidemic proportions in the eighteenth century, when the Lands of Overmaas were plagued by large, organized bands of robbers known as Goat Riders.[9] It required interstate diplomacy to deny them refuge—or to accomplish something as mundane as improving a road. Magistrates who presided over such small jurisdictions also had very limited resources. Those of Vaals, for example, had no courthouse or jail at their disposal, at least not at the beginning of our story. Taxpaying landholders were neither numerous nor rich enough to shoulder heavy expenses.

This effect was compounded by the rural character of the Lands, which provided no obvious place for the forces of law and order to concentrate. Maastricht to the west functioned as de facto capital of Dutch Overmaas, and there one could find government officials, attorneys, troops, and jail facilities. Yet not even Maastricht was fully under Dutch control, since the States General were forced to share sovereignty over it with the bishop of Liège. Besides, it was a small city with a population of only eleven thousand, and it lay a full five hours' travel from Vaals.

Aachen, by comparison, had twenty-seven thousand inhabitants and was practically next door. That is where people from Vaals went to consult a doctor, have a notary draw up a contract, or purchase, say, a clock or a gun. Irrespective of state borders, Aachen functioned as metropolis for all the villages in its vicinity, providing their inhabitants with a wide range of amenities. This fact points us to another characteristic of early modern borderlands: the intimate ties that joined communities belonging to different states. All kinds of activities and relationships straddled the political borders, requiring people to cross borders routinely in the conduct of their daily lives. Some people, for example, lived in one state but worked in another—like the sexton Martinus Buntgens, who lived in Aachen's Reich but served the Vaals parish church. This was an entirely natural arrangement given that the parish of Vaals included Aachen's Vaalserquartier, where a third of its members lived. Father Bosten and his brother commuted between states even more frequently, for the rectory where they resided actually straddled the border physically: situated right behind our familiar marker stone on the Vaals-Aachen road, the compound had its entrance on Dutch territory while most the house within it stood on Aachen's soil. When Dutch authorities began to blame Bosten for Cunegonde's crime, they were very unhappy to realize that the pastor could escape their jurisdiction merely by retreating to his bedroom.

Similarly, individuals and institutions in one state commonly held powers and properties in neighboring states. Consider, for example, the mighty canons of the Aachen Minster, the most important church in the city. They owned extensive estates in Dutch Overmaas and wielded a powerful vote at the annual meetings of the Vaals district taxpayers.[10] As patrons of the Vaals parish church and recipients of the parish tithe, they in effect appointed the Catholic pastor of Vaals. As seigneurial lords, they even appointed the sheriff of one Dutch village. In turn, though, the canons were subordinate to the bishop of Liège. This foreign prince, who held sovereign sway over the principality of Liège to the southwest, exercised episcopal jurisdiction over a much wider area that extended all the way to Aachen. All these relationships and overlaps undercut the territorial integrity of states. They made it very difficult for political authorities to exert effective control over their share of the borderland.

In some respects, then, life in the region of Vaals went on with scant regard to political borders. In other respects, though, the borders had a profound impact, recasting basic patterns of human activity. A good example of this dual dynamic is offered by the cloth industry.

In the eighteenth century, the region of Vaals was one of the heartlands of this, the largest and most important of all European industries. A dense network of business relationships connected producers of woolen cloth across a wide area from Aachen, via Burtscheid and Vaals, to Monschau in Jülich, Verviers in Liège, and Eupen in Limburg. From spinning and weaving to bleaching or dying, different phases of production were handled by specialists often based in different locales. The process was organized by merchants who imported the raw wool, mostly from Spain, and exported the finished product. Merchants, master craftsmen, and laborers all moved freely between locales and were not loath to change homes, as Sara's father, Mathias, did, when it met their interests. For a time, in the 1730s, Mathias was in fact on the cutting edge of economic development. Based at the time in Vaals, he and his employees produced cloth for sale to merchants in Aachen. In so doing, they undercut Aachen's own local craftsmen, who operated under the rules and restrictions set by the city's cloth guild and consequently charged higher prices. Mathias was one of many cloth producers who, over more than a century, clashed with the Aachen guild as it conducted a rearguard action to prevent the diffusion of cloth manufacturing across the region. To thwart Mathias and others like him, the guild persuaded Aachen's magistrates in 1737 to ban the "putting out" of cloth production. In the long run, though, the restrictions championed by the guild backfired, as they encouraged more and more of the industry to locate outside Aachen and its Reich.[11] Thanks to the political border that placed it just beyond the city's control, Vaals was a prime beneficiary of this development, and it won the ultimate prize in 1761 when the Aachen merchant Johann Arnold von Clermont (fig. 14) chose the village as the site for a new kind of industrial organization, one that would enable him to direct more closely all the phases of cloth production. After four years of construction, Von Clermont opened one of the earliest factories on the Continent in Vaals (fig. 15). He was enticed to the village partly by a Dutch official, the lieutenant governor of the Land of 's-Hertogenrade. This official convinced the Vaals magistrates to curtail the right of Von Clermont's workers to strike or protest. He also convinced the Dutch States General to waive a restriction on the sale of homes. As a result, Vaals took on the air of a boomtown and was soon transformed, physically as well as socially. It grew further when a manufacturer from Burtscheid followed Von Clermont's example in 1777, establishing a needle factory.

It's a familiar story to us in the twenty-first century: companies "offshoring" work to countries where labor is cheaper and less protected, governments vying to attract enterprises that will generate

14. Johann Arnold von Clermont (1728–95). Portrait by unknown artist, second half of eighteenth century.

employment and prosperity. Long before he moved his business to Vaals, though, Von Clermont had become familiar with the village and the advantages afforded by its location. For it was where he, as a Lutheran, had been going for decades to attend church. Just as many people in the region crossed borders in pursuit of their livelihoods, so they did the same in order to worship. And just as the borders played a key role in configuring economic activity, so they shaped religious life for both Catholics and Protestants.

To the north, in the heartland of the Dutch Republic, Catholics led a stunted religious life. To be sure, except for their exclusion from government office, they generally enjoyed full citizenship and could conduct most aspects of their lives as Calvinists did. But when it came to the exercise of their faith, Catholics, like other non-Calvinists, faced sharp restrictions. Officially, the only religious

15. Von Clermont's textile factory in Vaals. Constructed in 1761–64, it is known as the Stammhaus or Von Clermonthuis and is now used as town hall. Originally it formed a complete square with four sides and interior courtyard.

right they enjoyed was freedom of conscience. That meant they could believe as they pleased and were never coerced into attending Reformed services. But it did not mean they had a right to worship God as their faith prescribed. Only privately, within the confines of their homes, could they pray, meditate, and pursue other "domestic devotions." Strictly speaking, it was illegal for them to gather as congregations, and priests were forbidden to celebrate mass or administer sacraments. In reality, Catholics and other non-Calvinists were allowed to operate quasi-clandestine churches known as *schuilkerken*. These were mostly houses whose exteriors were left unchanged but whose interiors were adapted for use as places of worship. Their disguise was manifestly a pretense: crowds numbering in the hundreds thronged into some of these churches on a regular schedule, and music could sometimes be heard emanating from them, floating across the canals. Still, non-Calvinists had to maintain a fiction that these buildings were merely the secular structures they appeared to be. As long as they did so, they were usually left in peace. Toleration meant, in most parts of the Republic, that government officials—and ordinary Calvinists—turned a blind eye to what was going on. It was a form of connivance. It left Catholics able to worship discreetly, privately, behind closed doors.[12]

Not so in Dutch Overmaas. Here a religious settlement prevailed that was unique in the Republic, though familiar in certain other parts of Europe. It was called Simultaneum: joint use of the medieval parish churches by two religious groups. This remarkable arrangement was a product of geography and political calculation. When Stadholder Frederick Hendrick in 1632 led the Dutch army southward up the river Maas, he and the States General back in The Hague hoped that his early conquests would mark the beginning of a long string of victories. They imagined that the inhabitants of Brabant, Flanders, and the other southern provinces of the Netherlands yearned to cast off the oppressive yoke of their Habsburg masters and join their northern cousins in freedom. The Dutch recognized, though, that Catholicism was popular in the south and that the Counter-Reformation had made headway there; southerners would hardly welcome the Dutch army if its arrival meant the suppression, in any way, of their religion. Stadholder and States therefore extended a very special offer: if the southerners rose up in rebellion, they would be allowed to retain "the public exercise of the Roman Catholic religion." They could keep their churches and institutions, rites and clergy. All they would have to do is provide suitable places for Calvinists to worship as well. In the event, the offer did not suffice. Few southerners greeted the Dutch as liberators, and having seized first Upper Gelderland, then Maastricht and the Lands of Overmaas, Frederick Hendrick's army got only as far as Limburg before it was repulsed. To the very end of the Old Regime, most of the southern provinces remained under the Habsburgs—first the Spanish branch of the family, then from 1713 the Austrian one. In the lands they conquered and held, though, the Dutch kept their word, allowing Catholics as well as Calvinists to worship publicly.

Farther north, Dutch Calvinists enjoyed exclusive use of the old parish churches, and it was one of the chief privileges of the Reformed Church that it alone could hold fully public services, announced by the ringing of bells and conducted in buildings that looked unmistakably like churches. By contrast, in Dutch Overmaas the parish church buildings were either shared or, if there was no Calvinist congregation in a locale, simply left to the Catholics. This situation continued until the Dutch and Spanish signed their Partition Treaty in 1661, settling the status of Overmaas. Because the Spanish had suppressed Calvinist worship throughout their portion of the Lands, the Dutch now felt obliged to end public Catholic worship in theirs. For about a decade, Calvinists in Dutch Overmaas enjoyed the same monopoly of public worship as did their coreligionists farther north. But then in 1672 the tables were turned when the French army under Louis XIV invaded the Republic. Louis ejected the Calvinist congregations from all the shared churches in Overmaas, restoring the churches to the Catholics for their exclusive use. His forces finally departed in 1678. Remarkably, though, Dutch authorities did not seize this opportunity to restore the immediate status quo ante. Instead, they reverted to their original commitment to allow public Catholic worship. Initially they had made that commitment for its demonstration value, to make their rule more appealing to their southern neighbors. Now they honored it partly in response to diplomatic pressure, partly also because, had they again suppressed Catholic worship, the Catholic inhabitants of Overmaas would probably have erupted in anger. Crucially, though, they also found that they could afford to honor their commitment. The reason was simple. Viewed from Holland, Dutch Overmaas was a remote patchwork of tiny territories separate from the rest of the Republic. It was too small, too distant, too marginal to matter greatly. Special concessions for Catholics there (and in Maastricht, where Catholics similarly enjoyed the right to worship publicly) did not set any potent precedent or undermine religious arrangements farther north. Thus, even as they denied any legal obligation to do so, the Dutch States General allowed public Catholic worship in Overmaas to be restored. For the next hundred years and more, they permitted it to continue.[13]

Thanks to the location and prehistory of Dutch Overmaas as part of the Catholic south, few Calvinists ever lived there. When a Catholic Church official inspected the area in 1658, he found in most villages not a single "heretic." Over the following decades, Dutch rule encouraged Calvinist immigration as well as conversions, and eventually Calvinist congregations would form in fourteen out of thirty-two communities. Most, though, were tiny. Vaals was the exception that proved the rule. When Dutch authorities in 1649 organized Calvinist worship in Vaals, the village had at most just a handful of Calvinist inhabitants.[14] Seventy years later, the Calvinist congregation of Vaals still counted only ten or eleven members who resided in the village. Even if one includes the children of members and people who attended services without holding full membership, the number of Calvinists living in Vaals remained small.[15] Despite this fact, from the moment of its establishment the Vaals congregation always numbered in the hundreds. In all of Dutch Overmaas, only in Vaals did the number of Calvinist worshipers roughly match the number of Catholic ones. The large majority of them, though, were visiting foreigners.

It was for Calvinists living in neighboring Catholic states that the Dutch government in 1649 forced the Catholics of Vaals to share use of their parish church. These Calvinists performed a kind of reverse commute, traveling to Vaals on Sundays in order to attend services there. German-speakers had a special term for such travel: *Auslaufen*, which literally meant "walking out." In fact, they made their way by every means of transport available: foot, horseback, coach, carriage, wagon, cart. The term, though, referred to the general phenomenon of religious dissenters who lived in one state traveling to attend services in another where their worship was legal, or at least tolerated. The practice had existed since the sixteenth century, when the issue first arose in large parts of Europe whether communities with an official religion could accommodate dissent. Many rulers and ordinary, conforming Christians—many more than often recognized—were prepared, if grudgingly, to allow dissenters to live quietly in their midst. But far fewer were willing to stand by idly if confronted by any public manifestation of dissenting worship. The question then arose, What modus vivendi would enable dissenters to practice their faith while respecting the sensibilities of the orthodox? One answer was to allow dissenters to worship privately in quasi-clandestine churches, as they did in the Dutch Republic. Another was to allow them to go exercise their religion somewhere else, beyond the borders of the community. If dissenters traveled to another state, neither rulers nor people had to see their worship nor did they bear responsibility for it.[16]

Auslaufen was one of the most common arrangements in early modern Europe for the accommodation of religious dissent. From any perspective, it was far from perfect. It subjected dissenters to all the rigors of early modern travel. Foul weather and bad roads could prevent all but the healthy and strong from undertaking it, and the number of people performing Auslaufen invariably dipped in winter. As for the orthodox, it may have spared them the sight of dissenting churches and rituals, but they still had to confront troops of dissenters coming and going on a regular schedule for well-known purposes. The biggest limitation of Auslaufen, however, was practical: if dissenters were going to rely on it for weekly worship, they had to be able to travel to another state and return home the same day. Hence it was possible only if the community where they lived was located near the border of a state with a different official religion. The smaller and more fragmented states were, the more easily dissenters could perform Auslaufen. That is why the practice was so widespread in parts of the Holy Roman Empire and why it was so well suited to the Lands of Overmaas. For there was no place in Dutch Overmaas from which Catholics could not, by traveling less than two hours, reach a Catholic church or chapel on Habsburg soil, and conversely no place in Habsburg Overmaas from which Calvinists could not reach a place of worship on Dutch soil in an equal time. For most the trip was much shorter. Dutch authorities knew it would be thus when they agreed in 1661 to the partition settlement with the Habsburgs, and the fact did not displease them. To the contrary, once they conceded the piecemeal partition of all three Lands, they made a point of ensuring that religious dissenters on both sides of the border would find their religious needs conveniently accommodated. They made it a high priority to retain under their sovereignty communities that were reachable by Calvinists from other territories. For the benefit of their coreligionists in Liège, Limburg, and neighboring parts of the empire, the Dutch held on to three strategically located villages: Eijsden to the southwest, Olne to the south, and Vaals to the southeast. Surrounded by foreign soil, these enclaves served as religious outposts, islands of Calvinism in a Catholic sea.[17]

The Calvinists who went to church in Vaals came mostly from Aachen, Burtscheid, and Eupen.[18] Those from Eupen, in Limburg, had the longest trip to make: to Vaals and back was four hours each way for them. Such a trek pushed the outer limits of Auslaufen; only a few hardy souls had the commitment and endurance to make it week after week. Over the eighteenth century, though, their ranks grew as Eupen burgeoned into a major textile center specializing in the dyeing of fine cloth. Almost everyone in the industry there was Calvinist. Some had migrated from France after Louis XIV declared Calvinism illegal, revoking in 1685 the Edict of Nantes. Others had migrated from Aachen to escape the city's guild restrictions. Some Calvinist families, such as the Baumheuers and Fremereys, who ran major textile concerns, developed branches in both Eupen and Aachen, and traffic between the two places was intense.

By far the largest contingent of Calvinists lived in Aachen. Numbering in the hundreds, this group was the surviving remnant of a massive community that once constituted, together with Lutherans, a majority of the city's population. Over the seventeenth century the size of this community was greatly reduced by Aachen's economic decline, by fires that destroyed large parts of the city, and above all by fierce persecution. In 1648, though, the Peace of Westphalia guaranteed the right of religious dissenters throughout the Holy Roman Empire to live in their communities—and to perform Auslaufen.[19] Thanks to the peace, Aachen's Protestants could no longer be driven into exile, and even if they were still forbidden to worship in their own community, they could not legally be hindered from attending services elsewhere. This is what prompted Dutch authorities the next year to establish Calvinist worship in Vaals. To support their coreligionists in Aachen, they appointed a minister and agreed to pay his salary. This minister would henceforth live with his flock in Aachen, where he could provide pastoral care only privately, and travel with them to Vaals, where he preached and administered the sacraments.

Though it practically nestled under Aachen's walls, Burtscheid offered Protestants a more hospitable residence. The abbesses who ruled it were never as intolerant as Aachen's magistrates, and ironically, their religious calling even worked in Protestants' favor. Due to the vagaries of imperial law, the territory belonging to the Burtscheid abbey fell under the "guardianship" of a secular ruler, the duke of Limburg. When the Dutch briefly conquered Limburg in the 1630s, they claimed the duke's powers, on whose basis they granted Calvinists freedom of worship in Burtscheid and ordered the construction there of a Calvinist church. Building had proceeded as far as the roof when the Dutch army was driven out of Limburg. For the next seventy years the church stood unfinished, a testimony to frustrated designs, until the War of Spanish Succession gave control of Limburg once again to the Dutch, who ordered its completion. For a few years then, from 1707 to 1714, Burtscheid's Calvinists had their own place of worship and so were spared the necessity of traveling to Vaals. Aachen's Calvinists, too, availed themselves of its use. At the end of the war, the Habsburgs received Limburg back from the Dutch and promptly had the church demolished. Calvinists resumed their trek, and were joined in it by the increasing number of visitors who came from across Europe to "take the waters" in Aachen and Burtscheid, famous for their hot mineral springs.

The Calvinist congregation in Vaals thus comprised four distinct groups. Calvinists from Aachen, Burtscheid, Eupen, and Vaals attended services together, listening to sermons delivered by their ministers in rotation: the Aachen and Vaals groups shared a minister, who preached once every two weeks; Eupen and Burtscheid had their own ministers, who preached once every four weeks. Communion was received on successive Sundays by two groups at a time. Each group had its own governing board, known as a consistory. Relations among the groups were not always harmonious, and the Aachen and Vaals Calvinists in particular struggled bitterly in the 1710s over the power to appoint their shared minister and other issues. To resolve the dispute, a "combined consistory" was established with purview over all matters that affected the groups jointly. Most members of the congregation spoke German as their first language. That was true also of the group that came from Eupen, which today is capital of the German-speaking part of Belgium, known as the East Cantons. Services for the congregation were therefore conducted normally in German, not Dutch, despite the fact that the congregation belonged organizationally to the Dutch Reformed Church. French-speaking Calvinists established a separate Walloon congregation in Vaals. Some lived in Aachen and Burtscheid, and they were joined by others who performed Auslaufen from Limburg and Liège. Just a few Walloons settled in Vaals itself, one of them being Jean Renotte, the maternal grandfather of Sara Erffens.

At the beginning, Calvinists and Walloons had only the old parish church of Vaals in which to worship.[20] The two congregations shared the building with Catholics, each having use of it for specified hours. This three-way Simultaneum was neither harmonious nor comfortable, especially not for the Calvinists, who found the thirteenth-century building inadequate. To make even half their congregation fit into it, they enlarged its gallery, but despite some refurbishment the building remained "very run down, outmoded, and dilapidated." In any event, the Walloons were the first to move out, preferring to worship in a rudimentary barn, but they soon moved again into a more satisfactory structure that came to be known as "the French church." The Calvinist congregation was relieved when, after the Partition Treaty, Catholics were barred from using the old parish church. Still, it had an urgent practical need for a larger space. In The Hague, authorities acknowledged this need and were concerned to fulfill it. From their perspective, though, the matter also had symbolic importance: the largest, most prominent Calvinist congregation in Overmaas, they insisted, should have a place of worship that befit its status as embodiment of the Republic's official faith. Members of the Council of State visited Vaals to help draw up plans, and the States General agreed to foot most of the bill for the construction of a new church.

Erected between 1669 and 1672, the Reformed church of Vaals was (and still is) a modest but elegant neoclassical structure (fig. 16). The only purpose-built Calvinist church in Overmaas, it was designed by the renowned architect Pieter Post, whose previous commissions included a new city hall for Maastricht (fig. 17). Made of brick with white stone framing its door and windows, the church had few ornaments and a sober appearance. Its simple hall layout created a single, open space inside. Despite these facts, construction cost a whopping 13,000 guilders. The most remarkable thing about the church was that it did not replace the old parish

16. The Vaals Reformed church, designed by Pieter Post and constructed in 1669–72. Exterior view from the southeast.

church, which remained standing and was eventually returned to the Catholics for their use. Instead, the new church intersected with the old one at right angles, meeting it at the tower that rose at its western end. The two churches, Catholic and Reformed, thus formed a single complex, the Catholic one extending eastward from the tower, the Reformed one northward. Eventually, in the 1750s, Catholics enlarged and remodeled the old parish church. Its position, though, remained unaltered. In this extraordinary, entirely unique way, Catholics and Calvinists in Vaals got places of worship that were separate but conjoined. This was not Simultaneum in the ordinary sense, since the two groups shared only the medieval tower and its bells. One might say rather that the bitter rivals were joined architecturally at the hip (figs. 18, 19).

Calvinists and Walloons were not the only Protestants to perform Auslaufen to Vaals. Lutherans and Mennonites in the region also seized eagerly the opportunity afforded them by the proximity of the Dutch village, where their worship was tolerated. Under Dutch law, these Protestant dissenters could not have public places of worship. Ironically, then, while Catholics in Overmaas could have churches that looked like churches, Lutherans and Mennonites could not, though the amount of camouflage and pretense they had to maintain decreased markedly over time. The Mennonites who worshiped in Vaals were a small and shrinking group who could not afford a minister of their own. In any event, they believed in eschewing grandeur. They held their meetings in an ordinary house known as the *Verfhuis*, its name indicating that it was (or at least had been) used for dyeing cloth. The Lutheran congregation, by contrast, thrived and grew, counting among its members wealthy merchant families such as the Clermonts. Almost a century before Johann Arnold von Clermont moved his industrial enterprise to Vaals, his great-great-grandfather bankrolled the Lutherans' purchase of their first place of worship there. In the 1730s, a

17. Maastricht city hall. Designed by Pieter Post and constructed in 1659–84, a major piece of Dutch neoclassical architecture.

great-uncle donated much of the money for an entirely new church (fig. 20).[21] Octagonal in shape, this stately building did not really look like an ordinary house. Its windows, though, were not oversize, and crucially it lacked that ultimate mark of church-liness, a tower with bells. Ironically, the same Aachen magistrates who continued to forbid Lutheran worship contributed toward the cost of the new church. They did so to accommodate the Lutheran soldiers who, as part of an imperial army, had their win-ter quarters in the city. These soldiers joined the civilians on their weekly trek.

So it happened that one modest village acquired no fewer than five churches—all of them filled with foreigners.[22]

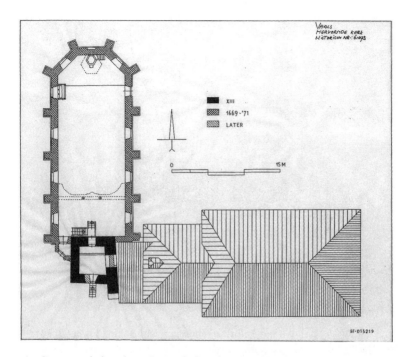

18. Connected churches. Ground plan showing the Vaals Catholic and Reformed churches before the demolition of the Catholic church in 1967. Solid = the shared tower dating from the thirteenth century. Cross-hatched = the Dutch Reformed church, constructed in 1669–72. Striped = the Catholic church, with sections dating (left to right) from the thirteenth century (but later rebuilt), 1751–52, and 1833.

Thanks to its location at the epicenter of an intricate borderland, Vaals had a unique religious profile. Catholics enjoyed greater freedom there than they did in the heartland of the Dutch Republic. They worshiped not in some quasi-clandestine schuilkerk but in the medieval parish church of their village. They did not have to practice Simultaneum, sharing their church with Calvinists: the two groups had their own, equally public churches. As members of a

19. The Vaals Catholic and Reformed churches, with shared tower. The section in the middle of the photo is a remnant of the Catholic church as rebuilt in 1751–52 under Father Bosten.

parish and diocese that spanned political borders, the Catholic inhabitants of Vaals worshiped in the company of foreign Catholics, under the spiritual authority of foreign prelates. Meanwhile, in an extraordinary spectacle, hundreds of foreign Protestants flooded into Vaals every Sunday, their vehicles so numerous that they damaged the churchyard where many parked. These subjects of Catholic rulers felt immensely grateful to the Dutch for giving them an opportunity to worship legally and—they hoped—safely. Without that opportunity, many would have found the repression they suffered at home unbearable.

Today we tend to think of political borders as restrictive—as tools that help states keep some undesirables out (impoverished

20. The Vaals Lutheran church, an octagonal structure, design attributed to the Aachen architect Johann Josef Couven. The church came into use in 1738 and is now used as a cultural center.

immigrants, threatening ideas) and prevent others from escaping (criminals, political dissidents). Yet the borders that divided Vaals from its neighbors clearly had a liberating effect, producing in religion as in economics a kind of deregulation. Just as the political fragmentation of the region defeated the protectionism of Aachen's guildsmen, so it defeated or at least mitigated their intolerance.[23] As the Catholics of Aachen, Burtscheid, Limburg, Liège and Jülich discovered, it was well-nigh impossible to suppress religious dissent in one community if another one with a different official faith lay near to hand. Through the practice of Auslaufen, political borders offered escapes from religious repression. More than that, they enabled dissenters to draw comfort and material support from core-ligionists in neighboring states. Protestant dissenters in the region of Vaals deftly exploited these opportunities.

It was not just dissenters, though, who exploited the borders for religious purposes. So did the Dutch States General when they paid for the construction of a new Calvinist church just a hundred and twenty yards from Aachen soil. That church symbolized the jurisdiction of the Dutch state over Vaals. It demonstrated concretely the official status of the village as Calvinist, and in this sense it clarified the distinction between the village and the Catholic states that surrounded it. This was not, though, the principal intention of the authorities in building that church. Rather, it was to support their foreign brethren. Dutch authorities used the church—used Vaals—to project their influence and promote their faith beyond the borders of the Republic. In the process they won the gratitude and loyalty of Protestants in neighboring Catholic territories, binding them to the Dutch state. In this sense, you could say they were purposefully blurring political borders and undercutting the territorial integrity of their neighbors. It is no wonder the Catholics of the region responded to the Protestant churches in Vaals not just as an affront but as an attack.

In response, they found other ways to exploit the borders surrounding the village. Although the Dutch could project their religious influence beyond those borders, they had no legal authority there. So, Catholics found ways to attack Vaals and those who worshiped there from behind the safety of the border. Cunegonde's arrest would provoke them to their boldest action ever.

CHAPTER FOUR

Flouting Authority

As the grim reality of her situation sank in, Cunegonde began to weep. Trapped and under arrest, the miserable girl explained between sobs to the stunned Calvinists in church that she was a sister of Hendrick Mommers from Würselen. When questioned, she briefly recounted her story. "She had been summoned by an unknown man," she told them, "to be godmother of her brother's child. This man had also shown her this church and ordered her to get the child out of it."[1] Guards then came and took Cunegonde away. Because Vaals had no jail, they brought her to an adjacent tavern named the Coul, where a watch was set.

A few hours later, Henricus Schmalhausen and his fellow magistrates convened in their capacity as judges of the local court. Under Dutch law, Cunegonde's arrest had to be ratified by the court, as it duly was, and the judges agreed to convene again the next morning so that Cunegonde could be formally questioned in their presence. From the moment of her arrest, though, the verdict of the Calvinist judges seemed a foregone conclusion. Cunegonde had invaded their church, desecrated their sacrament, and tried to kidnap a child who belonged to their religious community. Her "scandalous deed" blatantly violated the laws that protected the Dutch Reformed Church and could be construed as an attack on the official religion of the Dutch state. So of course the judges would condemn Cunegonde to receive "her condign punishment."[2]

As word of events spread across the border, though, Catholics in the territory of Aachen grew quickly enraged. From their perspective, the episode must have looked completely different. In their eyes, Calvinists had taken advantage of the power they enjoyed on Dutch soil to impose their own faith on the child of a Catholic father. Hendrick and Sara's baby rightly belonged to their community, it was the Calvinists who in effect had stolen it away, and Cunegonde was a heroine for attempting to rescue it. In Aachen some Catholics even claimed that Minister Pferdmenges had grabbed the baby out of the Vaals Catholic church in order to baptize it. Inverting the true story, this rumor cast Pferdmenges rather than Cunegonde as the real kidnapper.[3] Both religious communities, then, saw themselves as attacked by the other; both felt existentially threatened by the theft of their children. It is no wonder the community that had state power and the law against it resorted to violence. Catholics wanted to see the guilty Calvinists punished and the innocent Cunegonde rescued from her impending fate. To right the scales of justice, they would take direct action. In the process they would commit what a Dutch official called "one of the most serious [of all] crimes, punishable by death": the "violation of the territory and jurisdiction" of Their High and Mighty Lordships, the States General.

By the time Pferdmenges completed the baptismal ceremony for little Mathias Hendrick, an angry Catholic crowd had gathered outside the Vaals Reformed church. "From the unfriendly gestures of the embittered mob" Pferdmenges perceived "that he would not reach home without great danger."⁴ He therefore turned to the burgomaster of Vaals, Johan Frans à Brassard, who assigned four sturdy peasants to accompany him and his fellow church officers back to Burtscheid. The party decided to avoid the main road, striking out instead on a path through a wood. It proved a fortunate decision, for as the men later learned, they would otherwise have run straight into a party of Catholics from Aachen who intended to intercept the preacher and teach him a lesson.

Mathias Erffens did not share the preacher's luck. After the ceremony ended, he went to visit his daughter, who in accordance with custom had remained at home in bed. It was around seven in the evening by the time he left her and headed back to Burtscheid. He had been walking only a few minutes when he reached our familiar boundary stone at the edge of Vaals and the barrier gate opening onto Aachen territory. There, in front of the rectory, he encountered a hostile foursome: pastor Bosten, his brother the curate, the sexton Martinus Buntgens, and the sexton's father.

"So what happened this afternoon in your church?" asked Bosten, disingenuously.⁵

"You know well what happened," replied Mathias, "and I don't think I've ever heard of the holy sacraments being defiled in such a manner." To Mathias, the desecration of a solemn Christian rite seemed an act no fellow Christian, not even the clergy of a rival confession, could approve.

Bosten told his side of the story. "Your son-in-law visited me just a half-hour before the child was baptized and said that he would send the child to me for baptism. Either you are scum if you forced him against his will, or your son-in-law is scum for making me a promise he had no intention of keeping."⁶

"You must not use words like scum." Mathias would not have his honor or that of his family impugned.

"Mommers," Bosten repeated, "is scum, for he said to me that the beggars [a Catholic term of abuse for Calvinists] pestered him at every turn to have his child baptized in the Reformed church, [and that] if this weren't the case, he wanted to bring his child to [me] for baptism." Bosten told Mathias he could prove that Hendrick had asked him to baptize the child.

"If that was true," conceded Mathias, "such behavior, which might amuse some people, could not be approved."

At this point the curate began to heap abuse on Mathias and his fellow Calvinists, accusing them of using their wealth to buy off Catholics: "That [is] how the Reformed [go] about things, robbing people of their freedom through their bribes and gifts." It's "just like scum and beggars" to behave so.

Joining in, the sexton upbraided Mathias for an unmanly cowardice: "Erffens, what do you think you're up to? You ask the midwife and other women why I visited Mommers at the Groene Driesch? If you'd asked me, I would have given you an answer."

Mathias didn't recall questioning the midwife on this point, but now that they were discussing it, he wished the sexton would tell him.

"For one thing," Buntgens explained, "[it was] because the pastor sent me, [and] for another because Mommers, as he tells me, is a relative, and so I would have preferred to see the child baptized in the Roman [Catholic] religion than in another."

If the sexton was a relative, replied Mathias, he should have said so before Hendrick and Sara's marriage contract was drawn up.

The curate here interjected: "The contract [is] rubbish. The general laws prescribe that boys go with the father and the girls with the mother." Not only was this claim untrue, but the curate himself had heard and accepted Hendrick's promise to raise all his children Catholic.

At this point Mathias had had enough. He said he "wouldn't stay any longer for such abuse and was going home." And ending the conversation, he resumed his journey.

Buntgens accompanied Mathias a little way, for his own house lay in the same direction, about a hundred and twenty yards east of the Dutch border (fig. 21). Then, as the sky darkened, Mathias continued alone along the main road toward Aachen and Burtscheid. After some minutes he heard someone coming up quickly behind him. Turning around, he saw the menacing figure of a man apparently intent on catching up to him. Hoping to evade his pursuer, Mathias headed toward a nearby field. But the unknown man followed and, when he reached Mathias, struck him with a heavy wooden club. Then a second man joined the attack, and the two beat Mathias over his whole body until he lay motionless on the ground, wallowing in his own blood. Satisfied, the mysterious assailant and his accomplice returned to the road and hightailed it. For a long while, Mathias lay where they left him. Eventually he tried to stand, but the fifty-seven-year-old was too weak, and he sank again to the ground. Fortunately, a relative of Mathias happened that evening to be traveling along the same road and, in the dim twilight, saw him lying prostrate. Somehow this relative and his companion got the injured man to a nearby tavern—a landmark on the road between Vaals and Aachen called the Heumans-Häussgen. After spending the night there, Mathias was bundled the next morning into a sedan chair and transported back to Burtscheid. A medical doctor and barber-surgeon who tended to his wounds initially gave him little chance of recovering, but heal he did, eventually.[7]

Meanwhile, that same evening, Martinus Buntgens had just reached home when Magdalena, daughter of the blacksmith Conrad Wolff, came to fetch him. Buntgens accompanied Magdalena back to her father's house, where he found Wolff, his family and servants, and a couple of friends, all eager to hear from him what

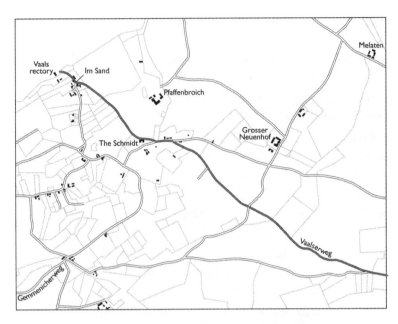

21. The Vaalserquartier, part of the Reich of Aachen. The Vaals rectory stands right on the border between Dutch territory and the Reich. The road from Vaals to Aachen runs diagonally from top left to bottom right. The area "Im Sand" is where Martinus Buntgens and Frans Hendrick Bosten lived and where Cunegonde's liberators congregated. "The Schmidt" was Conrad Wolff's house. The map also shows several of the principal farmsteads from which Cunegonde's liberators came: the Grosse Neuenhof, Pfaffenbroich, and (top right) Melaten, where Sebastian Gimmenich lived in 1762.

had happened earlier that day in Vaals. Over a few tankards of beer Buntgens spent an hour telling them the story of Hendrick and Sara's baby and Cunegonde's attempt to grab it. Wolff asked whether Cunegonde was related to Buntgens; if so, he said, she was related to himself as well. One of the servants present was a twenty-six-year-old named Hendrick Lotmans. According to testimony that Lotmans would later give, Buntgens told the assembled group that he "wished the woman could be gotten out of Vaals." To get her across the border to Aachen territory would be to rescue her from punishment. Father Bosten, Buntgens reportedly added, "would be greatly pleased, since the pastor also wished it."[8]

That night, after Buntgens had gone to bed, he heard voices in front of his house. A bunch of youths were hanging out on the road talking about Cunegonde. "Who's the woman under arrest in Vaals? Where does she come from? What shall happen to her?" he heard them ask. One member of the group told the others that she came from Würselen and added, "I've heard that she is going to be brought soon to Maastricht, where she'll be whipped and branded."[9]

The next morning, Thursday, 15 April, Vaals was awash with rumors: "The boys were in the village last night . . . but they didn't accomplish anything, the night-watch stopped them."[10]

After mass, Father Bosten decided to pay Cunegonde a visit. Taking his sexton Buntgens with him, he walked to the Coul, where the young woman was being detained. There he found the usher of the village court, Daniel Quet, standing at a door, controlling access to the prisoner. Quet allowed the two men into the room, where they found Cunegonde sitting quietly while her guards passed the time playing cards. She had already undergone interrogation earlier that morning.

"Have you had anything to eat?" Bosten asked her.[11]

A guard named Dirk answered in Cunegonde's stead: "Yes, Sir, she has already eaten a piece of bacon and bread, and there's her glass of beer."

Another guard, Herman, then complained: "Whoever brought this person here has caused great trouble."

To this the sexton replied, "My father brought her."

Intervening, Bosten excused Buntgens's father, Andries, and accepted some of the blame himself: "It shouldn't be held against your father, for I summoned her, and I take responsibility for that." Bosten struck his breast as he spoke these last words, which Dutch authorities would later fling back in his face, construing them as an admission of guilt. Then he continued, "But that she did what she did in the church, I suppose that was wrong, and I didn't ask her to do it."

Cunegonde began to cry. Moved, the priest tried to console her: "Be comforted, my child, you'll soon be out of here," and he gave her some money—coins worth six Aachen marks. Cunegonde thanked him. She would later use the money to buy a ribbon to wear around her neck.

Leaving the tavern, Bosten went to the house of his neighbor, Burgomaster Johan Frans à Brassard, whom he told about his visit to Cunegonde, expressing the hope "that it wouldn't be held against him."[12] The young woman, he said, had an innocent, simple look. Could À Brassard not arrange for her to be released from arrest? The burgomaster "was held in great respect or credit among the guards, [and] had only to say the word and it would be done." (In fact, one of the guards was À Brassard's brother-in-law Arnold Schiffers—a Catholic; take note: À Brassard's sister Anne Gertrude was in a mixed marriage.) Bosten pledged that À Brassard would forever have his "sincere friendship" if he were to help in this way. But the burgomaster replied that it was not within his power. Bosten returned home to his rectory.

About an hour and a half later, À Brassard found the priest again at his door. This time Bosten informed him that he had just received a letter from his ecclesiastical superior, the dean of the Aachen Minster, who ordered him to come that very afternoon to give a full report on yesterday's incident in Vaals. Bosten asked À Brassard's advice: Should he go? He feared that if he did and, "should a tumult or revolt occur in Aachen, he would fall under suspicion of having incited it."

"Sir," answered the burgomaster, "I have always regarded you as a sensible man, and so I'm not in a position to give you advice or assistance in the matter."

"Then I shall go to Aachen," declared Bosten.

That afternoon, Hendrick Lotmans, the blacksmith's servant, sent a message to one of his buddies, Sebastian Gimmenich, who worked on Melaten, one of the large farmsteads that dotted the countryside between Vaals and Aachen. Like Lotmans, Gimmenich was in his mid-twenties. His name suggests that his family came from the nearby village of Gimmenich, in the Habsburg Duchy of Limburg. He was a tough man, prone to violence, and not afraid of the law; in later years, he would get into trouble at least twice for committing assault. He was also a successful, or at least fortunate, man: by his early thirties he would have a farmstead of his own, called the Grosse Neuenhof (fig. 22), which he held in a sharecropping arrangement that was typical for the region. Though an illiterate farmhand, Gimmenich had the qualities of a leader. He, Lotmans, and another farmhand named Johannes Grommet would lead the assault to free Cunegonde from her arrest.

Gimmenich was plowing a field when a stable boy came with the message from Lotmans to come to the blacksmith Conrad Wolff's house that evening. When Gimmenich arrived at Wolff's, Lotmans recounted what Buntgens had told him and the others the previous evening about Cunegonde. While Lotmans and Gimmenich were discussing the matter, they were joined by Johannes Grommet and one Simon Knoop, and the four young men went together to Buntgens's house to speak directly with the sexton. They found him standing at his door. When they asked his advice how they might be able to speak with Cunegonde, he replied that it would be difficult since there was a watch guarding her. Knoop, though, might manage it because his sister Anna worked as maidservant

22. The Grosse Neuenhof. Modern photograph showing the former main entrance to the large compound, which was typical of the principal farmsteads in the area.

for the proprietor of the Coul and lived there with the proprietor's family.

The four headed toward Vaals. When they reached the barrier gate at the border, they were challenged by the village watch, who would not let them pass. Let us through, they warned, or "the fires of hell will strike the beggars and Christians in Vaals in their bones."[13] When they tried to force their way through, the watch repulsed them, and the four retreated, uttering curses and threats: "You and the beggars are all scum. You had better think twice before you ever show your face on this soil."

It was after ten at night when they arrived back at the sexton's house. There they found other youths milling about—the area "Im Sand" in front of the house was clearly a hangout. Recounting their clash with the watch, they told the others of their determination to rescue Cunegonde and asked them whether they'd help. Gimmenich exhorted those who agreed: "Come on, boys, let's go home and get our weapons." So the band broke up. Gimmenich went back to Melaten, where he picked up a pistol. Most of the others fetched clubs. Because it was illegal to carry guns or knives, clubs were the common man's usual weapon of choice. Long, heavy wooden things, fitted sometimes with metal studs, clubs could inflict terrible wounds. A strapping lad could bash someone's head in with one, and a common saying in the region advised precisely that: "Hit him in the head, then he won't limp."[14]

Gimmenich returned an hour or so later with four others from Melaten. By midnight, a crowd of about thirty had assembled. They were all stable boys, shepherds, farmhands, laborers, and other male youths who lived and worked in Aachen's rural Reich. In addition, there was a single French soldier. As an ally of France, Aachen provided winter quarters for many French troops, and the soldier in question was quartered at Melaten, where Gimmenich had recruited him for the night's venture. Dressed in a blue uniform and armed with a pistol and saber, he stood out from the other participants. So notable was his presence that some witnesses got the impression there was more than one of him.

Buntgens, so he later said, became aware of the crowd when someone knocked on his door and asked for a light. Rising from bed, he went to the front room of his house and lit a lamp. When he opened his door, Gimmenich and eight others, including the soldier, piled inside.[15]

"Damn it, boys!" said Gimmenich, "We've got to get that woman out of Vaals somehow, for I've heard that tomorrow she's going to be brought to Maastricht and is going to be whipped and branded there. I've heard," he confided, "that the magistrates [of Vaals] themselves wished she were gone, [and that] we won't have any trouble consequently with the watch."

"Boys," said Buntgens (still wearing no trousers), "you'll be doing me and the pastor a great favor, for that woman is related to me, and to the blacksmith, and to [the farmer] at St. Albert's."

With this encouragement, the band set off for Vaals. Buntgens shouted after them, warning about the French soldier, who spoke no German: "Boys, don't have an accident, watch out, what are you doing taking that bad man with you? You can't even understand him."

By the time the band approached the border, about half its members had gotten cold feet. Some hung back in the vicinity of the sexton's house, others went only as far as the barrier gate, while still others headed to a nearby brewery to quench their thirst. Pausing, the remaining half agreed solemnly "to help one another in case of accident or injury." Then they crossed into Vaals.

Nicolaes Welter, age thirty-three, was the sole member of the village guard keeping watch at that moment near the barrier. As he heard the group approach, he called out, "Who's there?"[16] When no one replied, he asked a second and a third time. Raising his musket, he tried to shoot at the intruders but found that the weapon wouldn't fire. Then his assailants were upon him. One grabbed him, knocked a knee out from under him, and seized his musket. Another assailant—probably the soldier—struck him several times with a saber. Crying, "Help, help," Welter fled. Hearing the attack, two of his fellow guardsmen retreated back into the brewery where they had just been enjoying some refreshment.

Making a great ruckus, the band headed to the Coul to liberate Cunegonde. "Open the door," they demanded when they reached the front of the tavern. "Let the young lady go!" "Open the door or we'll set the house on fire!" The guardsmen inside quickly hid or fled. One threw himself into a coal bunker, another cowered on the stairs to the cellar, while a third concealed himself behind some furnishings. Others simply bolted. Several took refuge in the brewery, which by this time was getting rather crowded. For her part, Cunegonde ran in fright to the bedroom shared by the proprietor's daughter and his maidservant, in whose company she hoped she might be safe. The two young women, though, wouldn't let her in. Johannes Dirricks, proprietor of the Coul, stayed in bed with his wife until it was all over.

With several heavy blows, the band burst the lock on the front door and forced their way into the tavern. Once inside, they worked swiftly and quietly. Cunegonde saw "a young, tall, strong fellow with a blue smock" bound into the room.[17] At first he didn't spot her in the dark, so he demanded of a remaining guardsmen to know where she was. Then he made out her figure. Grabbing her by the arm, he practically carried her outside. With Cunegonde in tow, the whole band then headed back to the border. As they went, they whooped and fired their weapons, while one of the young men jubilantly played a flute. Within just a few minutes they had reached the safety of Aachen territory.

When they arrived back at Buntgens's house, the sexton opened the door for them. "By jiminy, boys," he exclaimed," aren't you lucky you haven't had any accidents."[18] After they had entered and set Cunegonde down in a chair, Buntgens said to the group, "You've done well, and when the pastor hears about it, he shall be overjoyed." Buntgens did not want Cunegonde remaining in his house, though, and so the group left. They received a less nervous reception at the blacksmith Wolff's, where the mistress of the house and her daughter Magdalena greeted them. As the members of the band enjoyed a celebratory beer, Magdalena remarked happily, "You've done well, and you've done us a favor, and the woman is lucky to be free." Gradually the young men parted, leaving Cunegonde at the blacksmith's, where she slept the remainder of the night. The next morning, she had breakfast with her hosts. Buntgens's wife came by with Cunegonde's red pinafore and riding hood, which had been left behind in the Coul the previous night. Then, setting off by herself, Cunegonde walked home to Würselen.

Thus was Cunegonde, the would-be kidnapper of Hendrick and Sara's baby, herself "kidnapped": at least, that was the word used by Dutch authorities for what happened. Intent on rescuing the young woman from punishment, Catholics from across the border had invaded Vaals, overpowered the village guards, freed Cunegonde from arrest, and whisked her back across the border, beyond the authorities' reach. Thanks to the protection afforded by the border—and the faint hearts of the amateur guards—the perpetrators had been able to act with impunity. They and their supporters could scarcely contain their glee. That would teach the Dutch who was really master around there! That would teach the Calvinist "beggar dogs" whose faith was dominant and whose merely tolerated! To add insult to injury, Cunegonde's liberators returned to Vaals a few days later to celebrate their triumph and thumb their noses at the Dutch authorities. On Sunday, 18 April, at around six in the evening, a "band of peasant boys" from across the border again paid Vaals a visit. The band was led by Gimmenich, Lotmans, and Grommet, who this time brought with them two French soldiers. With great hoopla and to the jubilant tooting once again of a flute, the youths staged a mock-military parade. Playing the role of officers, the soldiers lined up the "boys" and marched them, clubs on shoulders, right up through the village, pausing for extra effect in front of Burgomaster À Brassard's house. Then they all went to the Coul and had a drink (talk about returning to the scene of the crime)![19]

With the "kidnapping" of Cunegonde by Catholics from across the border, what had begun as a religious conflict took on a political dimension. For unlike Cunegonde's own attempted violence, the actions of her liberators constituted a direct attack on the authority of the Dutch government. As Dutch officials saw the matter, an armed band assisted by foreign soldiers had invaded Dutch territory, assaulted the local militia, broken a woman out of jail, and thwarted the government's rightful power to try and punish a manifest criminal. Obviously the perpetrators had trounced the Vaals magistrates, but they had done much more. In effect, a group of German Catholics had challenged the sovereignty of the Dutch state over Vaals—first in practice with their daring nighttime assault, then symbolically three days later with their taunting parade. By these acts, fumed the magistrates, "the territory of Their High and Mighty Lordships and this jurisdiction have been tremendously violated."[20]

Sovereignty over Vaals was vested in the States General, who ruled the Dutch Lands of Overmaas both directly and through various officials, foremost among whom were the governors. In 1762 the governor (*hoog drossaard*) of the Lands of Dalhem and 's-Hertogenrade was Count Charles Bentinck, Lord of Nijenhuis, son of the famous Hans Willem Bentinck, who engineered the successful invasion of Britain in 1688 by the Dutch Stadholder William III. Compared to his father or elder brother Willem, Charles played only a minor role in Dutch politics, but he did sit for a time in the States General and lead the stadholders' party in the province of Overijssel. Thanks to his high connections, he received several preferments that supplemented the modest income he received from his estates. One was the governorship of Dalhem and 's-Hertogenrade, a sinecure that imposed few duties and did not require him to reside in those lands.[21] His subordinate, the lieutenant governor (*lieutenant drossaard*), conducted the business of government there in his name. Based in Maastricht, the lieutenant governor reported directly to the States General, implemented its orders, enforced the law, and prosecuted criminals. It was he who bore primary responsibility for upholding the sovereignty of the States General.

The man who held this key post in April 1762 was Abraham van den Heuvel. Like Bentinck, he belonged to a ruling elite, but a regional rather than national one. Like his father and grandfather before him, he held a law degree and served with distinction in the Maastricht city government. Proud of his erudition, he served also as the city's librarian and superintendent of its Latin school. It was he who, as a proponent of progress, enticed Johann Arnold von Clermont to Vaals and helped him establish his textile factory there. Van den Heuvel was a professional and, at the age of sixty-three, highly seasoned administrator with decades of experience as public prosecutor. In all his years, though, he had never encountered such outrages as those committed by Cunegonde and, even more, by her liberators. The exuberant insolence of that "band of peasant boys" was enough to make steam bellow from his ears. He found it particularly galling that one of the perpetrators had had the effrontery on both occasions to play a flute. Whoever had done so had "flouted" authority in the original, literal sense of the word. Van den Heuvel was determined especially to punish the flute-player.

Van den Heuvel and his subordinates had launched an investigation into Cunegonde's original crime the very morning after its commission, and the investigation of the night raid that freed her likewise commenced immediately. The village guardsmen were all questioned, as were the owner of the Coul and his family and the brewer Gillis Kreuwen and his clients that fateful night. Then on 24 April Van den Heuvel abruptly suspended the investigation. As he explained later, he would not have done so "if it were not feared that such legal proceedings, devoid of force, far from restraining these hoodlums, would provoke them to further acts of violence." If he pursued the case, Catholics on the Aachen side of the border would, he believed, wreak vengeance on the Protestants who traveled to Vaals to attend church, and they might even launch an attack on the village itself. So for more than a month, Van den Heuvel sat on his hands. He didn't even report to the States General what had happened in Vaals until 2 June, when he asked them to dispatch to Vaals a contingent of regular army troops. Because the guardsmen had proven so inadequate, a "detachment of the state militia" was necessary to protect Protestant worshipers and to free "the entire village of Vaals and the Protestant inhabitants and magistrates there from the wrath of these lawless malefactors." The troops would make it safe for him to prosecute the wrongdoers and would also help him catch them.[22]

After the necessary consultations, the States General responded favorably to Van den Heuvel's request, asking the effective head of the Dutch army, the Duke of Brunswick, to order that a detachment of sixty infantry and twenty-four cavalrymen, with their officers and full equipment, be dispatched from the Maastricht garrison to Vaals. The States General ordered Van den Heuvel to prosecute "with the full force of the law" all those who participated in the violent incidents of April, making "every effort" to apprehend the foreigners involved, as soon as they might come onto the territory of the Dutch state. They ordered the Vaals judges to "uphold the law and administer justice without any connivance." And they ordered the lieutenant governor to close the Catholic church in Vaals "until such time as Cunegonde Mommers . . . shall be returned again to detention in the control of the lieutenant governor, or put in the hands of the court there."[23]

Back in Maastricht, Van den Heuvel was pleased to receive the support and authorization he needed. He then pondered how he might best effect the capture of those Aachen "peasant boys." He could arrest them only if they came onto Dutch territory, but once he arrested one, the others would know not to cross the border. He therefore had to capture as many of them as he possibly could in a single ploy. In consultation with the military commander of the Maastricht garrison, Van den Heuvel came up with an ingenious plan. He then went to Vaals to oversee its execution.

Thursday, 24 June, was a Catholic feast day, the Nativity of St. John the Baptist. As Van den Heuvel anticipated, lots of Catholics who lived in Aachen's Vaalserquartier attended mass that morning in their parish church—that is, in Father Bosten's church, on Dutch territory. As they watched, listened, and prayed, the contingent of Dutch troops arrived. Having left Maastricht the night before under cover of darkness, they timed their arrival in Vaals to coincide precisely with morning mass, and as the service was performed inside the church, the troops surrounded the building. Those inside were trapped. When the service ended, the soldiers filtered the worshipers as they left. Conrad Wolff and his daughter Magdalena were arrested. Martinus Buntgens was locked up in the church tower, which the soldiers appropriated as a temporary jail. Van den Heuvel had all the church ornaments and ritual paraphernalia put away in the sacristy. Then Father Bosten and his brother the curate were brought before the village court and informed of the States General's order to close their church. They were forbidden to perform any pastoral functions until the lieutenant governor or the court once again had Cunegonde in their hands. On hearing this, Bosten flew into a rage, banging his fists on the table. His "impertinent gesticulations" would be neither forgotten nor forgiven.[24]

Basically, though, Van den Heuvel's ploy was a flop. Only two of his principal targets were caught in the dragnet, and both young men were able later to demonstrate that they had stayed behind on Aachen territory and not taken part in the actual kidnapping of Cunegonde. To the lieutenant governor's acute disappointment, none of the perpetrators were in church that morning. Afterward, Van den Heuvel wasn't sure whether bad luck had foiled him or his prey had gotten wind of his plan. What he did determine was that one of the Vaals judges, while chatting in a coffeehouse in Maastricht, had let slip the entire contents of the States General's orders.

The lieutenant governor's one major success was to secure Cunegonde's extradition back to Dutch soil, and this he could have achieved without the drama. In fact, he might have achieved it more easily had he not offended Aachen's magistrates by giving them no advance notice of his plan. He and the Vaals judges compounded their offense by addressing their request for extradition not to the Aachen magistrates but to a rival authority in the city, an official known as the Vogt-Major who represented the government of Jülich. Despite these insults, on the morning of 25 June, Aachen's burgomaster Peter Strauch dispatched some soldiers to Würselen, who apprehended Cunegonde and brought her back to the city. Strauch and his colleagues also obliged the Dutch authorities by taking steps to prevent any popular backlash against local Protestants in reaction to the previous day's events. They issued an ordinance (fig. 23) threatening anyone who molested the Protestants with corporal punishment, and they stationed soldiers along the road to Vaals to protect Protestants traveling to services there. Whether they should send Cunegonde back to face Dutch justice was a thornier issue that provoked debate in the Aachen city council. At first, Strauch and his colleagues tried to circumvent the

Verordnung.

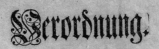

Von wegen Bürgermeister, Scheffen und Rath dieses Königl.

Stuhls und des H. R. Reichs freyer Stadt Aachen ꝛc. wird allen und jeden Bürgeren, Unterthanen, und Einwöhnern hiemit am nachdrucksamsten verbotten, sich bey Gelegenheit des Vaelser Vorgangs aller Thätlichkeiten und Rottirens zu enthalten, die Reformirten in ihrem Kirchen-Gang, noch auch sonsten zu molestiren, oder auch auf ein oder ander Art zu insultiren, mit der ausdrücklichen Wahrnung, daß nicht allein wider die hiergegen Frevelnde mit scharfem Obrigkeitlichen Einsehen, auch gar bewandten Umständen nach, mit Leib-und Lebens-Straf verfahren werden solle, sondern auch der oder diejenige, so wider dieses Gebott zu handeln sich unterstehen würden, denen zu Vorkommung derley höchstgefährlichen Unheils von Obrigkeits wegen vornehmenden Mitteln exponirt, und all dabey befahrende Unglück sich selbst zuzumessen haben würden, welches dann zu Jedermanns Nachricht durch offenen Druck zu publiciren, und an allen Ecken und Thoren zu affigiren verordnet wird. Aachen den 25. Junii 1762.

EX MANDATO
D. P. M. BECKER
Secretarius.

23. Ordinance issued by the Aachen city government on 25 June 1762 prohibiting the molestation of Protestants.

matter by informing Van den Heuvel of Cunegonde's arrest and asking him, disingenuously, on this basis to reopen the Vaals Catholic church. As they well knew, the arrest did not fulfil the condition set by the States General, so the lieutenant governor's answer was no. It was a week before the Aachen magistrates gave in, deciding formally that Cunegonde had no legal rights that might exempt her from the extradition request. Informally, what mattered was that the Dutch authorities were holding Catholic worship in Vaals effectively hostage to the girl's return. As anticipated, the decision was bitterly unpopular. "In order to prevent any rebellion by the wanton rabble," Strauch had a contingent of soldiers transport Cunegonde by night. They delivered her in Vaals before dawn on 1 July.[25]

Van den Heuvel had suffered a setback, but he remained angry and determined. Now that Vaals was properly guarded, it was safe for him to investigate the April events properly and bring all those implicated in them to justice. Over the following months, that is precisely what he and the Vaals judges did. Cunegonde was interrogated again about her attempt to kidnap Hendrick and Sara's baby. Martinus Buntgens and his father, Andries, were questioned, as were midwife Anna Olivier and the guardsmen who had kept watch over Cunegonde in the Coul. Father Bosten was summoned for questioning repeatedly. For more than a month the priest found one excuse after another to avoid appearing in court: he was away, he was "indisposed," his superior the bishop of Liège was "his only competent judge" and forbade him to recognize any other.[26] Finally, when he was going to be held in contempt of court, he and his brother appeared and were subjected to very hostile examinations.

What occupied the lieutenant governor and judges most, though, was the prosecution of the Aachen farmhands who had so egregiously violated Dutch territory and jurisdiction. Their crime was nothing less than a capital offense, under the legal code of the day, and the States General's instructions mandating their prosecution were clear and sharply worded. The officials already possessed, courtesy of the Dirricks family, a list of the impudent youths who drank in the Coul on Sunday, 18 April. Martinus Buntgens provided them with a list also of those who had piled into his house on the night of 15 April. Gimmenich, who had committed "many other misdeeds against inhabitants of this district and others," was the officials' number one target.[27] Again and again they issued summonses ordering him and the other malefactors to appear in court. Each time the court usher Quet posted the summonses on the doors of the parish churches and along the borders of the district. But these gestures were all too obviously futile: Gimmenich, Lotmans, Grommet, and most of the other perpetrators remained safely out of reach on the other side of the border.

Only two farmhands made the mistake of appearing on Dutch soil. One was a twenty-three-year-old named Pieter Koetgens.[28] Though he worked on a farmstead called Pfaffenbroich on Aachen territory, Koetgens came originally from Vijlen, one of the three villages that belonged to the Dutch district of Vaals. Buntgens had named him as a member of the band that had raided Vaals on the fifteenth, and two members of the Dirricks family identified him as one of the drinkers on the eighteenth. Moreover, Koetgens was known to all and sundry as the owner and sometime player of a flute.

Van den Heuvel and the judges were determined to make an example of whoever had so brazenly—and literally—"flouted" their authority. Two witnesses claimed that it was Pieter Koetgens's flute they had heard on the night of 15 April. So when Koetgens was apprehended in July and hauled before the Vaals court, he found himself in a very hot seat. The young man denied everything. He claimed he hadn't left Pfaffenbroich the night of the fifteenth, nor had he played his flute. He wasn't the only person, he noted, who had a flute. As for the following Sunday, he certainly didn't take part in the insulting parade, for he spent that afternoon and evening with a girl at the Burg (a favorite make-out spot for the local youth). Koetgens remarked indignantly that the behavior of which he was accused "would be entirely unbecoming to him as a native Hollander [that is, Dutchman] and as someone who had spent his childhood on Holland's [Dutch] soil."[29]

Under the circumstances, Van den Heuvel requested permission from the Vaals judges to have Pieter Koetgens tortured in order to extract a confession from him. However repugnant it may seem to us today, this request was completely in line with early modern norms. Not that judicial torture was employed lightly or carelessly—at least, not in the Republic. But when an accused person "dared adamantly deny" a heinous crime that seemed at least "half-proven," early modern law authorized prosecutors to extract by this means a confession.[30] In some parts of Europe, torture was deemed absolutely necessary in such cases because a person accused of a capital offense could be convicted and executed only if he or she confessed. This was the law in Overmaas, as it was in Holland, and in the Habsburg Netherlands. Originally the requirement was intended to protect suspects against unfounded accusations. The reality, notoriously, was quite different, and by the second half of the eighteenth century, many rulers and officials had developed serious qualms about the utility as well as ethics of judicial torture, which Frederick the Great of Prussia led the way in abolishing. In 1776, an official in Overmaas would lend his weight to the move toward abolition. Until then, however, judicial torture was still employed regularly in Overmaas. Between 1773 and 1776 alone, authorities there used torture to extract confessions from more than a hundred men accused of belonging to the Goat Riders.[31] In fact, then, it was not a discretionary matter but a legal requirement Van den Heuvel was fulfilling when he asked to have Pieter Koetgens tortured—"in omni gradu," as necessary.

Before granting the lieutenant governor's request, the judges followed best practice by seeking the opinion of two impartial jurists in Maastricht. The jurists' opinion came back that the judges should approve the use of torture if the witnesses against Koetgens confirmed their testimony in a "confrontation" with the accused. The confrontation was a common procedure in Dutch law. Whereas witnesses in a criminal case would initially give their testimony without the accused being present in the courtroom, in a subsequent "confrontation" they would be required to confirm their testimony in the presence of and facing the accused. The idea was that witnesses would thereby confirm the identification of the accused as the perpetrator of the crime, and judges would be able to assess the truth of the accusation from the comportment of both parties. On Tuesday, 27 July, therefore, Pieter Koetgens faced his accusers. According to the court secretary, Koetgens paled each time one of them entered the courtroom. All the witnesses confirmed their testimony. The judges hereupon approved Van den Heuvel's request, and since Vaals had no facilities for torture nor any person skilled in its application, they ordered that Koetgens be taken to Maastricht. There he would await his fate in a cell in the old city hall, which served as a jail. In the basement of the building was a torture chamber.[32]

The torture of Pieter Koetgens was an alarming prospect not only for Koetgens but for his family. Pieter's uncle took the lead in gathering evidence that might exculpate his nephew. He sent a notary to Pfaffenbroeck to take depositions from the sharecropper who ran the farmstead and from others there on the night of the fifteenth. According to these, Koetgens had been asleep in bed when all the action had taken place. The uncle also obtained depositions from two men who had seen the band of young men who gathered that night. According to the two, Koetgens hadn't been among the band. Members of Koetgens's family also took the step of threatening Martinus Buntgens that he had better change his testimony, or else.

Perhaps that is why Buntgens had an abrupt change of heart, or perhaps he was disturbed by the idea that he might be responsible for sending Koetgens to the torture chamber. In either case, he wasn't the only one suddenly to change his testimony: so did both members of the Dirricks family. All three witnesses traveled to Maastricht, where the Vaals judges convened in extraordinary session. All three were suddenly unsure of their identification. It was Buntgens, though, whose testimony was critical, for he alone had supposedly seen Koetgens on the night of 15 April among the band that kidnapped Cunegonde. With his change of heart, the case against Koetgens collapsed. The Vaals judges had no choice but to release their prisoner. It was a lucky thing: months later, the judges would hear convincing testimony that Koetgens had played no role in the kidnapping. They had almost tortured the wrong flutist.

CHAPTER FIVE

Beggar Dogs

As we all know, little sparks can light terribly destructive fires. So too in history, seemingly minor events sometimes trigger major conflicts. The dispute in Vaals over Hendrick and Sara's baby was just such an event. As we have seen, it originally involved only a small circle of people—family and clergy principally, who resorted to pressure and tricks, but no force. At stake was the religious fate of a child. But then came the baby's baptism, Cunegonde's attempt to "kidnap" him, and her arrest. In reaction to this drama, scores if not hundreds of people—rural folk living on Aachen territory, residents of Aachen, and inhabitants of Vaals—were swept up in the clash. Violence erupted on a scale that dwarfed Cunegonde's own futile act. First unknown assailants beat Sara's father, Mathias, nearly to death while enraged Catholics hunted Minister Pferdmenges. Then a band of armed youths invaded Dutch territory, stormed the tavern where Cunegonde was under arrest, and carried the young woman off. With this extraordinary assault, the dispute took on a political dimension. As the mock-military parade staged a few days later made explicit, Cunegonde's liberators challenged the sovereign control of the Dutch government over Vaals. In response, the Dutch sent in the army. From the local magistrates in Vaals to the States General in The Hague, Dutch authorities mobilized to capture and prosecute the Catholics who had attacked their religion and state. So eager were they to punish the guilty that they almost tortured an innocent man. Yet across the border, safe on Aachen territory, Catholics stood ready to perpetrate more violence in defense, as they saw it, of their community and church.

This conflagration could not have been lit had the fuel not already been primed for combustion. If the region of Vaals burst into violence in 1762, it was because it was ready to do so. Here we confront a paradox—a common one in the interwoven histories of religious conflict and toleration. On the one hand, Catholics and Protestants in the region usually got along well enough in daily life. It was perfectly normal for them to buy and sell goods to one another. Some maintained friendships, such as Father Bosten and the burgomaster, while a few intermarried, as did Hendrick and Sara. The two groups also shared common values, such as honor. Even their notions of the sacred overlapped, so that Mathias, for example, could expect Father Bosten to understand his outrage at the desecration of a sacrament. Yet at the same time, relations between Catholics and Protestants in the region were incredibly fraught in the mid-eighteenth century, and it took very little to provoke a breakdown in them. When Calvinists and Lutherans came to loggerheads in 1752 over the baptism of a mixed couple's child, leaders of the two Protestant groups could draw on a reservoir of fellowship and goodwill to douse the conflict. Not so Protestants and Catholics: whenever they clashed, their reactions were colored by a deep well of hostility and mistrust. That well had been dug long ago, in the sixteenth and early seventeenth centuries, when Protestants and Catholics in the region had struggled for religious and political supremacy, just as their brethren had done across much of Europe. The religious hatreds of that earlier era were still alive in the eighteenth century, and in the 1730s, after decades of relative calm, those hatreds had been reactivated. Against a background of enduring enmities and new strains, an incident had occurred in 1738 that plunged Protestants and Catholics back into violent conflict. This incident had inaugurated a period of renewed strife that was still going strong when the dispute over Hendrick and Sara's baby brought it to a climax.

The colorful, dramatic events of 1762 can only be understood as part of this longer history. Indeed, in some respects the events were not so singular at all. The year 1762 was hardly the first time Aachen's Catholics had fired guns in Vaals or assaulted Protestants traveling home from it. Nor was it the first time Dutch authorities had dispatched troops to the village. These actions fit well-established patterns.

To understand relations between Catholics and Protestants in the region of Vaals, we need to turn our eyes to the region's principal city. Anyone who visited Aachen in the mid-eighteenth century would have seen rising from its main square in front of city hall an imposing column (fig. 24). Erected in 1616, it was known as the *Schandsäule*, or column of infamy, and it stood there until a French revolutionary army pulled it down in the 1790s. Near the top, on its capital, it displayed on one side an allegorical figure representing justice, sword in one hand, scales in the other, eyes blindfolded. On the other side it showed the image of an executioner hacking with an ax the decapitated body of a naked man. The body was meant to be that of Johann Kalckberner, who in 1611 led Aachen's Protestants—Calvinists and Lutherans together—in revolt against their Catholic magistrates. Contrary to what the image suggested, Kalckberner was never actually executed. When Aachen's Catholic

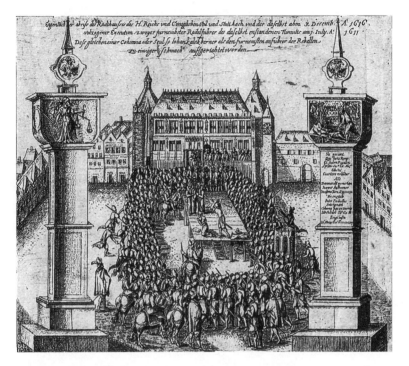

24. The *Schandsäule* (column of infamy). Seventeenth-century engraving showing both sides of the column, including the imaginary image of Johann Kalckberner's corpse being quartered. In the background, on a dais in front of Aachen city hall, two other leaders of the 1611 rebellion are being executed.

regime was restored to power in 1614, he and most other leaders of the revolt fled the city, escaping the capital punishment meted out to two of their associates. The image of Kalckberner's corpse being quartered thus did not represent a real event. It was an act of symbolic justice, intended as a perpetual warning and deterrent, as an inscription on the column explained: "Thus may they perish who, disregarding the edicts of his Holy Imperial Majesty, seek to destroy this state and royal seat. To the accursed memory of Johann

Kalckberner, leader of traitors in the last rebellion raised here in the year 1611, this column was ordered erected . . . by decree of the commissioners of his Holy Imperial Majesty." No mention of religion, but the potential traitors whom the imperial commissioners had in mind were Protestants.

Protestantism had come to Aachen in the middle decades of the sixteenth century, carried by refugees fleeing persecution in the neighboring Netherlands. These immigrants had received a warm welcome, and by the end of the sixteenth century more than half of Aachen's inhabitants had embraced the Protestant faith. Under the terms of the Peace of Augsburg (1555) they demanded freedom of worship, while under the terms of the city's medieval constitution (1450) they also claimed the right, as members of the craft guilds, to elect fellow Protestants to the city council. But the Habsburg emperors who were Aachen's overlords rejected these claims, and to impose their will, they had the help of Catholic princes in Jülich and other neighboring territories. Within the city the emperors could count on a segment of Aachen's Catholic elite who found it in their interest to exclude Protestants from government. So, in a manner typical of the era, religious divisions, social conflict, factionalism, constitutional disputes, and relations with outside powers all became intertwined. The results were explosive. Three times in thirty years—in 1581, 1608, and 1611—crowds stormed Aachen's city hall. Twice, in 1598 and 1614, the sitting emperor sent an army to purge Aachen's government of every last Protestant. After 1614, a coterie of Catholic magistrates maintained an iron grip on the city, and within a few decades fierce persecution, combined with economic decline (partly caused by the persecution), decimated the city's Protestant population.[1]

This early, formative experience of religious strife left deep scars and enduring myths. The *Schandsäule* contributed to the mythmaking by pinning blame for the 1611 uprising on an individual—as if

Kalckberner had not had scores of associates and thousands of supporters. Silent about the clash of faiths, the column cast the rebels as traitors pure and simple who had no religious motive or legal justification for their acts. What became the definitive Catholic version of events was written in 1631 by a magistrate and lawyer named Johannes Noppius. His vernacular chronicle of Aachen's history highlighted two interconnected things: Aachen's special relationship to the holy roman emperors and its character as a holy city (fig. 25). The special relationship to the emperors, whose figures adorned the facade of city hall, went all the way back to the first emperor, Charlemagne, who had made the city his capital and built there a glorious basilica, which became the Aachen Minster. Charlemagne became Aachen's patron saint, and three feast days dedicated to him were celebrated every year with a special high mass.[2] On three other feast days a figure of Charlemagne, twice the height of a man, was carried through the city streets in procession. It was Charlemagne, too, supposedly who had had four priceless relics brought from Jerusalem. Once every seven years pilgrims streamed to Aachen from as far away as Hungary to witness the salvific spectacle of the relics' display. Aachen was also the place where, for most of the Middle Ages, each successive holy roman emperor had been crowned king of the Germans. On this point Noppius did not need to exaggerate: Aachen owed much of its identity and prestige to its ties to the emperors, and an important part of civic life consisted in the celebration and confirmation of those ties through Catholic religious rituals. Turning to recent history, the chronicler attacked Aachen's Protestants for abandoning the religion "originally planted here by Roman emperors and kings" for the sake of "a foreign religion . . . of which their forefathers had not thought." In his book Protestants appeared as violent rebels whose faith was incompatible with loyalty to either emperor or city.[3]

Not only did Noppius's chronicle continue to be read in the eighteenth century, it was republished to meet unsatisfied demand.

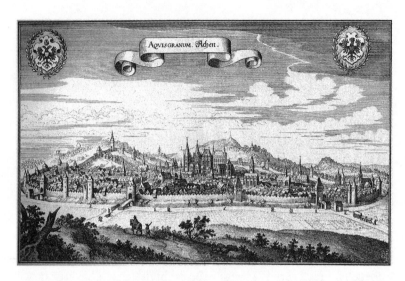

AQVISGRANUM. Aachen.

25. Aachen. View of the city from the south, with the coat of arms of the city in the top right and that of the holy roman emperors top left. Eighteenth-century engraving based on a seventeenth-century one by Matthaeus Merian.

A minor municipal functionary named Johannes Janssen copied long passages from it directly into a new chronicle that he began to write in 1739. Janssen expected the Protestants of his own day to behave just like the Protestants he read about in Noppius. He therefore took as an ominous sign what he perceived to be their rising numbers:

> Alas these days one sees here in our dear city of Aachen all sorts of sectarians—Calvinists, Lutherans, Anabaptists, Quakers, Freemasons, and more such heretics. Our dear Christian Catholic community had formerly to endure so much from this godless vermin. . . . [Earlier in my chronicle I described] the sorts of violence they committed against clergy and laity, church

and cloister, etc., and now the spiritual and temporal authorities let these people and their teachers once again live here in great numbers and enjoy freedoms. . . . Just wait and see, if a small uprising ever again occurs, whether or not a greater one again grows from it.[4]

Janssen was, to be sure, a moaner, the sort of person who constantly decries the state of the world. His suspicion of Protestants, though, was typical of most eighteenth-century Aachen Catholics, who harbored an anachronistic fear of a group that had long ago been reduced to a small, politically impotent minority. Deprived of full citizenship, Protestants in Aachen were barred from the craft guilds. They could not vote, sit in political bodies, or serve as municipal officials. Yet in the eyes of Aachen's Catholics, Protestants were still seditious "beggars." This derogatory label from the sixteenth century referred originally to the Netherlanders who rebelled in the 1560s against their ruler, Philip II of Spain. Unlike those original rebels, who had worn the label as a badge of pride, Aachen's Catholics used it as an abusive epithet, elaborating it often into "beggar dogs" to make it even more dishonoring. As late as the 1760s, it was how they referred in casual conversation to Protestants.

Aachen's magistrates shared the same historical consciousness. In 1763, they were outraged to find themselves the objects of a suit brought in one of the imperial supreme courts (the Reichskammergericht, or Chamber Court) by their Calvinist subjects. Where did the magistrates turn for evidence to support their side of the case? To Noppius, of course, whose account of events back in the sixteenth and early seventeenth centuries they (or their lawyer) summarized in a legal brief. Thanks only to one "atrocious rebellion" after another had Calvinists ever obtained a right to worship in Aachen. They therefore did not constitute a legal community or church, the argument went. Under the laws established in 1614, when order was finally restored, these "peace-hating people" were no more than "individuals granted residency" in the city. Those laws still remained in force; therefore, those who claimed to act as leaders of Aachen's Calvinist community had no standing to bring the suit.[5]

Aachen's Calvinists were well acquainted with Noppius's chronicle, but naturally they rejected its construction of events: what Noppius wrote, they argued, "was by no means any Gospel." They told a very different story, about "religious differences" that had arisen with the Reformation itself and for almost a century and a half had caused terrible turmoil not only in Aachen but across "our German fatherland." Thankfully, in their eyes, the turmoil had been laid to rest in 1648 with the Peace of Westphalia. At least, it should have been laid to rest: to them it seemed bizarre that Aachen's magistrates would dredge up this ancient history, as if it "had any bearing on the present matter." The Peace of Westphalia had guaranteed religious dissenters extensive rights, and a follow-up conference had formally registered the claim of Aachen's Protestants to enjoy those rights. So now the Calvinists insisted that they were fully entitled to sue their magistrates for violating the terms of the peace, which more than a century later remained a fundamental law of the empire.[6]

One of the rights which the Peace of Westphalia guaranteed dissenters was the freedom to perform Auslaufen—to travel to neighboring states to worship in accord with their faith. Less than a year after the peace was signed, the Dutch States General exploited this new right in order to alleviate the dire situation of their coreligionists in Aachen. They hired a preacher and arranged for Calvinist worship to begin in Vaals. From the moment of its inception, though, this worship was bitterly opposed by Catholics in Aachen and its rural Reich.

On the Monday before Easter in 1649, two Calvinist ministers came to Vaals accompanied by a Dutch military escort. One
was Philippus Ludovicus, the "Nestor" (most senior member) of
the Calvinist ministry in Maastricht. The other was Georgius
Ulricus Wenningius, whom Ludovicus installed as the first Calvinist
minister in Vaals. The ceremony was conducted in the Vaals parish church, where formerly only Catholic services had been held:
the soldiers broke open the doors of the locked church to give the
Calvinists access to it. After the ceremony, Ludovicus proceeded
alone to Aachen. Word of events had reached the city before him,
and in anticipation of the minister's arrival, a crowd had gathered
atop the city walls around the gate facing outward toward Vaals.
Among the crowd were students from the local Jesuit college, who
were invariably among the most anti-Protestant—and uninhibited—
Catholics in the city. As they watched, two sergeants, on orders from
the Aachen magistrates, barred Ludovicus from entering the city.
From above, the crowd heaped verbal abuse on the minister. Then
people began to hurl stones down on him (stoning was, of course, a
highly symbolic act, prescribed in the Bible as punishment for blas-
phemers). By luck, Ludovicus escaped mostly unharmed to nearby
Burtscheid.[7]

In the following decades, the Protestants who worshiped in Vaals
endured persecution and violent attacks. The Catholic ecclesiastical
court in Aachen prosecuted those who were married by a Protestant
minister or had their children baptized by one. Aachen's magistrates
ordered the city gates shut some Sunday mornings to prevent Protestants from traveling to services in Vaals. Bands of soldiers—mostly
Spanish ones in the 1650s and 1660s, French ones in the 1670s—
attacked Protestants en route, robbing them, stripping them of their
outer clothes, and handling them with a roughness that terrified and
sometimes injured. The soldiers attacked only Protestant travelers,
not Catholic ones. The Dutch garrison in Maastricht dispatched

military escorts to protect the Protestants on their Sunday commute, and the States General sent remonstrances to Aachen and
Brussels. Despite these measures, the trip to Vaals was sometimes
too dangerous to undertake, and services there had to be suspended.
With all this action by authorities and soldiers, it seems that ordinary lay Catholics themselves did not feel a great need to take the
initiative.[8]

Beginning in the 1680s, the Protestants who traveled to Vaals
seem to have been left to worship in peace. At least, the surviving
records of their churches do not mention incidents of persecution or
attacks. Instead, they show the Protestants quarreling a lot among
themselves, a luxury groups can usually afford only when secure
from external threats. The Peace of Nijmegen, concluded in 1678,
had brought stability to the region, demilitarizing and at least partly
depoliticizing relations between Catholics and Protestants. The
War of Spanish Succession brought temporary changes to the situation, but with its end in 1713 came a return to the status quo ante.
Then suddenly in 1738, a particular dispute triggered a resumption
of violence. The dispute concerned a life-sized figure of Christ on
the cross that hung above the entrance to the Vaals Catholic church.
The battle over this crucifix is worth recounting, for it inaugurated
a new phase of religious conflict; looking back later, Aachen's Protestants saw it as the beginning of the troubles that climaxed in the
1760s.[9] In this new phase, encompassing the middle decades of the
eighteenth century, Catholic peasants and burghers took the lead
in violently attacking Protestants and Protestant worship in Vaals.

The crucifix had hung on the outside of the Vaals parish church
"from time immemorial," according to Catholics.[10] At any rate,
it had been there since before the partition of Overmaas in 1661,
by which Vaals had been formally incorporated into the Dutch
Republic.[11] Despite a 1663 order for the removal of Catholic sym-

bols from public places, Dutch authorities had always turned a blind eye to the crucifix and allowed it to remain. Turning a blind eye to this particular symbol was not easy, given its size and prominence: it could be seen clearly from a nearby road, and even worse, Calvinists had to pass close to it every time they entered and exited their own church. They thus had to witness the reverence paid to the crucifix by Catholics, who would kneel and cross themselves. This behavior amplified the "offense" that the crucifix caused the Calvinists. Nevertheless, most Calvinists who worshiped in Vaals favored leaving the offending object where it was, not out of some warm embrace of toleration, but out of fear. Around the year 1698, when members of the States General happened to pass through the village and see the crucifix, a local magistrate conveyed to them the keen sense of vulnerability he and other Calvinists felt. The village, he explained, was "an enclave [surrounded] on all sides by papist lands." If the crucifix were removed, Catholics from those lands would take revenge on the Calvinists who worshiped there. Only after hearing repeated pleas did the visiting regents consent for the crucifix to be left "in statu quo."[12]

Some forty years later, the crucifix caught the attention of another outsider, someone who like the regents was not vulnerable to Catholic attacks, nor was he as enmeshed as were local Calvinists in the compromises and complicities that coexistence entailed. This person was Baron Eger Tamminga, then-governor of the Dutch Land of 's-Hertogenrade. How the crucifix came to his attention is not clear, for like his successor, Tamminga did not reside or spend much time in the territory he supposedly governed. We know why it came to his attention, though: in July 1737, Petrus Rademacker, Father Bosten's predecessor as Catholic pastor of Vaals, had the figure of Christ replastered and repainted. The figure had been "very mauled and damaged by worms" and, in Rademacker's view, badly needed maintenance.[13] The repair work must have been thorough, for some Calvinists gained the impression that Rademacker had replaced the old figure with a new one. Tamminga ordered his lieutenant governor to investigate and take action.

This put the ball in the court of Abraham van den Heuvel, who in 1737 already held the post he would occupy in the spring of 1762. Van den Heuvel knew the crucifix. In his own defense, he claimed that he had tolerated it only because he saw that it was "very old and broken and was going to fall into decay by itself soon enough."[14] In Van den Heuvel's mind, at least, toleration of the crucifix had always been a temporary accommodation that merely postponed, for however long, the day when such open manifestations of Catholicism would no longer be seen in the public spaces of Vaals. Now, though, he had to report that things were moving in the opposite direction: "The romanists [that is, Roman Catholics] in Vaals grow more impudent by the day as they see the brethren of the true Christian Reformed religion in the vicinity being thwarted and oppressed." The lieutenant governor's investigation unleashed a torrent of Calvinist complaint. Catholics, he was told, had begun "without the slightest caution, publicly before the eyes of the entire world, to perform their superstitious ceremonies for the burial of the dead, even on the Heeren Street and in the public cemetery, likewise also to carry the so-called 'venerabile' [the viaticum] to the sick more or less publicly along the streets." In January 1738, Van den Heuvel warned Rademacker to put a halt to all such "offensive innovations" and ordered him to remove the crucifix.[15]

The old priest demurred. Now seventy-eight, he noted, he had served the Vaals parish "peaceably" for thirty-six years. He had not intended with the repair work to make trouble. Years earlier, he claimed, he had once had the crucifix repainted without receiving any complaints and his predecessor had done likewise, so he hadn't expected any now. Given these past precedents, Rademacker felt he had done nothing wrong in having the crucifix repainted, and he denied introducing any "innovations" in ceremonies.[16] Was the priest telling the truth—the whole truth? It's difficult to say. In response to his claims, the lieutenant governor collected statements from some of the oldest Protestant residents of Vaals (Mathias Erffens helped with the collection; among those questioned was his mother-in-law, Anne Calefie, wife of Jean Renotte). All of them declared that in the entire time they lived in the village, the crucifix had never been repainted.

When Tamminga heard that the priest refused to comply, he ordered Van den Heuvel to initiate proceedings against him. That entailed applying for an injunction from the Vaals district court. At this point, though, the leaders of Aachen's Calvinist congregation intervened. Trembling at the thought of the vengeance Aachen's Catholics might wreak on the city's Protestants if the crucifix were removed, they convinced Van den Heuvel to postpone requesting the injunction. This bought them time to try to change the governor's mind, but they failed to do so, and in June the court issued the injunction. With the dreaded danger much closer, the Calvinists of Aachen and Burtscheid now pulled out all the stops, doing everything they could to halt or at least delay the proceedings. But again the governor refused to yield, and so at the end of July, the injunction was finally served on the priest. It gave Rademacker eight days to remove the crucifix, and on the last day permitted he did so.

Aachen's Calvinists knew they would be blamed for the action of the Dutch authorities. They knew they would be the object of reprisals, and indeed they received warning that, when they set off for Vaals the following Sunday, they would be attacked. Anticipating the attack, Aachen's magistrates strengthened the watch on the city gates. They also admonished the Jesuits to forbid their students to commit any "insolences" against the Protestants. These preventative measures were insufficient. On Sunday, 10 August, at around eight or nine in the morning, a crowd of several hundred Catholics massed in the vicinity of Aachen's Jakobskirche. Many members of the crowd lived on the adjacent Jakobstrasse. Home to some of the most bigoted Catholics in the city, the Jakobstrasse (fig. 26) was a major thoroughfare that Protestants had to traverse to leave the city for Vaals. That Sunday, the crowd blocked the way to the city gate, creating a gauntlet so intimidating to Protestants that most turned around and went home. When Minister Gerhard von Hemessen tried to run it, he was stoned but managed to get through. A lawyer's apprentice inserted himself between some soldiers passing through

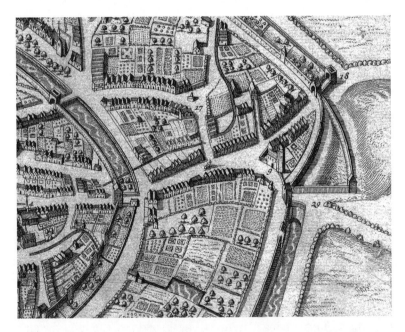

26. The gauntlet. Detail from an eighteenth-century map of Aachen showing the Jakobstrasse, through which Protestants traveling to Vaals had to pass. It is the main road from the center of town toward the right (west). The Jakobskirche is marked on the map with a number 9, the St. Jakobs gate number 18, and the alternative Junckers gate number 29.

the crowd, but instead of protecting him, the soldiers ended up wounded as well. A resident of Burtscheid who suffered from epilepsy was beaten with clubs until he sank to the ground; then he was kicked, dragged by the hair, and finally left lying there. Throughout all this, the watchmen at the city gate stood by, unable or unwilling to confront the crowd. Protestants who made it to Vaals faced similar assaults later in the day, when they found the road homeward filled with enraged Catholics. Some of the returning worshipers were badly wounded. A Catholic man who accompanied two little Protestant boys for their safety was not spared either, but was beaten on the arms until they were almost rendered lame. When a Lutheran maidservant dropped her hymnal, her attackers engaged in a sort of Catholic iconoclasm: they "tore up [the book] with their teeth and then ground the pieces into the earth with their feet, all the while making all sorts of godless expressions."[17] Few Protestants dared attempt the trip to Vaals the following week, and those who did were again assaulted.

The response of Aachen's magistrates to the riot seemed sincere and substantial, on the surface. When leaders of the Protestant community came to city hall, the magistrates expressed their sorrow, protested their innocence, and promised protection for Protestants traveling in future to Vaals. They also issued an ordinance threatening anyone who molested or assaulted the Protestants "with an ineluctable severe punishment." But their subjects in the city and countryside apparently knew they could pay the ordinance scant heed, perhaps because, as Van den Heuvel heard, the functionaries who went around publishing the new ordinance would "point over their shoulder as a sign that one needn't comply with it."[18] Or perhaps it was because those whom the magistrates arrested never received the promised punishment. Meanwhile, Aachen's magistrates urged the leaders of the Protestant congregations to press the Dutch authorities not to undertake any reprisals for the riot. Otherwise, the magistrates warned, the government "would not be able to restrain the raging populace any longer" (as if they had done so previously). The magistrates repeated their warning in a letter to the States General: should the legal proceedings against Rademacker continue, the magistrates could not be held responsible for the "manifold very dangerous inconveniences" that might arise.[19] The thinly veiled threat suggests that the magistrates did not find their subjects' illegal violence really so inconvenient. In fact, it gave them leverage when dealing with a far more powerful neighbor.

Not that the magistrates were lying: hundreds of Catholics in Aachen and its rural Reich stood ready to perpetrate further violence against the "beggar dogs." Rumors reached Van den Heuvel in Maastricht that the Aachen rabble "had threatened to ransack the houses of the Reformed in the village of Vaals, yea to set the entire village . . . on fire and cut to pieces some of the Reformed of Vaals." The burgomaster of Vaals and his family received threats, as did the lieutenant governor himself. In response, Van den Heuvel had a contingent of thirty soldiers dispatched to Vaals, where they set up a twenty-four-hour watch. This countermeasure proved effective. Although "crowds of rabble had appeared in troops in the village of Vaals and its vicinity on various days," Van den Heuvel could report at the end of August that no major incidents had occurred.[20] Still, the threat remained and the issue of the crucifix had to be resolved. For their part, the Calvinists of Aachen and Burtscheid continued their lobbying campaign, and in early September they finally convinced Dutch authorities of the wisdom of discretion. After investigating the affair, two commissioners of the States General ordered that the case against the priest be dropped and the crucifix returned to its former place.

With this concession, peace was restored—but not entirely. From that time on, Protestants later recounted, whenever authorities in

Vaals punished any of their Catholic subjects "for any offense they committed . . . the common folk [of Aachen and its Reich] did not fail thereafter on each and every occasion . . . always in the same way to pounce upon [the Protestants] and repeat the excesses described above."[21] That is precisely what happened in 1756, when the Catholic sexton of Vaals, Martinus Buntgens, got into trouble for ringing the bells of the village church tower during a Calvinist service. In revenge, a crowd in the Jakobstrasse harassed Von Hemessen and prevented him and his flock from traveling to Vaals.[22]

The 1750s in particular saw a whole variety of incidents: attacks on houses belonging to Protestants in Aachen and Burtscheid, attacks on Protestants traveling to Vaals, and attacks in Vaals itself. In 1750, three cloth workers were ambushed right in the middle of the village by a group of Catholics from across the border. The incident occurred on a Catholic feast day, which the cloth workers had spent weaving wool: one assailant later explained that his companions had wished to "teach" the Protestants not to work on such days. The assailants were all farmhands, and most of them lived on the same farmsteads as Cunegonde's liberators did twelve years later. One of their victims died of his head wounds. In 1757, a man shot one of the wings off the figure of an angel that served as weathervane on top of the Walloon church. The perpetrator, one Matthys Krieger from the Jakobstrasse, was amusing himself in Vaals along with a group of friends after taking part in a shooting competition. When the village burgomaster tried to arrest him, Krieger ran across the border onto Aachen territory and from there fired another round at the angel. That evening, after assaulting the Lutheran minister Zacharias Ennighman, Krieger and his buddies sent a message to the burgomaster of Vaals that they would "get" him. In response, Van den Heuvel launched a prosecution of the whole group and— once again—had a contingent of soldiers from the Maastricht garrison sent to Vaals for protection. Neither measure deterred the group from appearing in the village a month later to demand that their names be removed from the church doors, where as wanted men their names had been posted. On this occasion they attacked a village guard and his son, threatened a lawyer who acted on behalf of the lieutenant governor, and vowed that if their names weren't removed, "a bunch of [Jesuit] students" would soon pay Vaals a visit. In reprisal, Dutch authorities blocked commercial traffic to Aachen and threatened to confiscate properties on Dutch soil that belonged to Aachen burghers. Unable to catch the perpetrators, the district court could only condemn the men in absentia for "violation of the territory of Their High and Mighty Lordships, and sacrilege."[23] This incident anticipated closely the events of 1762.

Beginning in the late 1730s, then, Vaals, Aachen, and the area between them were once again seething with religious strife. The obvious question is why: Why did the dispute over a crucifix trigger large-scale, popular religious violence? Why did the violence continue sporadically thereafter? However incendiary the dispute was in itself, one cannot help suspecting that an underlying shift was afoot that altered the tenor of relations between Protestants and Catholics. If that is correct, we can point to two possible factors.

One was the economic decline of Aachen. This decline was nothing new: since its medieval heyday as one of Europe's premier centers of cloth production, Aachen had already descended far. Nor was the decline total; the city continued to attract immigrants and to play an important role in the more geographically distributed system of textile manufactures that flourished in the eighteenth century. That said, many of Aachen's inhabitants were afflicted in the eighteenth century with poverty. Many craftsmen in the textile industry in particular suffered unemployment as the merchants who controlled their industry had more and more of the work of cloth production done outside the city. Not coincidentally, the craftsmen were Catholic, while most of the merchants were Protestant. This polarization was a product of the exclusion of Protestants from Aachen's crafts guilds, which had left commerce as one of the only ways local Protestants could earn a living—and a good one it turned out to be. Protestant merchants not only favored craftsmen outside the city, whom they could pay less; they were accused of favoring Protestant over Catholic ones, bringing some into the region as new immigrants. This struck the craftsmen in the city hard. The economic situation for them reached a nadir precisely in the middle decades of the century, when Catholic journeymen in Aachen and Burtscheid repeatedly went on strike, boycotted workshops, rioted, and destroyed the equipment of Protestant craftsmen. Sara's father, Mathias Erffens, was one of the craftsmen whom Catholics bitterly resented. In 1737, the year the crucifix dispute began, he was barred from bringing wool he had purchased in Aachen to Vaals any longer for weaving.[24] Of course, the greatest loss to Aachen's textile industry was the construction in Vaals of Johann Arnold von Clermont's factory. Initiated in 1761, Von Clermont's move to Vaals formed part of the background to the events of the following year. Even Protestant masters like Erffens who were far from wealthy wielded economic power over impoverished journeymen like Hendrick Mommers. They did so not only by giving or denying them employment but informally as well. As we have seen, Erffens and his family were able to offer Hendrick much-needed clothing and furniture if he would acquiesce in the Calvinist baptism of his child. It was an example, complained Catholics, of "how the Reformed [go] about things, robbing people of their freedom through their bribes and gifts."[25]

The other factor exacerbating tensions was not specific to the region of Vaals. It was a wider rise in Protestant-Catholic tensions that can be observed, starting in the 1720s, across many parts of the Dutch Republic. These tensions were intensified by news of foreign events, in particular the persecution of Protestants in Poland, Austria, and Piedmont. On the Protestant side, they manifested themselves in a storm of protest over the appointment in 1732 of a new apostolic vicar for Dutch Catholics, in a panic two years later about Catholic plots, and in new restrictions on mixed marriage, among other phenomena. For their part, Dutch Catholics seem around the same time to have grown more secure and self-confident, thanks partly to a series of placards that extended to them a greater measure of official recognition. One of the placards, issued by the States General in 1730, recognized the right of Catholics in the Lands of Overmaas to worship publicly.[26] The result, at least in Overmaas, was more assertive behavior by Catholics. As Father Rademacker was accused of doing in Vaals, so in other nearby villages and towns ruled by the Dutch, priests began to carry the viaticum more openly through the streets on their way to performing last rites for the dying. Priests and mourners began to carry crosses, candles, and other symbols more commonly at funerals. The number of Catholic processions rose. It also became the custom increasingly for Catholics to kneel and pray at the ringing of the Angelus bell. In short, Catholics in Dutch Overmaas became less shy about performing their rituals in the public sphere. Synods and other Calvinist bodies complained repeatedly about such "papist impudences," which they said "were not decreasing but rather increasing daily."[27] Protestants reacted to such assertive behavior as Baron Tamminga had to the restoration of the Vaals crucifix, by taking countermeasures. Simultaneum, the shared use of church buildings and cemeteries, offered Calvinists and Catholics in Overmaas countless opportunities to harass one another. Above all, the two groups clashed over the ringing of church bells, whose use, too, they shared.[28]

These new frictions exacerbated the enduring religious enmities inherited from previous centuries. They seem in particular to have given a new impulse to the deep-rooted intolerance of Aachen's Catholics, who gained a reputation in the eighteenth century for being militantly anti-Protestant, more so than their counterparts in most other German cities. This special local animus against Protestants was a product partly of Aachen's unique history. It was also a testimony to the character of Catholic piety in the city and surrounding area. While the picture was far from uniform, Baroque Catholicism showed many signs of vitality in Aachen, as it did throughout the German Rhineland, in the mid-eighteenth century. Aachen's Jesuit college continued to expand until perhaps as late as 1750. New confraternities were founded while old ones remained active. New pilgrimages and processions joined an already rich repertoire. The number of masses commissioned for the souls of the deceased continued to rise, peaking in the 1760s.[29] The mentalities of many Catholics were as traditional as their practices. One of the tenets of Enlightenment thought held that nature operated according to physical laws without the intervention of supernatural forces (at least, not since the early days of Christianity). Yet most Catholics in the region of Aachen and Vaals continued to spy the hand of God in extraordinary occurrences, like the appearance of a comet. They trembled at the threat of divine punishment and, when misfortune struck, rushed to placate God to avert his wrath. Epidemics of cattle plague in the 1740s occasioned swarms of processions. When rain and cold threatened crops in the summer of 1763, thousands flooded into the churches for special services and prayers. When the bad weather failed to let up, Janssen blamed it on "the wicked morals of us humans": because of them "God shuts his ears and will not listen to our prayer." To be sure, Janssen was constantly decrying the sins of his fellows and predicting their baneful consequences; "every indication," he wrote, "is that the end of the world must be near."[30] Janssen's mentality was typical, though, of most Catholics in the region, a fact attested by the number and scale of rituals occasioned by communal misfortunes. Of these misfortunes, none provoked reactions as strong as an earthquake that shook the region on 26 December 1755. Janssen's account of the episode captures the horror and hysteria that gripped people in Aachen who woke at night to a series of shocks that cracked houses and toppled chimneys:

> Then everyone began to pray, weep, scream, lament—there's never been the like. Hundreds and hundreds of people ran to all the monasteries, sought a confessor—everyone wanted to do penance. People who hadn't confessed in six or seven years went to confessors. . . .
>
> All the good preachers in all the churches preach, cry out, call: cease your evil passion, godless slander, persecution; do right by those unjustly treated, put away such great hate and envy. . . . All this calling and preaching by all the preachers in the city was for nothing and in vain. But then the great, almighty God began to climb the pulpit and when he just set foot on the pulpit stairs the whole earth began to shake and move in a frightful way. Before the infinite God and Lord had even spoken, the streets were too narrow, the places of worship too small for the crowd of sinners, men and women, who wished to do penance—then they saw the might of God's arm. . . .
>
> Finally on St. John the Apostle's Day [27 December] in the evening Brother Michael on the hill comes with his entire neighborhood on the hill [and] they go in public procession with praying and singing through the whole night, and many other people accompanied them, [and] even though the weather was dreadful and rainy they continued through the entire night until the next day through the whole city, which then everyone in the city followed and [the procession] continued until Three Kings' Day [6 January], and no one paid any attention to rain, wind, or cold. All the parishes of the city went through the entire night.[31]

As more earthquakes struck over the following months, Aachen's pious Catholics threw themselves frenetically into further acts of individual and communal penance.

To be sure, the practices and mentalities described above had their critics, and not just among Protestants. As one of the most important cities in northern Germany, Aachen was not cut off from the new cultural currents that circulated with people and books. To the contrary, every year the city received swarms of educated visitors who came from near and far to take the baths. French army officers quartered in the city likewise influenced its cultural climate, and it was probably they who founded Aachen's first masonic lodge. Among Aachen's native population, though, Enlightenment culture began to spread only around the middle of the century and seems not to have penetrated beyond elite circles. Part of the effect of its spread, and the sociability that went along with it, may have been to increase the gap between the city's elites and ordinary burghers.[32] An examination of last wills and testaments shows that doctors, lawyers, magistrates, and other educated men began around the 1750s to abandon the idea of a God who intervenes in the world, either with vengeance or with mercy. Artisans, by contrast, held fast to traditional forms and customs for several decades longer. The same divergence split different segments of the city's clergy. One hears an echo of it in Janssen's chronicle, where under the year 1760 it is noted with disapproval that the canons of the Aachen Minster seemed no longer to believe in miracles. Across the German lands, a growing number of educated Catholics condemned the "superstitions" and "excesses," ignorance and bigotry in which they saw plebeians and, above all, peasants mired. The alienation ran in both directions. Attempts by "reasonable" Catholics to reform popular religious practices met massive resistance.[33] In Aachen, some manifestations of Enlightenment culture became themselves objects of popular attack. In 1765, word spread that certain Catholics had begun to study the Bible critically and had ceased to observe the prohibition against eating meat on Fridays. After several preachers denounced these Catholics from the pulpit, Jesuit students went from house to house seizing the Bibles and other suspect books. In 1779, mendicant friars in the city preached against Freemasonry. Inspired by their sermons, a group of Catholics attacked a Freemason. In reaction, the city council outlawed masonic lodge meetings. Where did Aachen's Freemasons reconstitute their lodge? Across the border, of course, in Vaals. Only after the prince-bishop of Liège (himself a mason) forbade the friars' preaching and the king of Sweden (also a mason) interceded with the city magistrates could the lodge move back to the city.[34]

The events of 1762 can only be understood in this context of enduring religious enmities, new frictions, and the persistence of Baroque Catholicism. This combination goes some way toward explaining the great propensity shown in the mid-eighteenth century by Catholics in the region of Vaals, especially the peasants and burghers of Aachen, to perpetrate acts of religious violence against Protestants.

Given how lopsided the violence was, it might be tempting to blame Catholics for all the religious strife in the region. Such a once-sided judgment would be mistaken. In the first place, Protestants had their own history of religious violence; it's just less recognizable to us today as violence or is seen as a lesser form of violence. As historian Natalie Zemon Davis was the first to point out, Protestant and Catholic violence in early modern Europe tended to take different forms.[35] Catholics usually attacked those whom they considered heretics in their persons and bodies: they injured, killed, and in the course of religious wars mutilated the corpses of Protestants. The archetypal form of Protestant violence, by contrast, was iconoclasm: Protestants mostly attacked images, symbols, and other objects associated with Catholic worship, especially those which Catholics venerated. But when Protestants destroyed, say, a crucifix or trampled on a consecrated eucharistic wafer, they were perpetrating in Catholic eyes an act of violence against God himself—arguably a far worse offense than attacking a human being. Dutch Calvinists committed widespread iconoclasm in the 1630s when they first gained control of parts of Overmaas. They did so again in the 1660s when for a time they suppressed Catholicism there, and again around 1680 after they regained control from the French.[36] True, most of this iconoclasm was committed by soldiers rather than civilians, or by magistrates in an orderly fashion rather than by rioting crowds. But that was because Calvinists had the Dutch state to act on their behalves, so they did not need to resort to violent action themselves. The same dynamic operated in 1738 when Dutch authorities ordered the removal of the Vaals crucifix: this, too, counted as iconoclasm in the eyes of Catholics, even if their own pastor had been forced to remove the symbol. When violence erupted in reaction, Calvinists relied on the army of the Republic for protection. They did so in 1738, 1757, and again in 1762. Local Calvinists were simply too weak and vulnerable to dare commit iconoclasm most of the time, even when they wanted to: they tolerated the crucifix mostly out of fear, not principle. Similarly, Aachen's Catholic burghers and peasants did not resort to violence much in the 1650s through 1670s, when officials and soldiers were actively persecuting local Protestants. They did not need to. In 1738, by contrast, it seemed that their faith was under attack in Vaals and that the authorities in Aachen were doing nothing to prevent it. Then they stepped in, initiating a sequence of attacks on Protestants and Protestant worship in Vaals.

Under the circumstances, Aachen's Catholics felt that their actions were legitimate in a political and moral as well as religious sense. The history of their city, in the version they learned of it, demonstrated that Protestants were a seditious lot who, if given half a chance, would again seize power, just as they had done in 1581 and 1611. While in reality Aachen's Protestants wanted nothing more than greater toleration, in the imagination of many Catholics they still aspired to overturn the city's religious establishment. In 1757, for example, a rumor circulated that Protestants were boasting that within a year one of their ministers would be preaching in the minster. But Catholicism was one of the foundations of the city's government, identity, status, and security. In committing violence, Catholics believed they were defending their civic community as well as their religious one, a duty that in their view Aachen's magistrates were now failing adequately to perform. This is again a pattern of behavior that Davis found more widely: crowds stepping in to assist civil authorities who were incapacitated or negligent, doing what they felt the authorities should have done themselves. Aachen's Catholics believed that their magistrates should have done more to suppress Protestantism, and it is possible that the magistrates would have done so had they not felt hamstrung—by the Peace of Westphalia, by the crucial contribution of Protestant merchants to the local economy, and above all by the patronage and protection extended to Aachen's Protestants by the Dutch state. These obstacles to official action did not stand in the way of unofficial, popular violence. Neither did the magistrates, who either were impotent to halt popular attacks on Protestants or did not want to do so. Protestants suspected the magistrates even of encouraging the attacks with the early modern equivalent of a wink and a nod. In the latter case, the attackers would have had even more reason to feel they were doing right. Alternatively, one might speculate that the magistrates' ambiguous behavior was the product of an inner, psychological conflict. Perhaps the magistrates retained some of the anti-Protestantism of their subjects, even as they accepted the new, eighteenth-century values that condemned persecution as a barbarous act. Few peasants or craftsmen, though, would have felt such a conflict, given the limited spread in Aachen of Enlightenment culture.

If many local Catholics hated and feared Protestants, the sentiment did not go entirely unreciprocated. Like their coreligionists elsewhere, Protestants in the region—even highly educated ones such as Abraham van den Heuvel—subscribed to anti-Catholic opinions. These opinions were not, for the most part, directed against the persons of ordinary lay Catholics, for whom Protestants, in a religious context, mostly felt contempt and pity. Rather they excited hostility against Catholic institutions, practices, and agents. Protestants continued in the eighteenth century to deny the legitimacy of Roman Catholicism by calling it "popery" and its adherents not Catholics but "papists" or "romanists." They suspected Catholics of putting their allegiance to a foreign potentate, the pope, above loyalty to their own fatherlands. With a sense of superiority, they dismissed Catholic rituals as "superstitious ceremonies" and branded the Catholic veneration of images and objects a form of "idolatry." When they witnessed public manifestations of Catholic piety, they denounced such demonstrations as "scandalous" and "offensive."

This anti-Catholicism might, on the surface, seem anachronistic, even archaic. After all, by the mid-eighteenth century, the Enlightenment had had a major impact on Protestant religious culture. Even bulwarks of the Calvinist establishment, like the Leiden theologian Johannes van den Honert, with whom Gerhard von Hemessen had studied, accepted many of the ideas of John Locke. Boasting that theirs was a reasonable religion, they attached greater importance to morality than dogma and urged Protestants of different churches to tolerate one another.[37] Enlightenment thought mixed in complicated ways, though, with traditional Protestantism, and an enlightened benevolence toward people of other faiths did not simply supplant anti-Catholic opinions. To the contrary, in many respects Enlightenment influence had the effect of reinforcing prejudice. Protestants had always condemned Catholicism for its "superstitions"; now Enlightenment thinkers construed superstition as irrational and primitive. Protestants had always said that Catholicism thrived on ignorance and fear; now education was proclaimed to be a social cure-all. Protestants had always accused Catholic clergy of tyrannizing the laity and crushing Christian freedom; now freedom of thought and expression became the credo of the avant-garde. And when Enlightenment campaigners elevated toleration to the status of an essential virtue, they simultaneously condemned the Catholic Church as a breeding ground of fanaticism. Thus eighteenth-century Protestants faced an internal conflict of their own: on the one hand, both faith and reason urged them to treat Catholics with tolerance; on the other hand, the edifice of Catholicism seemed to them inherently opposed to the progress of civilization and welfare of society.[38]

For the many ills they believed Catholicism caused, Protestants blamed the Catholic clergy. Back in the sixteenth century, Protestant polemicists had cast monks and priests as minions of Satan and agents of Antichrist. It had become an article of faith that Catholic clergy—all too human in their vices, despite their claims to sanctity—were the self-interested beneficiaries of their malign teachings. In the myths of Protestant culture, Catholic clergy loomed as immensely powerful figures, able to enthrall minds with their rhetoric and counsel and to command the laity's obedience with the weapons of penance and inquisition. No wonder Catholic clergy formed the chief exception to the patterns of violence described above: in Europe's religious wars, Protestants did attack Catholic clergy in their persons and sometimes kill them. By contrast, Protestants were inclined to excuse Catholic laity, at least partly, as acting at their clergy's behest or out of ignorance. Since the earliest days of the Dutch Republic, when Catholic laypeople committed a religious offense, Dutch authorities had usually suspected clergy of putting them up to it. They continued to do so in the mid-eighteenth century. In 1738, Van den Heuvel portrayed Father Rademacker as the sole instigator of the conflict over the crucifix and blamed the priest for all the "innovations" his investigation had discovered. Likewise, in the spring of 1762 he quickly came to suspect Father Bosten of being the "author or stirrer" of all the new troubles in Vaals.[39] Bosten's arrest later that year would trigger a new wave of violence more terrible than any before.

CHAPTER SIX

Reprisals

Through the high summer months and into the autumn of 1762, Dutch authorities pursued their investigation of the April malefactors. After the drama of 24 June, when Van den Heuvel had sprung his ingenious but ineffective trap, the lieutenant governor had little success apprehending the youths who had "kidnapped" Cunegonde. He only caught two youths on Dutch soil, Pieter Koetgens and Martin Mullenders. The one was almost tortured before the case against him fell apart. The other was released after questioning and, for unknown reasons, was never prosecuted.[1] The remaining suspects, more than twenty of them, remained safely across the border on Aachen territory. Three times the Vaals court summoned them to appear before it, but they never did.

Cunegonde remained locked up in the church tower—now under military, not village, guard. She presented the authorities with a different sort of dilemma, for there was a real question whether she could be held culpable for the crime she had committed. It was manifest to all that Cunegonde suffered from a mental disability—

what kind and how severe were matters of dispute, but not the fact of the disability. It was common knowledge in Würselen, Cunegonde's village, as the local pastor there attested in a letter to Aachen's magistrates. Cosigned by several villagers, the letter stated that "the said Cunegonde has been utterly simple and feeble-minded since her childhood and is scarcely able to distinguish between good and evil." The pastor and villagers ventured to assert that Cunegonde "could not consequently be subject to any criminal punishment." The Aachen magistrates, who questioned Cunegonde before returning her to the Dutch, took the same view. In a letter to the Vaals district court, they remarked that the court would no doubt notice the young woman's "idiocy and great feeble-mindedness" and hoped that the judges would "take them into due consideration." Upon Cunegonde's return, therefore, one of the first things Van den Heuvel did was send for three highly reputed medical doctors—two Calvinist, one Catholic—to examine her. After questioning the young woman, they found unanimously "that the said Cunegonde Mommers [is] not entirely witless but [is] an imbecile and stupid."[2] The meaning of the doctors' finding, Cunegonde's mental capacities, and their legal consequences would long be contested.

Even before questions arose about Cunegonde's culpability, though, Van den Heuvel had concluded that someone else bore at least as much responsibility as Cunegonde did for her attempt to kidnap Hendrick and Sara's baby. There was no doubt in the lieutenant governor's mind that someone had put her up to it, and that someone was Father Bosten. In his report to the States General at the beginning of June, Van den Heuvel laid almost the entire blame for the April events at Bosten's door. He claimed that Bosten had tried to force an unwilling Hendrick to have his child baptized Catholic. When Hendrick stoutly resisted, Bosten had been "driven so mad by this rebuff" that he had sent Andries Buntgens to fetch Hendrick's sister Cunegonde "in order for her to carry off the said child of her brother when it was presented in the Reformed church for baptism." This account contained several inaccuracies that would subsequently be corrected, as well as assertions that would be hotly debated. But regardless of the details, from this time on, from the lowest levels to the highest, Dutch authorities were convinced that Father Bosten had incited, instructed, and indeed ordered Cunegonde to snatch the baby out of the church. That made him, in legal jargon, "mandans criminis." When Cunegonde was found to be disabled, Bosten was deemed all the more responsible for her actions. After her examination by the doctors, the "general talk" in Vaals (among whom Van den Heuvel doesn't say, but clearly he means Protestants) "is that the pastor, who had this stupid, foolish woman summoned and used her, deserves greater punishment than she."

The lieutenant governor's accusations against the priest went further. When he described the "kidnapping" of Cunegonde by Catholics from across the border, Van den Heuvel said that he "ventured to surmise that all of this had occurred on the incitement and with the knowledge of the Roman pastor and his associates." As reason for his surmise he explained that Bosten "at the time of the tumult and violence could not restrain himself from appearing that same night on the street close to the place [where it all occurred]."[3] Van den Heuvel thus portrayed Bosten as playing literally in this second crime the role he played figuratively in the first: that of a shadowy figure lurking in the background, a gray eminence who used Catholic laypeople as tools to carry out his evil designs. Again, the details of the account would later be questioned. No matter: from this time on, Dutch authorities never doubted Bosten's role as the instigator of Cunegonde's liberation. Having gotten this simple woman into a fix, the story went, Bosten was determined to get her out of it. But in doing so, he committed a crime far worse than his first offense. For in using foreign civilians and soldiers to violate

Dutch territory and break Cunegonde out of "jail" (though it wasn't literally a jail), Bosten, a Dutch subject, had arguably committed the most heinous of all crimes: *laesae majestatis*—treason.

This narrative, whose key points Van den Heuvel sketched as early as June, was elaborated by Dutch authorities over the following months as they put leading questions to a series of witnesses and, finally, to Father Bosten himself. By November they had lost interest in prosecuting either Cunegonde or the farmhands who had kidnapped her. Cunegonde now seemed to them relatively inconsequential, and her limited responsibility for her actions, one may surmise, made her less satisfying as an object of retributive justice. The Aachen farmhands, meanwhile, were simply beyond the reach of justice. The most important factor, though, was that the authorities were now intent on frying a much bigger fish.

This crucial shift occurred, not coincidentally, when a new lieutenant governor replaced Abraham van den Heuvel, who died suddenly in August. Like his predecessor, Guillaume-Frédéric de Jacobi de Cadier belonged to the regional elite of Dutch Overmaas. His grandfather had been a tax collector and with the earnings from this post had purchased two estates in the Land of Dalhem, where French was the predominant language. His father had lived as a nobleman. His younger brother Christian married one of Abraham van den Heuvel's daughters and made a career in the Maastricht city government, which he headed for twelve years as burgomaster. Guillaume-Frédéric, or Willem Frederik, as he was known in Dutch, took a law degree at the University of Leiden, specializing in criminal law. After returning home, he was appointed to several government posts in Maastricht and Overmaas. He was, among other things, sheriff of Vaals when, with the approval of the States General, he was elevated in the autumn of 1762 by Count Bentinck van Nijenhuis to the lieutenant governor's office. At the time he was thirty-four years old.

De Jacobi de Cadier was much less experienced than Van den Heuvel had been. He was also, as we shall see, less judicious and less scrupulous. Soon after taking office, he took two decisive steps. First, he sent Cunegonde for safekeeping to Maastricht, where he had her locked up in a jail cell in the old city hall (fig. 27). There she could be "employed, through further questioning and confrontation, to convict and confound the . . . pastor."[4] The new lieutenant governor claimed to fear that, should she stay in Vaals, a further attempt might be made to free her. Second, he convinced the States General to grant immunity from prosecution to three of the farmhands involved in her "kidnapping" back in April—on condition that they testify against Bosten.

Thus armed, on 8 December the new lieutenant governor requested that the Vaals district court issue a warrant for the corporal apprehension of Father Bosten. It was immediately granted. That evening, the unsuspecting priest was summoned to the house where the court met. There, Bosten later recalled, "Having been detained under a pretense of friendship until around ten o'clock, he was then immediately apprehended and brought that same night, escorted by a detachment of soldiers and armed peasants, like a rogue and a crook, sitting on a horse tied firmly to another [prisoner], from Vaals to Maastricht, where, having arrived on the 9th at four o'clock in the morning in front of the city gate, and having had to wait until after the opening of the gate, he was then at eight o'clock towed in the same ignominious fashion, in view of the entire city, to prison in the new city hall."[5] The unsuspecting Bosten was given no chance to flee and his fellow Catholics were given none to free him.

Bosten's arrest was a turning point, not just in the pursuit of the April malefactors, but in relations between local Catholics and Protestants. Catholics reacted to the arrest with a series of reprisals against Protestants, Dutch authorities responded with counterreprisals against Catholics, and a cycle of violence was activated. As

27. Old City Hall in Maastricht, where Cunegonde and, later, Father Bosten were imprisoned. Their cells were in the attic; in the basement was a torture chamber. The building was also known as the Dinghuis.

we have seen, popular religious violence had been recurrent in the region since the 1730s. Now things got seriously out of hand. The result was a kind of religious war—popular, undeclared, but no less nasty for that.

The term *reprisal* means of course an act of retaliation. One thinks of it especially in the context of war, where one of the parties to a conflict seeks to avenge an injury or defeat. While the object of retaliation might be an enemy's military force, all too often in the history of war it has been noncombatants, third parties suspected (rightly or wrongly) of sympathizing with the enemy. These third parties are made to pay for the actions of others. Alternatively, they are sometimes used as hostages, in the hope that the threat of reprisal against them will deter an enemy from acting in the first place.

The term came to figure very prominently in the religious politics of early modern Europe. By some point in the seventeenth century, a majority of European rulers (though by no means all) had reconciled themselves, more or less grudgingly, to the presence of religious dissenters in their states. Even those who found the situation repugnant, like the magistrates of Aachen, often felt constrained by a variety of circumstances and needs, and found themselves either unable or unwilling to pay the price for imposing total religious uniformity on their subjects. Some, like the regents of the Dutch Republic, never tried. Thus Catholic states like Aachen ended up with Protestant minorities, while Protestant states like the Republic ended up with Catholic ones. But early modern rulers invariably cared about the fate of their coreligionists in other lands. This situation created on the level of international politics a rough balance of power between states with different official faiths, or at least a degree of mutual vulnerability. By treating dissenters in their own lands well, rulers created an expectation that their coreligionists in other lands would likewise be well treated; this was the principle of reciprocity. Inversely, rulers knew that if they treated dissenters badly, other rulers might punish their own dissenters with reprisals. Reciprocity and the threat of reprisals became common currency in the practice of religious politics. Some rulers made frequent use of them, the kings of Prussia perhaps more than any others. Frederick I and Frederick William I of Brandenburg-Prussia repeatedly threatened reprisals, and in some cases carried them out, against Catholics in their lands in response to actions by Catholic rulers in the Holy Roman Empire and beyond. The mere threat of reprisal turned dissenters into useful tools of diplomacy: when the archbishop of Salzburg decided, for example, to expel some twenty thousand Lutherans from his domains in 1732, Prussian Catholics begged him to desist after Frederick William spelled out the consequences for Catholic institutions in Prussian lands.[6] To be sure, the threat of reprisal sometimes failed to have its intended effect. Still, the fact that so many states held dissenters in effect as hostages tended to turn persecution into a zero-sum game that could yield no net benefit. In some cases, it demonstrably inhibited states from persecuting religious minorities.

Reprisals always factored in the calculus of religious conflict in the region of Vaals. As early as the 1630s, Calvinists asked the Dutch States General to close all the Catholic churches in Overmaas in order to persuade the Spanish to stop persecuting Calvinists there. They suggested a similar countermeasure in 1650. In 1663, when the Dutch removed all the Catholic altars and ornaments from the Vaals parish church, Aachen's magistrates closed their city's gates on Sundays to stop Protestants from traveling to worship in Vaals. In 1713, when Calvinist worship was terminated in Burtscheid, where it had briefly flourished, and the Calvinist church there was razed to the ground, the States General threatened to confiscate all the incomes owed to the Burtscheid abbey from properties located on Dutch territory. And in June 1762, when Dutch authorities demanded that Aachen's magistrates extradite Cunegonde, they closed the Vaals Catholic church and threatened to keep it closed until she was returned to them.[7]

Rulers and magistrates were not the only ones, though, to resort to reprisals. Just as ordinary people exploited the borders between states to pursue religious goals, so they used reprisals to pressure their religious opponents. This is not to say that such reprisals were rational acts performed by coolly calculating actors, but it does mean that they sometimes had a purpose beyond the immediate expression of religious hatred. The riot that erupted in 1738 on the Jakobstrasse is a prime example. Like other reprisals, the riot and the attacks that followed it made local religious dissenters—Aachen's Protestants—pay for an action taken by a foreign government, namely the removal of the Vaals crucifix. The Protestants were forewarned, the purpose of the threat being to create a disincentive so that Dutch authorities would not remove the crucifix in the first place. The threat was also intended to mobilize the Protestants to lobby the Dutch, which they did but to no avail. Although the violence obviously expressed anger and was a means for Catholics who felt that their religion was under attack to lash out at its enemies, it also succeeded in getting the Dutch to restore the crucifix. And like some official reprisals, the popular violence threatened to provoke counterreprisals: Aachen's magistrates urged the Dutch not to respond to the riot by taking any action against Father Rademacker, the pastor at the time. Otherwise, they warned, they would be unable to prevent their subjects from perpetrating even more violence in turn—a vicious cycle of tit for tat.

The arrest of Rademacker's successor in December 1762 triggered just such a cycle. By the time it petered out, the religious conflict in and around Vaals had taken on the proportions of a minor international incident.

Even before Father Bosten's arrest, all had not been quiet on the road between Aachen and Vaals. Protestants had been verbally harassed almost weekly, and in November, when Cunegonde was transported to Maastricht, Catholics responded with an attack that left two men seriously wounded. This was nothing, though, compared to the storm that burst when news of Bosten's arrest reached Aachen. To Calvinists it seemed "as if all the devils had been released from hell and had united with the rabble in Aachen and peasants in the Reich to force the Protestants here by every sort of molestation to get the dismissed priest set free."[8] Word went around that the Calvinist ministers in particular would pay dearly for Bosten's treatment. In the event, it was mostly laypeople who paid, one of them with his life.

Anticipating violence, few Protestants attempted the trip to Vaals on Sunday, 12 December. Some who did had stones thrown at them by Jesuit students and other Catholics as they attempted to leave Aachen; others were driven back by peasants with the warning that "they would not go to Vaals until they had freed the pastor of Vaals." The small, frightened group that made it to the village received at the end of the morning sermon a message from Burgomaster Strauch: they should keep together on the trip home but would be safe, as Strauch had dispatched a contingent of eighty soldiers to protect them. When the Protestants set out, though, instead of the promised eighty they found only eighteen or nineteen soldiers, and these "were so drunk that one had almost as much danger to fear from them as from others." A Calvinist later recounted the ordeal that awaited them when they arrived back in Aachen:

> Finally the poor troop of Protestants, escorted by these drunken guardian angels, reached the Jakobs gate, where they had to pause for a while and, like poor sinners, await their fate. Finally the officer of the watch came and informed them that it was

beyond the power of him and the entire watch to get a single Protestant through the city alive. Not only were the streets filled with enraged people, but the Jakobstrasse was barricaded by carts that had been shoved against one another. Everyone had supplied himself with a rich load of rocks in order to stone the so-called heretics.

The armed crowd did not flinch from facing down both the watchmen and the drunken soldiers, whom they chased along with the Protestants back out of the city with a hail of stones.

Just in time, the rabble was held back in the city by the closing of the gate. The little troop of Protestants had to put up with going, under the aforementioned escort, around the city to Burtscheid. To be sure, the soldiers shot at the mob that gathered on the rampart and city walls, but since they shot with blanks, as ordered, the Protestants had to continue on their way under a continuous rain of stones and offensive insults. However, God graciously averted all mishaps.[9]

Shaken by the day's events, a Protestant delegation rushed to city hall to complain to the city magistrates, whose reaction as always seemed sympathetic. Strauch and his colleagues protested "their powerlessness to control the raging rabble," but promised with soothing words to do their best to provide better security in future.[10] They also promised that if the ringleaders of the riot could be identified, they would receive an "exemplary" punishment. Protestants didn't think that identifying the ringleaders could present any difficulty. Hundreds of residents of the Jakobstrasse had stood in front of their houses looking on as the riot took place. The magistrates' own soldiers had witnessed it, as had officers of the city watch. The Protestants themselves denounced by name several people, including a "burgher's son" whom they accused of leading the riot.

Nevertheless, the magistrates made no arrests. Later they claimed that their diligent investigations did not turn up sufficient evidence to arrest anyone until March 1763. Coincidentally—or not—that was soon after the accused "burgher's son," a well-known trouble-maker, had been killed in a brawl with two Jesuit students. By the time they were in a position to prosecute, the magistrates claimed, the malefactor was dead. Protestants were furious. After the riot, Aachen's magistrates had reissued their ordinance threatening anyone who molested the Protestants with corporal punishment. But if the notorious leader of the riot could walk the streets freely and boast of his deeds over drinks at a tavern, why should any Catholic fear punishment? Under the circumstances, not a single Protestant dared venture out from Aachen or Burtscheid on the road to Vaals.

If they were not to be robbed permanently of their right to wor-ship, Protestants had to do something. But what? Opinions on this point differed sharply. Finally in February, a joint commission was formed to act on behalf of the three Calvinist congregations in Aachen and Burtscheid. To forge a united Protestant front, the lo-cal Lutheran congregation was invited to participate (it declined) and local Mennonites were asked for advice and financial support. The commission submitted a petition to the Aachen city council, complaining that local Protestants were being made scapegoats for the arrest of Bosten and other events in which they had had no part. Appealing to the council's sense of honor, the commission asked it to put an end to violence and disorder that would damage the "good name" of the city. In response, the council ordered burgomasters to investigate whether the Protestants faced any danger and, if so, to "take legal action, in accordance with the edicts, against disturbers of the public peace."[11] After receiving assurances, Protestants de-cided to test the waters, and on 13 March, for the first time in three months, a party set out for Vaals. En route, the party was attacked by a large group of Catholic peasants. Hiding behind some hedges lining the road, the peasants launched a volley of stones and excrement at the coaches and carriages in which the Protestants were riding. Windows were shattered, passengers injured, vehicles befouled. After this incident, the commission again submitted a protest to the city council. This time it used stronger language. "The extremely vexatious violence of the unbridled mob" was in effect robbing Protestants of their right to travel to Vaals to worship. This was a "blatant violation of the religious peace of Westphalia, [which had been] sworn at such a cost."[12] If effective action weren't taken, the commission warned, it would sue the city government in the Imperial Chamber Court, one of the two supreme courts of the Holy Roman Empire. The threat prodded the council into greater action. Not only did the council reissue its ordinance against molesting Protestants, but it offered a handsome reward of 100 reichsthaler for information leading to the arrest of anyone who violated it. Resolving to deploy "soldier-guards," it mustered the militia captains and ordered Captain Wolff of the Vaalserquartier (the blacksmith Conrad Wolff) to patrol the road. So on 27 March a group of Protestant coaches, carriages, and pedestrians once again set out. Not only did they meet the same treatment, but a Protestant traveling on foot was badly beaten. After this, Protestants again stopped traveling to Vaals.

As it had threatened, the Calvinist commission now took the step of suing the city government. On behalf of "all the merchants and other Protestant inhabitants of Aachen and Burtscheid," it requested that the Imperial Chamber Court issue a "mandatum de exequendo propria decreta"—an injunction requiring the Aachen magistrates to translate their ordinances into effective action.[13] By seeking the intervention of this higher, outside power, Protestants were escalating the local religious conflict dramatically, but not violently. The nature of the intervention was to be peaceful, its form judicial. This was the genius of the Holy Roman Empire, which for all its apparent weakness and dysfunction was good at conflict management. Imperial institutions like the Chamber Court offered mechanisms by which conflict could be directed into judicial channels and transmuted from physical violence into legal strife. At the same time, they performed the crucial function of offering protections to the weak against the strong. This was especially true of the Chamber Court in Wetzlar, which did not show the same aversion as the other supreme court to supporting subjects in cases against their rulers. On religious grounds as well, the Protestants may have expected a more sympathetic hearing in Wetzlar than in Vienna.

The Chamber Court was not known for its speedy handling of cases. In fact, one of the ways it helped pacify conflict was by drawing out its proceedings. This had the effect of keeping parties engaged with one another legally and thus with any luck not otherwise. The case of "All the merchants v. Aachen," though, did not have a pacifying effect. The court took less than a month to issue the requested injunction, ordering the Aachen magistrates to appoint a special prosecutor to investigate, apprehend, and bring charges against the Protestants' attackers. It also required the magistrates to deploy an adequate military force to protect the Protestants en route to Vaals. But the magistrates refused to obey the injunction, and it remained too dangerous for most Protestants to risk making the trip. This forced the commission, even as it continued its suit in Wetzlar, to seek a different solution. Escalating the conflict, it sought the intervention of another outside power.

In May 1763, the Protestants asked their historic patrons, the States General, to protect and secure for them "unhindered free access and transit to and from Their High and Mighty Lordships' church in Vaals." Not known any more than the Chamber Court for quick deliberations, the States General took until October to decide anything. Over the intervening summer, three more Protestants were badly beaten and the Aachen magistrates failed to arrest anyone. Based on information provided by De Jacobi de Cadier, the States General concluded that, however much responsibility the Aachen magistrates bore for the situation, someone else was ultimately to blame. The attacks on the Protestants, they judged, all "have their origin in the incitement of the Roman clergy there." The most effective course of action, they decided, was to threaten reprisals: if the Protestants who worshiped in any of the Lands of Overmaas were in future obstructed or harmed in any way, the lieutenant governor of the land in question was to close all the Catholic churches in his jurisdiction.[14]

For a while the threat seemed to work, as the Protestants of Aachen and Burtscheid enjoyed three months of peaceful travel to Vaals. On 15 January 1764, though, what Protestants had always feared finally happened: a Protestant youth was killed. The victim was an eighteen-year-old Lutheran named Gerhard Matthis Ullendahl who was walking home to Burtscheid with his brother and two friends after attending a service in Vaals. They were within hailing distance of the Aachen city gates when they encountered four "peasants" walking in the opposite direction. One of the peasants hit Gerhard hard on the head with a club (fig. 28). Gerhard collapsed to the ground, where he lay motionless. As quickly as they could, his companions "partly dragged, partly carried" him back to his home. Gerhard's distraught father summoned two surgeons and a doctor, but no ministrations could alter the fact that the young man's skull had been smashed. He died two days later of a contusion and heavy hemorrhaging.

Manslaughter was too serious a crime for Aachen's magistrates to brush under the carpet. They knew too that it might trigger reprisals by the Dutch. The magistrates therefore launched a thorough investigation of the incident. They soon got a detailed

MISHANDELING DER GEREFORMEERDEN OMTRENT VAALS,
TEN JARE 1764.

28. "Mistreatment of the Reformed Around Vaals in the Year 1764." This engraving from the *Vaderlandsch Woordenboek* (1793) shows Protestants being clubbed by Catholics while a friar lurks behind a tree directing the attack.

description of the perpetrator. They traced his doings earlier on the day of the crime (which included stops at two taverns to drink brandy). They quickly surmised that Ullendahl's killer might be a farmhand who worked on the Grosse Neuenhof. But then the magistrates managed to let the killer slip through their fingers. They brought in the farmer who ran the Neuenhof, a man named Werner Ortmans, and asked him about the seven hands who worked for him. Ortmans claimed that he "couldn't name or describe them without getting further information." Strangely, the magistrates accepted this answer and allowed Ortmans to go home, where it seems likely that he warned his employees that the magistrates were on their trail. One of them, Peter Hahnbucken, was indeed the killer. Along with his brother Johannes, Hahnbucken had participated two years earlier in the armed raid that freed Cunegonde. Hahnbucken's behavior at this point was as odd as the magistrates'. Popping up in Aachen, he arranged for several witnesses to hear his confession that he had indeed killed Ullendahl. Hahnbucken emphasized that his companions had not been accomplices and bore no responsibility for what he had done. Aachen's magistrates got wind of this extraordinary confession only two days later, but they didn't attempt to arrest Hahnbucken for another five days while they gathered further evidence. By the time they went after him, he had fled Aachen territory, reportedly taking refuge "in the French-speaking lands."[15] On the basis of Hahnbucken's confession, the magistrates decided not to prosecute his companions. Consequently, no one was punished for the killing, just as no one had been for the riot of December 1762. To Protestants it all reeked of collusion, although formally they accused the magistrates only of negligence. To aggravate the situation further, on the day Ullendahl died three Dutch soldiers traveling on the Aachen road were pursued and one was beaten bloody by a group of peasants.

With one Protestant dead and their own soldiers under attack, Dutch authorities did not wait for the Aachen magistrates to conclude their investigations. At the end of January 1764, De Jacobi de Cadier closed all the churches used by Catholics in the Land of 's-Hertogenrade. Those Catholics would now have to perform Auslaufen, just as Protestants in neighboring lands did except in reverse: in order to hear mass or receive the sacraments, they would have to travel from Dutch territories to churches and chapels in adjacent ones. They would have to continue doing so, resolved the States General, until the Aachen city government made amends, giving "adequate satisfaction" for the attacks.[16] It was a classic act of religious reprisal: since just 1750 the States General had ordered the closure of Catholic churches in the Generality Lands at least six times in response to Catholic "offenses." To close seven at once, though, may have been unprecedented.

The closure of the churches had international repercussions, albeit modest ones. Besides the magistrates of Aachen, two neighboring rulers found themselves affected: Charles-Nicolas d'Oultremont, Prince-Bishop of Liège, and Franz Jozef von Plettenberg, Imperial Count of Wittem. As bishop, d'Oultremont was in charge of the closed churches and their clergy, while as sovereign prince, he had state-to-state relations with the Dutch Republic. In March 1764 he instructed his ambassador in The Hague to protest the closure. The ambassador made light of the Protestants' complaints, suggesting to the States General that the whole fuss was about some "insults" to which the Protestants had been subjected. He pointed out that the Catholic parishioners whose churches had been closed had "nothing in common" with the magistrates of Aachen and were not the ones who had "insulted" the Protestants. It was therefore unjust, he argued, for the States General to punish the parishioners, whose freedom of religion, he claimed, was guaranteed by treaty. Their High and Mighty Lordships were not moved. If the prince-bishop wanted the churches reopened, they suggested, he had only to use his authority over the clergy of Aachen, who could easily convince the Aachen magistrates to make the roads safe for the Protestants, and had better do so soon if they wished "to forestall further decisions [by the States General which they would find] disagreeable."[17]

The Count of Wittem was affected on a smaller scale but more personally. He owned a castle in the district of Gulpen, and like most castles, it had a chapel. The count's secretary wrote to commissioners of the States General protesting that the chapel was private and was only used for worship by the count and members of his household. Consequently, he argued, it did not fall under the remit of the States General's order, which De Jacobi de Cadier had exceeded. The lieutenant governor easily rebutted this claim. If the count's wife had rheumatism and could not travel to services elsewhere, he added, that was just too bad: all the communities whose churches were closed had elderly and sick members who couldn't travel. The secretary protested further that the Catholics of Gulpen had played no part in any harm or hindrance done to the Protestants of Aachen and Burtscheid.[18] This argument, too, cut no mustard: it was precisely in the nature of religious reprisals that the suffering of innocent parties was used as leverage.

In the meantime, a third international figure intervened in the conflict, on the side of the Protestants. One of the sisters of Frederick the Great, the mighty king of Prussia, passed some weeks in Aachen, presumably to take the waters, in the latter part of 1764. While there, she and her retinue joined the local Reformed congregation on its trips to worship in Vaals. Aachen's magistrates could not ignore her demand for protection en route for herself and her coreligionists, as it would have been a political disaster had anything untoward happened to her or in her presence. The magistrates saw to it that nothing did.[19]

It was a plaintive letter from the burgomasters of Gulpen and Margraten that finally moved the States General in March 1765 to rescind their order. At that point, attacks on Protestants had ceased for several months. The States General wrote their good neighbors the Aachen magistrates informing them of their decision to reopen the churches and expressing their "reasonable expectation that the said magistracy would henceforth not neglect to enact such measures, and have them implemented with all due seriousness and vigor, that the insults and excesses to which the [Protestants] had been subjected would not occur again and remain unpunished." At the same time, the States General threatened new reprisals "of greater urgency and more direct application" should the attacks recur: in that eventuality, Dutch authorities would sequester the considerable income that the clergy of Aachen derived in the form of tithes from properties in 's-Hertogenrade. After all, remarked Their High and Mighty Lordships, it was the clergy "who are usually the cause of such disturbances."[20]

Judging by events, the reprisals undertaken or threatened by the States General were largely but not wholly effective. After De Jacobi de Cadier closed the Catholic churches, the sporadic attacks on Protestants grew rarer, but not even the threat to hit the Aachen clergy in their pocketbooks put a complete end to them. Whatever responsibility the clergy may have borne—and there is no evidence of any direct responsibility—for inciting the violence of their lay followers, it was unrealistic of Dutch authorities to think that the clergy could turn the violence on and off like water from a spigot. The reprisals failed also to spur the Aachen magistrates to fulfill the States General's "reasonable expectation." The magistrates did increase the watch on the city gates and dispatch armed men to patrol the road to Vaals regularly. The small patrol, though, could not make the entire road safe. Protestants complained that the men on patrol were desultory and often drunk. Given the part played by Captain Wolff and his family in the events of April 1762, it is hardly surprising that he and his subordinates did a poor job of protecting the Protestants. In Wetzlar the Protestant commission argued that the Aachen city government was failing in its legal duty to maintain order, keep the peace, and provide its subjects with "defense and protection." If the city's own military forces did not suffice, the government had an obligation to get help from the ruler of Jülich (the Elector Palatine) and the other princes who led the Imperial Circle of the Lower Rhine–Westphalia; this was an institution that bore some responsibility for upholding imperial law and maintaining peace in the region. The Wetzlar court agreed and ordered the city government to bring in outside troops if necessary, but it never did, and no wonder: the magistrates of any imperial city would have viewed such troops as a humiliating admission of incapacity and a threat to urban autonomy. Troops from Jülich would have altered decisively the relationship between Aachen and the ducal government, whose agent in the city, the Vogt-Major, was always looking to extend his influence. Protestants didn't mind. Their constant crossing of borders, along with the influence of Enlightenment ideas, made them less attached than their fellow burghers to local autonomy and privileges.

What most infuriated Protestants was the failure of the Aachen government ever to prosecute a single one of their attackers. In an effort "outwardly to appease and placate" them, Protestants accused, the government displayed a "pretended fake zeal" for punishing their attackers, while "in reality it left unused the means of enforcement that lay to hand." This was to make a mockery of justice and give as good as a green light to their persecutors.[21] Aachen's magistrates protested that they did their best in every case to investigate the Protestants' complaints and that in the two gravest incidents, the December 1762 riot and the killing of Gerhard Ullendahl, only circumstances beyond their control had prevented them from punishing the guilty parties. In all other cases, they claimed, their investigations had not yielded sufficient evidence to warrant arrests. Protestants didn't believe it, and their fury finally boiled over in December 1766, when for the first time they met force with force. The occasion was an attack on the master of the Lutheran school in Vaals, a decrepit man "whose behavior and build couldn't do harm to a child." The incident occurred one dark Sunday night when the schoolmaster was walking home from Aachen. The assailant who beat him with a club was twenty-six-year-old Wilhelm Schmitz, a member of the family that farmed the Grosse Neuenhof. Headed since the death of Werner Ortmans by Schmitz's brother-in-law Sebastian Gimmenich, the members of the family were "known to everyone as true zealots in the persecution of the beggars." The next day, Protestants in Vaals did not dare travel to Aachen except in a large group. Such a group was making its way home that evening when it encountered a drunken Schmitz with several companions. Schmitz reportedly attacked the group, but he and his party lost the bloody fight that ensued after one of the Protestants drew a hunting knife. Schmitz was badly wounded in an arm and a hand, from which he ended up losing two fingers. Having overpowered their opponents, the Protestants decided it would be futile to press charges against them in Aachen, so instead they dragged Schmitz and one of his companions back to Vaals to face justice there. But of course in so doing they committed a "violation of Aachen territory," giving Aachen's magistrates valid grounds to complain to the Dutch authorities. Two months later, De Jacobi de Cadier reluctantly agreed to extradite Schmitz and his companion, Peter Bischoff, back to Aachen. Sure enough, the magistrates let the two men off scot-free. Aachen's magistrates took the opportunity nevertheless to get even with the Dutch by demanding "satisfaction" from the States General.[22] Sebastian Gimmenich would later get even in his own brutal way.

According to Protestants, the violence against them would have ended if the Aachen government had only punished their attackers. Surely this claim was true at least to the extent that punishment would have had some deterrent effect. Events in Burtscheid seem to support the Protestants' case. In 1765 Catholic cloth shearers attacked and destroyed the house and workplace of a Protestant shearer named Wilhelm Ludwig, a recent immigrant to whom manufacturers were giving lots of work, leaving them unemployed. When Catholic shearers threatened to do the same to another Protestant immigrant, the abbess of Burtscheid did exactly what Protestants wanted Aachen's magistrates to do: she appealed for help to the princes of the Imperial Circle, who dispatched a contingent of twenty-four good soldiers. A combination of patrols, arrests, and sincere threats of punishment ensured that the riot was not repeated.[23]

To be fair to the magistrates, preventing attacks in Aachen and its Reich was far more difficult than doing so in little Burtscheid. Aachen was a troubled city in the eighteenth century with a well-deserved reputation for disorder and violence. Riven by factional strife between "Old" and "New" Parties, its politics were thoroughly corrupt, and when bribes did not suffice to win them elections, burgomasters employed henchmen to beat sense into the guildsmen who voted. Some guildsmen needed those bribes to help feed their families, as the restructuring of industrial production had left them unemployed. Strikes and other industrial actions were frequent in the 1750s and 1760s. It did not help that the government of Jülich, in its disputes with the city, used embargoes as a weapon, making the price of food skyrocket. A wealthy international elite periodically filled the city's baths and lodgings, bringing money to the city but also creating a huge market for gambling and prostitution and offering tempting targets for theft. Aachen also had a large contingent of students, never the easiest group to restrain even when they were not taught by Jesuits. Deference to authority was reportedly nil. The chronicler Janssen recorded, on the occasion of a labor strike, that "the common folk have made it known that if the court or mayor should try to punish anyone for it, they'd stone the [members of the] court itself to death." Janssen recounts numerous incidents in which crowds faced down magistrates and fought off troops—a daring perhaps less extraordinary than it seems, given that the army at the magistrates' disposal was a small, undisciplined force of some two hundred men who, as everyone knew, were forbidden to fire live ammunition at the city's inhabitants.[24]

For their part, Aachen's magistrates were furious, too. Not that the Protestants' lawsuit fazed them greatly: they had gone to court often enough in their conflicts with clergy, guildsmen, Jülich, Burtscheid, and other parties; the lawyers and judges in Wetzlar sometimes joked that if the empire had two cities such as Aachen, they would have all the work they could handle.[25] Like other local Catholics, though, the magistrates held a deep, historic grudge against the Protestants, whom they blasted as "peace-haters" who were guilty in the past of atrocious violence and rebellion. In the magistrates' construction of history, the Counter-Reformation had succeeded in purging the city entirely of non-Catholics. The Protestants who currently resided in the city therefore had no rights under the Peace of Westphalia and were tolerated only by the magistrates' grace and goodwill. In one submission to the court, the magistrates did not shrink from threatening to get even with the Protestants if they did not drop their suit.[26] Undeterred, the Protestants went on to win it. In July 1764 the Chamber Court issued a provisional judgment and in February 1768 a final one, both in their favor.

The government's threat of reprisal was not an idle one, though, and Protestants paid a price for their victory. No sooner had the court issued its first judgment than the government escalated the conflict in a new way by charging the Protestants a fee for their *Auslaufen*. Known as a "road charge" (*Weg-gelt*), the fee had existed for at least a century and was owed by anyone who traveled to or from the city in a wheeled vehicle. It was originally established to pay for maintaining the roads through Aachen territory, but recently the city government had begun to use it to repair the city's finances. Previously, Protestants had enjoyed a special exemption from having to pay on Sundays for their trips to Vaals. Now suddenly the so-called tax farmers who collected the fee on behalf of the city (and made a hefty profit doing so) began charging the Protestants two marks per horse.

It was not the first time the road charge had been used as a weapon of religious conflict. In September 1738 the tax farmers had begun to charge Protestants on Sundays in reprisal for the removal of the Vaals crucifix. The tax farmers had done the same in 1757 after another incident, until the burgomasters stopped them. This time, it was the burgomasters who instructed the tax farmers to begin collecting the fee, and they did not back down from their demand. So the Protestants filed yet another lawsuit in Wetzlar.[27] In this second suit the Protestants protested their willingness to contribute bountifully to the public purse, but not by means of an exaction that fell exclusively on them, for of course Catholics did not need to travel in order to attend mass or receive the sacraments. They claimed a continuing exemption on the basis of the Peace of Westphalia, long-standing custom, and the principle of fairness. Aachen's burgomasters, they claimed, had previously allowed them not to pay "partly to maintain equality between Catholic and Protestant fellow burghers . . . ; but partly also, since it already costs Protestants great effort, expense and hardship to travel such a long way through all sorts of bad weather, especially during winter, to go to church, in order to sweeten and lighten such effort and adversity for them somewhat by freedom from the charge in question."[28] This was not nearly as strong a basis for a suit as the one that undergirded the Protestants' demand for protection against violent attacks. Perhaps then it was not surprising that the court did not find in their favor. In fact, the court never rendered a final judgment: as both sides racked up legal fees, the case went on and on, and in 1788, when the Protestants' chief attorney, Dr. Carlier, retired at the age of seventy-three, he bequeathed the case to his lawyer son. This last remnant of the religious war triggered in 1762 had still not ended when a French Revolutionary army marched into Aachen three decades later.

CHAPTER SEVEN

A Moral Certainty?

While all this was going on—the attacks on Protestants, the reprisals by Dutch authorities, the court cases in Wetzlar—back in Vaals Father Bosten was being prosecuted on the charge of treason.

In the summer of 1762, Lieutenant Governor Abraham van den Heuvel had confidently called Bosten the "sole and principal cause of all the troubles [in Vaals] and their consequences." He had assured the States General that he had "enough material and proof to hand" to launch a successful prosecution of the pastor and, with their encouragement, had pursued the case.[1] His successor, Willem Frederik de Jacobi de Cadier, made the prosecution of the pastor his first and foremost business on taking office. Some initial inquiries sufficed to convince him of the priest's guilt, and in November he informed Their High and Mighty Lordships that he had discovered "various well-founded presumptions and indications . . . sufficient to create a moral certainty" that the pastor and his brother, the curate—or at least the pastor—had been the "authors" of Cunegonde's attempted baby-snatching, and "that the assembled mob of foreign residents of the territory of Aachen had been prompted by their instigation" to kidnap Cunegonde.

One might well ask, what is a "moral certainty"? De Jacobi de Cadier never explained the phrase, but clearly it meant to him something different from a certainty based on demonstrable facts. For however well founded his presumptions and indications might be, the new lieutenant governor had to concede that they "would not be of such evidence and weight as to stand the test of a judicial proof." That is why he needed the States General to grant immunity and safe-conduct to the three Aachen Catholics who had led the assault that liberated Cunegonde: Sebastian Gimmenich, Johannes Grommet, and Hendrick Lotmans. Without such assurances the three men would never give testimony in a Dutch court—indeed, they would not dare cross the border into Dutch territory—and without their testimony, De Jacobi de Cadier did not think he would be able to secure a conviction. And so he made the three men an offer: turn state's evidence, testify against the priest, and receive in return immunity for their crime. It was too good an offer to refuse, especially since the men had property and interests on the Dutch side of the border. De Jacobi de Cadier still had to convince the States General to approve the deal. To this end he claimed that the three men had not been leaders of the assault but merely "accomplices" who had acted "only rashly out of a blind zeal," without considering the seriousness of their wrongdoing; now they were prepared to testify "to exonerate their consciences."[2] This was, to put it mildly, stretching the truth.

A fundamental precept of law in the Dutch Republic, as in other parts of Europe, held that a suspect could not be arrested for a crime unless law enforcement officers satisfied a court that they had sufficient evidence to make a credible case—like satisfying a grand jury today.[3] It was this precept that prevented Aachen's magistrates, or at least gave them an excuse, not to arrest some of the worst perpetrators of violence against Aachen's Protestants, and in the Republic too the same precept gave many criminal suspects ample opportunity to flee. Flight was especially easy in the fragmented borderland of Overmaas, which was how it happened that many Goat Riders, members of the robber bands that plagued the region, evaded prosecution.[4] De Jacobi de Cadier reasoned that Gimmenich, Grommet, and Lotmans were sure to give him ample evidence to arrest Father Bosten, but if the priest heard that the three men had testified against him, he might well flee. So the lieutenant governor did not wait to take depositions from the men: no sooner had he received the States General's grant of immunity for them than on 8 December he had Father Bosten arrested and transported to Maastricht. As Bosten's attorneys later observed, this was arguably a violation of due process.

So commenced the prosecution of Father Bosten. Driven forward by De Jacobi de Cadier's unshakable certainty of the priest's guilt, the case was beset from the beginning by difficulties and marred by much chicanery.

On 27 December, Gimmenich, Grommet, and Lotmans came to Vaals and testified under oath. Following standard procedure, the Vaals magistrates put a series of questions to the three men that had been drafted by the lieutenant governor or one of his attorneys. In reply, the men provided detailed accounts of the events of 15 April and named some thirty participants. They clarified matters of special interest to the prosecutor: who had recruited the French soldier, who had used a firearm, and who had played the flute (not Pieter Koetgens, it turned out). Above all, De Jacobi de Cadier wanted to know who had put them up to the act. He dared Lotmans to deny "that he was not capable of bringing together so many youths and of talking them into such a dangerous undertaking." Therefore, Lotmans was asked, "by whose proposal and instigation" did it occur that he got Gimmenich, the French soldier, and "an entire troop of peasant boys" to gather on the evening of 15 April at the house of his master, Conrad Wolff? Lotmans denied that he had been instigated by anyone other than the sexton, Martinus Buntgens. All three witnesses were asked, did they not hear Buntgens "say publicly that the pastor Bosten and the curate Bosten had declared that the boys could do them no greater favor than if they got the arrested woman out of Vaals, and that he himself, the pastor, couldn't ask them, the boys, to do it and have them come to his house because of the scandal and danger [it would cause], for otherwise he would do so, and that they, the boys, would get something [that is, some money] from them for their troubles, and he, the pastor, was willing to take responsibility for whatever might come of their enterprise?" On this crucial question, the three men gave completely different answers. Lotmans denied it "per totum," noted the court's secretary. Grommet could say "only that the sexton had said, 'boys, you'll be doing the pastor and curate a great favor if you get the woman out.' " Gimmenich replied "affirmative per totum." So it went with question after question that laid responsibility at the pastor's feet: Lotmans denied, Grommet recounted specific words, and Gimmenich, the unscrupulous thug, sang sweetly to the prosecutor's tune.[5]

Until this point, neither the Vaals magistrates nor De Jacobi de Cadier had had any idea of the crucial role in Cunegonde's kidnapping played by Martinus Buntgens. In fact, it was Buntgens who had told Lotmans on 14 April that he "wished the woman could be gotten out of Vaals" and that the pastor wished it too. It was he who, the next night, had advised Lotmans, Grommet, and Gimmenich on how they might get access to Cunegonde and gave them a pep talk just before they led an armed band across the border. The testimony of Lotmans, Grommet, and Gimmenich also revealed that it was from Buntgens's house that the band had set out and to the same that it had returned with the hapless girl. When questioned during the summer, Buntgens had said not a word about any of this, nor had the Dutch authorities thought to ask. They had trusted the sexton and relied on his testimony to prosecute Pieter Koetgens, and now they learned the depths of his silence. "On account of his being related [to Cunegonde] as well as the pastor's incitement," concluded De Jacobi de Cadier, Buntgens had been "the organizer . . . of the criminal conspiracy, . . . the instigator of the forcible violation of Their High and Mighty Lordships' territory and jurisdiction, [and] . . . the leading figure in its administration and management."[6] The outraged lieutenant governor soon obtained a warrant for Buntgens's arrest.

Even after the three youths' revelations, though, the magistrates and lieutenant governor regarded the sexton less as a malefactor in his own right than as an agent of Bosten and a means by which they could bring down the pastor. The attempt they now made to use him as such constitutes one of the murkiest episodes in the prosecution of Father Bosten. It is murky partly because the protocols of the Vaals district court, which constitute a log of the court's activities, have a gap for the period 6 to 25 January 1763. It is a highly irregular gap in the court's records. Why the protocols were never registered for that period may just be down to accident. At the time, the court was meeting in Maastricht rather than Vaals, and the court's secretary, Isaac Daniel Fellinger, kept his notes on loose paper. Fellinger never transcribed his notes into the ordinary protocol book, perhaps because he subsequently became ill and died. That, at least, was the explanation offered by De Jacobi de Cadier when a very unhappy States General inquired after the missing protocols. The timing, though, seems wrong since Fellinger did not die until June 1764 and no subsequent protocols went missing. A more likely explanation is that members of the court did some very improper things in January 1763, things of which they wanted no record. Whatever the truth, it seems fairly certain that one magistrate, in his determination to convict Father Bosten, did, precisely in this period, perpetrate a grave abuse: he coerced Martinus Buntgens into giving false testimony. That magistrate was Bosten's next-door neighbor, the burgomaster of Vaals, Johan Frans à Brassard.

The account that follows of À Brassard's malfeasance incorporates testimony by Buntgens himself, his wife, his brother, and his brother-in-law—not impartial witnesses, obviously. But their story is consistent and credible, and although the accounts of their conversations with the burgomaster cannot be corroborated, the rest of the story was confirmed several years later when the States General demanded an inquiry.

The warrant for Buntgens's arrest authorized De Jacobi de Cadier to bring the sexton to Maastricht and lock him up. Even with a military garrison, Vaals was considered too vulnerable to attacks from across the border to keep prisoners there securely, and both Cunegonde and Father Bosten were already being held instead in the city. That meant that whenever a prisoner had to be questioned, the Vaals court met in Maastricht, where it convened in a chamber of the "new" city hall—the one constructed in the seventeenth century to a design by Pieter Post. The day the court issued its warrant, its members were in Maastricht, and À Brassard was with the lieutenant governor when De Jacobi de Cadier ordered that the warrant be brought to his attorney in Vaals, Hasenclever, for execution. At the time, À Brassard did not express two concerns he had about the execution of the warrant: Buntgens would have to be extracted somehow from Aachen territory, where he lived, and transported on the way to Maastricht through the County of Wittem, where an attempt might be made to free him. À Brassard also did not mention the feelings that Secretary Fellinger had confided to him. Fellinger, who resided in Aachen, shuddered in fear when he anticipated the wrath of his Catholic neighbors should the sexton be arrested; he and his wife would be "exposed to the greatest dangers."[7] Instead, À Brassard offered his services to the lieutenant governor, proposing to bring the warrant himself to Hasenclever. Later he claimed that he brought the warrant but the attorney refused to accept it. This was a lie. In fact, as À Brassard eventually admitted, he kept the warrant as a backup to use if necessary, but returned to Vaals with the intention of convincing Buntgens to come to Maastricht and testify of his own accord. In this way the burgomaster hoped to obviate the dangers that he and Fellinger foresaw.

The next day, À Brassard summoned Buntgens to his house and told him that "the boys" had testified against him.[8] Lotmans, Grommet, and Gimmenich had told the court that Buntgens had persuaded them to rescue Cunegonde. Bosten too had laid all the blame on the sexton. "I'd like it very much," continued the burgomaster, "if you would go with me tomorrow to Maastricht, as the lieutenant governor wishes to question you. What shall I ask you? Can you not say that the pastor himself told you to help get the arrested woman out of detention?" À Brassard ended his proposition with a promise: "If he [Buntgens] could say something against the pastor, he [À Brassard] would help him."

In reply, Buntgens declared "that the pastor had given him no advice on the matter, nor had he spoken to the boys." The sexton had qualms about agreeing to the burgomaster's proposition, "for I know that I would be pressured in Maastricht. I shouldn't go there with you, for I don't have anything to say against the pastor."

"Do not fear," reassured À Brassard, "I guarantee: you shall come home with me."

In a decision he would soon regret, Buntgens agreed to go with the burgomaster to Maastricht.

The following morning, 10 January, Buntgens's wife, Anna Margaretha Goesgens, accompanied her husband to the burgomaster's house. Fearful, she asked À Brassard, "What did it mean that her husband should go with him to Maastricht? Had the boys given some testimony against him?"

"A little," was the reply, "but the pastor puts the entire blame on your husband. But don't worry, we'll tell him what he should say, and then he'll get out and come back with me." À Brassard promised to pay Buntgens's travel expenses.

With this assurance, Anna Margaretha went home and the two men set off for Maastricht. When they arrived, they proceeded directly to city hall, where À Brassard gave one of his fellow magistrates a very incomplete account of events: "I've brought with me the sexton, [who has come] at my request and on my word that I would bring him back home a free man."[9] This was enough to elicit a reprimand; À Brassard's colleague told him his behavior had been very imprudent. Buntgens was then interrogated by the Vaals magistrates. However, he did not answer the questions put to him "as resolutely as expected." He conceded that the pastor had said to him "that he wished the woman could be freed." He admitted saying on the evening of 15 April, "Boys, you're doing me and the pastor a big favor." But he denied that the pastor had ever said "that the boys could do them [the pastor and his brother, the curate] no greater favor than by getting the arrested woman out of Vaals." And he denied that the pastor had ever charged him "with the planning and execution of that undertaking." At the end of the hearing, the frustrated magistrates told Buntgens he would do well to reconsider his testimony. The lieutenant governor then had Buntgens thrown in a cell, where he spent the following night with nothing to eat but bread and water. It was bitter cold in the cell that midwinter night.

The next morning, Buntgens received a visit from À Brassard, who asked him how he was.

"Not well," was the answer.[10]

"I've had a big argument about you. I've been to see all the gentlemen [of the court] and spoken on your behalf. If you could say something, anything, against the pastor, I shall help you, but otherwise you're going to take the rap for everything."

"If I had known that, I wouldn't have come here. I'm going to die of cold here."

"Figure out something, anything, [to say] against the pastor and I'll help get you free."

Then Buntgens made another decision he would regret. He sat down with pen and paper and wrote a statement that directly contradicted his previous day's testimony. Recounting the events of 14 April, in the afternoon after Hendrick and Sara's baby had been baptized, he declared that Father Bosten had said to him,

"I wish the woman could be gotten out of [the tavern where she was being held under arrest]." I said, "I'm afraid the woman may become unwell from it, but there's a watch guarding her." "Don't you know the boys in the Reich" [of Aachen, asked the pastor]? I said "no"—I said, "I have no close acquaintance with the boys." "I mean, [said the pastor,] couldn't you speak with one or another of them about their seeing whether they couldn't quietly get the woman out? It'll have to be done quietly, though. Go arrange it."

Later that day, Buntgens continued, he was summoned by the daughter of the blacksmith Conrad Wolff to come to her parents' house.

I was asked by the [blacksmith's] wife what had happened in Vaals. I told her everything that had happened. During our conversation, the servant [Hendrick Lotmans] came in. He heard me say that . . . the pastor had summoned [Cunegonde to come from Würselen]. He too wished she were free. The servant said, "If I had a few men I could make it happen, I'm not afraid, I'll arrange it. [Otherwise] it would be too bad. The wife said, 'I'd like to see that, go arrange it, yes, that would [otherwise] be too bad.'"[11]

This statement was dispatched to De Jacobi de Cadier, who quickly reconvened the court, before which Buntgens first read the statement, then confirmed its contents point by point. A day later, a confrontation was staged between Buntgens and the man whom he had betrayed. To the court's satisfaction, Buntgens confirmed every accusation to the pastor's face.

The next question was what to do with Buntgens. De Jacobi de Cadier was inclined to keep him locked up, but À Brassard and Fellinger pleaded for his release. Telling the lieutenant governor of the assurances he'd given, À Brassard explained that if he didn't bring Buntgens "back to Vaals a free man," he feared that the sexton's family members would "go after him."[12] Living as he did "on the frontiers," he "would be afraid every day for his life and of other dangers." À Brassard averred that, if he were allowed to bring Buntgens home as promised, he would be able to bring Buntgens back to Maastricht any time it should be necessary. Then it was De Jacobi de Cadier's turn to make a decision he would regret: he authorized Buntgens's release.

Several days later, the lieutenant governor thought better of his decision and sent a letter to Vaals ordering that Buntgens be returned to Maastricht, voluntarily if possible, but if not, with the aid of troops. À Brassard's claim was now put to the test.

Upon his return home, the sexton had initially resumed his duties in the Vaals Catholic church. After hearing a rumor about the letter, though, he had begun to avoid the church and the village. À Brassard thus found that the sexton had disappeared. He therefore approached members of Buntgens's family, including his wife, Anna Margaretha.[13] "Let your husband go [to Maastricht]," he asked her, "I promise and oblige myself to provide for you and your children for as long as he remains away, and I promise too that he'll get out, as long as he sticks to what he has declared against the pastor." When she replied that her husband would not enter Dutch territory, the burgomaster asked her to tell Buntgens to meet him at six o'clock that evening by the embankment dividing Vaals from Aachen's Reich.

That evening, the two men spoke to each other from just across the border. "Why are you avoiding our territory?" asked À Brassard. Buntgens said he had heard that everyone involved in Cunegonde's kidnapping was to be arrested. Dismissing the rumor, À Brassard claimed that the letter merely required Buntgens to answer some further questions. The burgomaster made a vow: "I promise you, you shall get out of this business, just stick to what you have declared against the pastor."

"This I cannot, nor may I, do," replied the sexton, "for my declaration was forced and contrary to the truth."

A few days later, À Brassard showed up at Buntgens's house. If the sexton would not come to Maastricht, asked the burgomaster, would he at least come to Vaals and ratify his previous testimony before the court there? He made a further request: "Sebastian Gimmenich should come too, and he should speak to [Buntgens] so that he and Sebastian agreed [in their testimony]."

Buntgens next did precisely the opposite of what the burgomaster had requested: he went to Aachen and made a declaration before a notary in which he formally recanted the statement he had made incriminating Father Bosten. The pastor, he declared, had never asked him whether he knew the boys in the Reich, and so on, nor had either the pastor or curate in any way "cooperated in such violence, directly or indirectly, with advice or otherwise." He had spoken differently on 11 and 12 January only "out of dread of the prison in which he then had sat for two days."[14] De Jacobi de Cadier would later claim that this recantation was as good as purchased by the clergy of Aachen in order to protect Father Bosten. What is certain is that Buntgens, who could no longer perform his duties in Vaals without being arrested, was appointed a few months later as sexton of Orsbach, a parish in the Reich of Aachen. He never again set foot on Dutch soil.

The whole sordid episode came to light only a year later, when Bosten's defense attorneys got wind of it. Collecting testimony from Buntgens and his relatives, they demanded that À Brassard, who by then was no longer burgomaster but remained a magistrate, recuse himself from the case against the pastor. The former burgomaster obfuscated and denied everything. Nevertheless, two expert jurists agreed with Bosten's attorneys. If the claims made about him were corroborated, À Brassard could not be considered an impartial judge on the case. In any event, the jurists advised the court, it would be wrong for him to serve as both judge and witness. The court felt impelled to take À Brassard off the case, "salvo tamen honore et juribus."[15] For the time being, the former burgomaster's honor was intact, but it would suffer severe damage from the inquiry into the missing protocols. Under pressure from The Hague, three of À Brassard's fellow magistrates would contradict him, the lieutenant governor would reveal his improprieties, and À Brassard himself would make damaging admissions.

Without corroborating testimony from Buntgens, De Jacobi de Cadier did not have a watertight case against Father Bosten. With such testimony he could have justified the use of what was called "extraordinary" legal procedure, which despite its name was the most common procedure followed in criminal trials. As part of it he could have had the pastor tortured to extract a confession, and a conviction would have been almost guaranteed. Without such testimony, the lieutenant governor faced the arduous task of collecting evidence that was less certain and piecing together a case that would hold up to scrutiny in "ordinary" court procedure. Although the prospect did not deter De Jacobi de Cadier, it may have caused him to pause. Perhaps he still hoped to obtain Buntgens's cooperation, or perhaps he was just distracted by other business. In any event, from February through July 1763 almost nothing happened in the case. Finally in August the lieutenant governor conceded that the priest had a right to defend himself in an ordinary procedure and submitted his indictment. The trial of Father Bosten now got under way.

Both parties to the case had highly qualified, well-connected legal teams. The lead barrister representing Bosten was H. J. Wilkin, a Catholic who for many years held high office in the Maastricht city government as representative of the prince-bishop of Liège (who ruled the city jointly with the Dutch States General). Bosten's solicitor had to be a Protestant, since only Protestants were admitted as solicitors in Dutch Overmaas. The brief went to none other than Stephan Arnold Schmalhausen, the man whom Cunegonde had almost knocked down when she had tried to snatch Hendrick and Sara's baby. Schmalhausen was deacon of the Calvinist congregation in Vaals. In his capacity as lieutenant governor, De Jacobi de Cadier functioned himself as public prosecutor, taking all key decisions on the case while his attorneys did most of the work. His barrister, based in Maastricht, was J. J. Levericksvelt, who like his counterpart held high office in Maastricht, but on the Dutch side.[16] As his solicitor in Vaals the lieutenant governor employed Hasenclever. For a time the Lutheran Hasenclever wore two hats in the case, working simultaneously as solicitor for the prosecution and clerk to Secretary Fellinger. Upon Fellinger's death, Hasenclever became court secretary. From attorney for the prosecution he thus became an official of the court that was supposed to decide Bosten's fate.

The lieutenant governor and his team charged Bosten with three crimes. The first was trying to force Hendrick Mommers to have his baby baptized in a Catholic ceremony instead of a Calvinist one, as Hendrick had purportedly agreed with his wife. According to the prosecution, these efforts violated the laws protecting the free exercise of the Dutch Republic's official faith. Bosten's second crime was commanding Cunegonde to snatch the baby out of the Vaals Reformed church, by which the priest had launched a violent assault on a Reformed service—the administration of a sacrament, no less. Bosten was held directly responsible for Cunegonde's act of sacrilege, which the prosecution construed as a capital offense. Finally, the pastor was accused of inciting Catholic peasants from across the border to conduct the armed raid that freed Cunegonde. At his urging, claimed the prosecution, foreigners had violated the Republic's territory, attacked a "jail," and freed a prisoner. Even if he hadn't taken part himself in the enterprise, the pastor had hereby committed "no less than a complete and qualifying crime of lese majesty," which in early modern law stood as the ultimate capital offense.

Naturally, prosecution and defense disputed the facts of the case. Had Hendrick and Sara agreed before their marriage to have their children baptized Calvinist or Catholic? Had Bosten really ordered Hendrick to use force if necessary to seize from his wife the baby she had just borne? Whose idea had it been to fetch one of Cunegonde's relatives from Würselen? When Bosten visited Cunegonde while she was in detention, had he spoken any words that admitted responsibility for her act? Had he revealed an intention to arrange the armed raid that freed her the following night? Had he or had he not instructed Martinus Buntgens to round up "the boys" to rescue Cunegonde? Calling between them thirty-eight witnesses, the prosecution and defense produced tons of conflicting testimony on all these questions.[17]

The most important question was whether on the afternoon of 14 April 1762, Father Bosten had really ordered Cunegonde to go into the Vaals Reformed church, snatch Hendrick and Sara's baby out of it, and bring it to him for baptism. The only witness to their conversation, other than the pastor and Cunegonde themselves, was the sexton's father, Andries Buntgens, who had fetched Cunegonde from Würselen. Between 1762 and 1764, Andries gave evidence three times, and on each occasion he testified that Bosten had advised Cunegonde to go to the Reformed church merely in order to speak to her brother, who he presumed would be in the church to attend the baptism of his baby. Bosten, he insisted, "had not said anything at all [to encourage], nor arranged for [Cunegonde] to get the child out [of the church]." The charge of sacrilege against the pastor, therefore, rested exclusively on the testimony of Cunegonde, who over two years gave evidence no fewer than seven times. It was on 5 July 1762 that she first recounted how Bosten had said to her: "The child is already in the beggars' church to be baptized. Young lady, you must go get it out of there. Then bring it to me, and we'll take it to the Catholic church to baptize it." When questioned subsequently, Cunegonde never deviated from this account. She maintained it steadfastly on 19 April 1763, when for the first and last time she and Bosten faced each other in court. It was a dramatic confrontation. When Bosten denied instructing her to snatch the baby, Cunegonde jumped to her feet and cried out, "I want to speak the truth. I do not want to bear the punishment for you."[18] When Cunegonde confirmed her account of the conversation, Bosten, according to the prosecution, ranted, raged, and tried to browbeat the young woman.

So it was Cunegonde's word against the two men's. Was she to be believed? In its concluding arguments, the prosecution cited Cunegonde's "constancy and candor" in confrontation with Bosten as evidence of her honesty. It portrayed her as "an innocent dummy" whose simplicity and faith the priest had taken advantage of. The defense, by contrast, cited Cunegonde's words during the confrontation as proof that she was testifying against Father Bosten "ex horrore carceris et metu poenae." It argued it was obviously in Cunegonde's interest to shift the blame for her manifest crime onto the pastor. Defense attorneys accused the prosecution of using threats and inducements to suborn false testimony from Cunegonde, just as it had from Martinus Buntgens. Above all, Bosten's attorneys insisted that Cunegonde's testimony could not be considered reliable and should not be deemed admissible in court: after all, the woman was an "imbecile." In rejoinder, the prosecution conceded that Cunegonde had a mental disability. Nevertheless, it held that even if Cunegonde's faculty of judgment was impaired, that didn't mean she was incapable of recounting past events accurately. To the contrary, it suggested, people like her "are usually endowed with an incomparably strong memory."[19]

A fundamental point in the case against Father Bosten thus came to rest on an assessment of Cunegonde's mental capacities. The assessment that counted for legal purposes was the official evaluation performed in court when three doctors had examined Cunegonde and declared her "not entirely witless but . . . an imbecile and stupid." It was therefore an astounding development in the case when the doctors' written statement went missing. Sometime in 1763, their evaluation of Cunegonde disappeared from the secretariat of the Vaals court along with two other crucial documents: the transcripts of the very first testimony Cunegonde gave, on 15 April 1762, and of the testimony she gave on 5 July 1762. When it was revealed that these three documents could not be located, Father Bosten's trial degenerated into a slanging match: prosecution and defense angrily accused each other of stealing them, and the Vaals magistrates found it necessary to open an inquiry into their fate.

Of course, everyone knew that the doctors had evaluated Cunegonde and everyone had at least a rough idea of their conclusions. The wording of their statement, however, mattered greatly:

according to Bosten's defense attorneys, the doctors had declared Cunegonde an imbecile and stupid "and thus incompetent to testify."[20] This was untrue, though if the attorneys were not lying when they denied having seen the statement, they could well have believed their claim. In May 1764 they set in train a search for the doctors' statement by demanding that all documents relevant to the trial be inventoried. In the course of producing the inventory, the Vaals magistrates discovered that the two transcripts were missing as well. They immediately dispatched the court usher, Daniel Quet, to the Aachen home of Secretary Fellinger with an order requiring Fellinger to return the missing pieces to the court secretariat in Vaals. Quet found Fellinger too ill to do anything. His wife, though, dropped a bombshell when she told Quet that her husband had sent the documents to De Jacobi de Cadier in Maastricht. When they heard this, Bosten's attorneys went into a rage: they denounced the surreption of the documents as an "abominable misdeed" of which they threatened to inform the States General. Claiming that the documents "demonstrated principally and absolutely the innocence of the accused," they demanded their immediate return "intact, unfalsified and in the same state as the same were filed *in initio* with the acta [of the case]."[21] By this time, Fellinger was so ill that it was clear he would not live much longer. Bosten's attorneys dispatched to Fellinger's home a notary and two witnesses, who heard the court secretary declare from his deathbed that on 6 January 1763, on the lieutenant governor's order, he had sent all the documents relevant to the case against Father Bosten, including the missing ones, to the lieutenant governor himself. On the basis of this declaration, Bosten's attorneys accused De Jacobi de Cadier of suppressing the documents and suggested that the lieutenant governor himself deserved to be prosecuted.

De Jacobi de Cadier did not take kindly to this "highly defamatory proposition."[22] Vehemently denying that he possessed the missing documents, he suggested that it was rather Father Bosten or his attorneys who must have them. It served the case of the defense very well, he noted, for the documents to be missing, since it enabled Bosten's attorneys to make false claims about their contents. Initially the lieutenant governor accused Schmalhausen of stealing the documents, but then he heard a rumor about Bosten's brother, the curate Frans Hendrick Bosten, who often visited the Vaals secretariat to pick up copies of documents needed for his brother's defense. Someone had heard Frans Hendrick gloat that on one such visit he had received more documents than he had asked for. De Jacobi de Cadier demanded that the Vaals magistrates investigate whether the documents in question were in fact the missing ones. So, in a highly irregular procedure, the magistrates hauled both Frans Hendrick and Schmalhausen—the solicitor for the defense—into court for questioning. Flatly denying the lieutenant governor's accusation, the curate identified certain other documents as the additional ones he had received. Schmalhausen, though, had a very different story to tell.[23] According to him, when he had asked Frans Hendrick some time ago what the additional documents were, the curate had, "with a very happy heart or face, answered the witness, we are pleased with them, without naming the same." Schmalhausen had found Frans Hendrick's behavior on another occasion equally mysterious. As he recounted to the magistrates, the curate had once confessed that he knew the doctors' statement was not in the secretariat, and that he knew how to get a hold of it.

"How do you know that, and where would it be then?" asked the surprised lawyer.

"A gentleman visited our barristers—he told them that this document was no longer in the secretariat."

"What gentleman was that?"

Frans Hendrick was silent.

"It must surely be a gentleman from the Vaals court or someone else who had access to the secretariat."

Refusing to confirm or deny the lawyer's suspicion, the curate had merely repeated, "We can get a hold of it."

On the basis of this testimony, the prosecution accused the defense of having the documents, courtesy of a secret supporter on the bench who had made off with them. The defense, meanwhile, continued to insist that De Jacobi de Cadier had the documents. Each side charged the other with lying and bad faith. Who really had the three documents will never be known for sure, as the originals never resurfaced. On 30 July 1764, though, De Jacobi de Cadier presented the court with copies of them. These copies were official, authenticated ones by Secretary Fellinger, whose signature they bore. De Jacobi de Cadier claimed to have found them when he and his attorneys conducted a thorough search through his papers for the originals. Bosten's attorneys would always question whether the copies could be trusted given their provenance, but considering their mixed contents, it seems unlikely anyone would have forged them. For if the copy of the doctors' statement did not declare Cunegonde unfit to testify, as the defense claimed, it still raised questions about the prosecution's reliance on her as principal witness against the pastor.[24] As for the copied transcripts, on the one hand they showed that on 5 July 1762, Cunegonde had blamed Father Bosten for ordering her to snatch the baby. On the other hand, the transcripts revealed that, when questioned on 15 April, the day after her attempted baby-snatching, Cunegonde had mentioned no such command—at least not by Father Bosten.

By the autumn of 1764, the case of "Governor of 's-Hertogenrade v. Johannes Wilhelmus Bosten" had generated more than a thousand pages' worth of complicated, conflicting documentary evidence. The final challenge for the prosecution and the defense was to knit this evidence into a convincing story that would secure a favorable verdict. The story had to be comprehensive, explaining not only the events of April 1762 but their prehistory, context, and consequences, including the twists and turns of the trial itself. It had to be coherent, tracing connections between events and offering a consistent set of explanations for them. Above all, it had to explain why people had behaved and spoken as they did. To do that, it had to portray Hendrick and Sara, Cunegonde, Buntgens, and all the other figures in the story as characters with comprehensible mindsets and motivations. Most important, it had to offer convincing accounts of the character and motives of the two chief protagonists: the accused, Father Bosten, and his prosecutor, De Jacobi de Cadier. In their final arguments, the lawyers for the prosecution and defense attempted to do just that. Each side appealed to the prejudices and preconceptions of its audience, the Vaals judges, to lend its story credibility.

As his attorney Wilkin portrayed him, Father Bosten was a cultivated man of the cloth, a gentleman who shared the norms and values of the educated elite to which he and the judges belonged. Reasonable, moderate, and tolerant, he embodied the virtues that his contemporaries associated with progress and civilization. In short, though the defense never used these terms, he was an Enlightened man of the eighteenth century. Would such a man ever behave as the prosecution had accused Father Bosten of doing? Wilkin entreated the judges to use their common sense and to attribute the same good sense to the pastor:

> It is, after all, repugnant to common sense [to suggest] that the defendant [literally: the detainee], an educated and cultivated, clerical, honorable man (against whose previous behavior no one had previously said the slightest thing) would give such a foolish and foolhardy counsel or order to an imbecilic and stupid woman to undertake and effectuate something that was absolutely beyond her power and in fact impossible, namely that she, alone

by herself, should go and snatch out of the hands of many people a child who'd been brought into a church for baptism in their presence, and, *nota bene* what's even richer, then bring the child to the defendant to be baptized, which the defendant indubitably knew *ab ovo* could not possibly happen [and] would result in the embarrassment of Cunegonde and himself. Indeed, to attribute such a crazy and mad counsel or command to one who not only has his ordinary five senses but to an educated and cultivated, honorable man (as the defendant is), as is attributed *ab adverso*, must strike everyone as improbable, unbelievable, and as pure madness—otherwise the prosecutor must maintain that the defendant is an ox and much more imbecilic and stupid than the prosecutor's wretched, stupid witness Cunegonde Mommers.

Wilkin made the appeal to class prejudices even more explicit in his rebuttal of another charge against the pastor. It was utterly incredible, he argued, to suppose "that the defendant would have incited and instigated the scum and rabble of Aachen and Aachen's Reich" to break Cunegonde out of her detention. These riffraff "are always, as is notorious, stirring one another up all by themselves with a very indiscrete fervor to [commit] on the slightest pretext of religion all sorts of rebellion and insolence (and thus need no author)." Bosten neither consorted with such base folk nor shared their fanaticism. As for his admonishing Hendrick Mommers to have his child baptized Catholic, Father Bosten had merely been the good shepherd performing his pastoral duty. He had never uttered the imperious words attributed to him or ordered Hendrick to use force.[25]

In the story told by the defense it was the lieutenant governor, not the pastor, who had acted unreasonably. Avarice had driven him to launch his prosecution of Father Bosten, and a "blind animosity" had led him to commit during it a whole series of procedural violations, excesses, and "crimes of falsification." In his determination to convict the pastor, De Jacobi de Cadier had even orchestrated the discharge and release of Buntgens and Gimmenich, "the real rascals and perpetrators" of the raid that freed Cunegonde. The consequences of such immoderate zeal in a case involving a religious dispute had been tragic: "Precisely because the matter of religion has had some influence on this business, the prosecutor should have proceeded all the more softly and with the greater moderation *propter publicam utilitatem*, namely to prevent further unrest and tumults, which only followed thereupon as a result of the prosecutor's own unlawful and violent actions." Wilkin alluded here to the attacks on Protestants perpetrated by the common folk of Aachen in reprisal for Bosten's arrest and imprisonment. By persecuting the good father, argued the attorney, De Jacobi de Cadier had triggered the religious conflict that had convulsed the region.[26]

For its part, the prosecution presented a mirror image of the contrast between the two men. Attorney Levericksvelt tapped the anti-Catholicism of the judges to present a very different portrait of Bosten. In telling of the struggle to determine the religious fate of Hendrick and Sara's baby, he reminded the judges of the "forcing of consciences and indecent procedures which the Romanists . . . are accustomed to employing." He denounced "the tricks of their casuists" that allowed Catholic clergy to lie without scruple. In explaining why Cunegonde had obeyed Bosten's order, Levericksvelt mocked the false authority that even "the most minor *sacredostuobularis* and village priest" exercised over the Catholic laity, especially "in places where blind popery rules." Recounting the attacks on Protestants traveling to Vaals, he quoted the States General, which had blamed the Aachen clergy as "the usual cause of such disturbances." Through such indirection, the prosecution presented Bosten not only as a man who *did* commit certain crimes but as one who *would* do so. Bosten was no gentleman; he was a priest who had behaved just like the other priests who were constantly whipping up the rabble of Aachen. As for the idea that such a "cultivated, educated" man would never have advised Cunegonde to attempt something so rash and foolish, De Jacobi de Cadier himself dismissed this as a red herring, citing "daily experience of the old saying, *Quod aliquando bonus dormitat Homerus* [Sometimes even the good Homer dozes—Horace], particularly when someone, driven by fury or an all too immoderate zeal, is so carried away that he doesn't know, or at least doesn't consider, what he's doing." In other words, Bosten had been gripped by religious fanaticism.

In the story told by the prosecution, De Jacobi de Cadier was the party doing his duty. In prosecuting Father Bosten he was merely executing the laws of the Republic, which of course required him to punish the perpetrator of the treasonable crime of "vis publica et fractae pacis ac seditionis." Viewed dispassionately, Bosten's interference with Calvinist worship had to be treated as treason too. Religion, declared Levericksvelt, was rightly regarded as "the basis, foundation, support and fundament of the well-being and enduring growth and flourishing of the substance of the state, which, if it is not properly maintained and, as is notorious, if it is upset and unsettled in its fundament, must inevitably be caused the greatest disorders, upset, and shaking." An attack on the official religion of the state was thus an act "tending toward sedition and disturbance of the peace." For the good, therefore, of the Dutch state and welfare of its people, it was incumbent upon the lieutenant governor to protect "the true Christian Reformed religion" against all hindrances and disruptions. True, for pragmatic reasons Their High and Mighty Lordships had allowed Catholics to worship, within limits, in accord with their faith. But Catholics enjoyed this freedom only "by the toleration and connivance of the authorities, who [demand] from them above all a humble acknowledgment of that goodness and connivance, and a special modesty and respect for the Reformed religion." In other words, Catholics had to respect the religious hierarchy of the Republic, in which they were subordinates.[27] Father Bosten had signally failed to do so.

Who then was the zealot, Father Bosten or De Jacobi de Cadier? With its counteraccusations against the lieutenant governor, the defense tried to shift the focus of judgment away from its client. Ultimately, though, it was the pastor, not the lieutenant governor, who stood on trial. The question posed by the case thus came down to this: Was Bosten an Enlightened gentleman or a fanatical priest? Was he reasonable or driven by religious passion? To De Jacobi de Cadier the answer had always been a "moral certainty," but it was not for him to render judgment. As things turned out, neither was it for the magistrates of Vaals. So great was the commotion over the case, and so intimate the involvement of higher authorities, that the official answer to these questions would be formulated not in the borderland of Overmaas but in the capital of the Republic, The Hague.

CHAPTER EIGHT

Their High and Mighty Lordships

People generally think of the Dutch Republic as a very decentralized state, and so it was. After all, it was the local magistrates and nobles of the seven United Provinces who ruled the Republic. These so-called regents did not cede sovereignty to higher bodies such as the provincial States or the national States General. Rather, they themselves composed those assemblies, and decisions of the weightiest import, such as whether to declare war or make peace, were decided by them after being debated in the councils of local government. Gathered together in their provincial assemblies, local authorities promulgated laws and levied taxes, which varied from one province to the next. Only a core of common affairs was handled by the States General, where the regents representing their provinces could not vote without specific mandates from their principals. Each province had an equal vote in the States General, and the great wealth of Holland, and within it Amsterdam, did not translate into a concentration of formal authority. The Republic had no king or queen, and the closest Dutch equivalent, the stadholder, was a pale shadow of a proper ruling prince. To be sure, the stadholder wielded enormous influence—increasingly so over time—as highest noble in the land, as captain- and admiral-general of the Republic's military forces, and as top official in each province. Thanks to his role in selecting magistrates and appointing officials, he disposed over great powers of patronage. Yet constitutionally he was a servant of the provincial States, not their master, and there were extended periods when the provinces did without a stadholder altogether.[1]

People often forget, though, that almost a quarter of the Republic's territory consisted not of provinces but of Generality Lands (fig. 5). These territories, most of which had been seized by the Dutch army in the course of the Eighty Years' War (1568–1648), were never enfranchised or granted much autonomy. Instead, they fell under the sovereignty of Their High and Mighty Lordships the States General, who ruled them from The Hague. The result was paradoxical: precisely because of their status as conquered borderlands (which they retained regardless of size), the Generality Lands had direct ties to the Dutch capital, where power over them was exercised. Consider, for example, Dutch Overmaas: its laws were issued, taxes set, and chief officials appointed all by the States General. Its lieutenant governors reported directly to the States General, carried out their orders, and did not dare take important decisions without their authorization. Other bodies in The Hague assisted the States General in governing Overmaas: the Council of Brabant heard appeals from lower courts, while the Council of State administered a wide range of affairs, including the upkeep of church buildings, hiring of Reformed ministers, and supervision of military garrisons. In alternating years, the States General and Council of State sent commissioners to the regional capital of Maastricht. And of course it was these two bodies, not local officials, who handled the relations with neighboring states that so impinged on life in the borderland.

Ironically, like other Generality Lands, Overmaas was doing far better economically in the 1760s than was the Republic's heartland. While Holland's cities watched their industries collapse and their paupers multiply, rural Overmaas reaped the harvests of a flourishing agriculture and was seeded with new industries, such as Von Clermont's textile factory. Yet despite its prosperity, Overmaas remained to the very end of the Republic in the 1790s a subject territory. As people in other countries petitioned their kings, so the inhabitants of Overmaas peppered Their High and Mighty Lordships with requests for legal exemptions, financial relief, and help in obtaining justice. This relationship of dependency and obligation extended even beyond the Republic's borders to the Protestants of neighboring lands, who employed attorneys in The Hague whenever they needed to lobby for support or protection.

It should come as no surprise, therefore, that authorities in The Hague decided the fate of Father Bosten, as well as that of Cunegonde and the other Catholics involved in the events of April 1762. These authorities acted at the request of the Vaals magistrates, who as the trial of Bosten approached its conclusion grew understandably anxious. The magistrates recognized that the case against Father Bosten was one "of great weight." They had observed "the commotion which the [case] was making throughout the Land [of 's-Hertogenrade]"—how could they not, given that the pastor's arrest had triggered something resembling a religious war? Given the sensitivity of the case and the mass of complex evidence it had produced, they felt that ruling on it would be "very thorny."[2] Even before the prosecution submitted its final argument, therefore, they resolved to do as Bosten's attorneys were asking and leave judgment of the case to outside experts. Over the course of the trial, the magistrates had sought more than once the advice of jurists in Maastricht. Now they turned to experts of even greater repute and authority: the "government attorneys" (*'s lands advocaten*). This was a group of attorneys who worked directly for the States General, offering them legal advice. Their judgment, issued with the authority of that sovereign body, would command obedience and protect the magistrates from the potential backlash that might follow a guilty verdict. And so, writing in September 1765 to Their High and Mighty Lordships, the magistrates asked them to instruct their attorneys to examine the records of the case and tell the Vaals court how to rule on it.[3]

Thus the case against Father Bosten went for judgment to The Hague. What happened next offers a lesson in the configurations of power, authority, and cultural influence in the Dutch Republic in its latter years. First the case went to the States General, who passed it on to the government attorneys and ratified their recommendations. Then it went to the young stadholder William V, Prince of Orange-Nassau, who had the authority to grant pardons. Finally there intervened a personage who has figured in our story so far only in absentia: Count Charles Bentinck van Nijenhuis, Governor of 's-Hertogenrade. All these high authorities accepted without question the charges leveled against Father Bosten. They insisted that Cunegonde and those who had kidnapped her be convicted of their crimes too. At the same time, they distanced themselves from the zeal of their local agent, the lieutenant governor, and lightened the punishment inflicted on the pastor. Their judgments were not only executed but also imitated by their subordinates in the borderland, who internalized the ambivalent mix of religious antagonism and Enlightened sensibility that swirled in the political heart of the Republic in the middle decades of the eighteenth century.

For authorities in The Hague, judging the case against Father Bosten meant returning to complete an old business, for they had been involved in launching the case to begin with. The States General themselves had instructed Abraham van den Heuvel back in

June 1762 to prosecute "to the full extent of the law" everyone complicit in the events of the previous April. Suspecting perhaps that local magistrates, for the sake of maintaining peace, might be too soft on the perpetrators, the States General had demanded that the Vaals court administer justice "without any connivance."[4] After consulting the Council of State and Duke of Brunswick, who commanded the Dutch army on behalf of William V, who at the time was still a minor, they had authorized the dispatch of a contingent of troops to help catch the perpetrators. Later they had granted immunity to the three leaders of the raid that freed Cunegonde from detention, to induce them to testify against Bosten.

Of course, the States General had done all these things based on information provided by their lieutenant governors, whose judgment they relied on and whose recommendations they usually endorsed. Normally, the States General placed great confidence in lieutenant governors and presumed that they would carry out their orders diligently. Although they had less confidence in local courts, they still tended to assume that the courts would follow the procedures prescribed by law. Their High and Mighty Lordships therefore received a shock when they heard in January 1766 the preliminary report of their attorneys. The States General were "very disturbed to learn that . . . various original documents have been mislaid and are missing, among others in particular all the proceedings and decrees relating to the case [against Bosten] in Maastricht from 6 to 25 January 1763." They ordered that De Jacobi de Cadier and the Vaals magistrates "make every effort" to locate the missing protocols, giving them only four weeks to report back. At the same time, they demanded answers to a series of embarrassing questions: Why hadn't the prosecution of Cunegonde Mommers been brought to a conclusion? Why had the former sexton Martinus Buntgens been released from jail? How far had the prosecutions progressed of the Aachen farmhands who had "kidnapped" Cunegonde?

They also asked whether the lieutenant governor had initiated any proceedings against Bosten's brother Frans Hendrick or the sexton's father, Andries.[5]

After investigating frantically, De Jacobi de Cadier and the magistrates wrote back in February informing T.H.M.L. that, although they had been able to reconstruct the events of January 1763, they could not locate the missing protocols, which Secretary Fellinger had possibly never written up. For his part, De Jacobi de Cadier had to admit that he had never submitted an indictment against Cunegonde. His plan had been first to use her to prosecute Father Bosten and then, only after his conviction had been obtained, to prosecute her. It had seemed to him that the charges he brought against Cunegonde would be determined partly by the evidence produced in the course of Bosten's trial. If the evidence proved that the priest had induced Cunegonde to kidnap Hendrick and Sara's baby, the lieutenant governor implied, she might be deemed less culpable for her act. Regarding the release of Martinus Buntgens from jail, De Jacobi de Cadier had to admit that he had been "weak" in yielding to the importunements of À Brassard and Fellinger. As for the prosecution of the Aachen farmhands, the lieutenant governor reminded his masters that they themselves had granted immunity to the farmhands' "principal leaders," a description he had not used for Gimmenich, Grommet, and Lotmans previously. He had begun to prosecute the other farmhands but had suspended proceedings for lack of the "conclusive proofs" needed to convict them. Part of the problem, he explained, was his dependence on the testimony of Martinus Buntgens, who had turned out to be a vacillating, unreliable witness. Similarly, the lieutenant governor said he lacked sufficient evidence to prosecute the curate or sexton's father successfully and so had not initiated proceedings against them.[6] De Jacobi de Cadier must have believed these to be reasonable rationales for his conduct or he would not have dared write them to his masters.

Understandably, he never confessed the essential truth: so consumed had he been by his desire to convict Father Bosten that the prosecution of everyone else had become a mere afterthought.

About five months later, De Jacobi de Cadier and the magistrates received word from their agent in The Hague (they too, as occasion required, employed an attorney in the capital): the government attorneys were finally ready to advise the States General. As customary, though, the government attorneys would not release their opinion until those who requested had paid for it. Thus it was September 1766 before Their High and Mighty Lordships received their attorneys' opinion, which they immediately adopted. In a devastating resolution, T.H.M.L. dismissed De Jacobi de Cadier's excuses and blasted him for not doing his duty. They were "very disturbed to learn" that the lieutenant governor had "been so imprudent as to consent, on the purported intercession of other persons using frivolous excuses," to the release from jail of the man whom he himself had called the "instigator of the criminal plot." Such informality and carelessness was "incompatible with the duty of an officer of high justice." They found it almost unbelievable that Cunegonde Mommers had never been indicted despite having sat in jail for more than four years and that the prosecution of the farmhands had been discontinued long ago. This state of affairs, "in an affair of such great weight, [causing such a] commotion, and of such great consequence for the Reformed religion," was unacceptable, and T.H.M.L. "very seriously recommend[ed]" that De Jacobi de Cadier set about correcting it as quickly as possible. He was to bring all the prosecutions to a swift conclusion, and the Vaals magistrates were to seek approval from the States General for their verdicts in each and every case.

At the same time, the States General sent the magistrates a draft verdict prepared by the government attorneys for the case against Father Bosten. They ordered the magistrates to adopt the verdict without the slightest alteration, have the sentence it prescribed properly executed, and report back when done. A week later the magistrates of Vaals "opened and read with reverence" their orders from The Hague. Obediently they converted the draft verdict against Bosten into a final one, and on 22 September two of them traveled to Maastricht to pronounce sentence on the imprisoned priest. Though couched in the legalese of the day, the sentence was relatively brief and direct. Without rehearsing his offenses or using emotive language, it found Bosten guilty, condemning him to perpetual banishment from Vaals, Dutch Overmaas, and all the Generality Lands. It also required him to pay the "charges and expenses [incurred in administering] justice, as well as the charges for the trial." Bosten was to remain imprisoned until he paid up.[7]

News of the sentence reached Aachen even before it had formally been pronounced. The reaction on the street was fury, made all the more ferocious by a rumor that Cunegonde too had been condemned by the States General, supposedly to be whipped and branded. Anonymous placards appeared in the Jakobstrasse and elsewhere calling on the peasants in Aachen's Reich to come to the city the following Sunday with hooks and other implements that could be used as weapons. The peasants were to join with the Jesuit students "to welcome the Protestants, should the latter get it in their minds to try to go to church." Vigorous steps by the city magistrates, including a stern warning to the students' Jesuit masters, prevented any violence, but the prospect of it had the predictable effect of deterring most Protestants from attempting the trip to Vaals that week. Some Catholics directed their rage also at former burgomaster Strauch, who it was said had extradited Cunegonde back to the Dutch on his own authority. Threats were also made against Johann Arnold von Clermont and another leading Protestant manufacturer, who purportedly had guaranteed personally that Cunegonde would be delivered back to Aachen "free and unpunished." The two manufacturers ran a notice in the local newspaper, the *Aacher Zeitung*, denying any involvement in the matter and offering a reward of 100 ducats to whoever would report the author of this libel. The *Zeitung* refused to run a similar notice that Strauch wanted to place, so the former burgomaster resorted instead to having a defense of his actions printed in Düsseldorf at his own expense.[8]

Meanwhile, De Jacobi de Cadier resumed the prosecutions he had initiated in 1762 against the farmhands. At the time, he had known the names of only some of them, but Gimmenich, Grommet and Lotmans had subsequently named many more in their confessions. Now all of them (except the three ringleaders, who remained immune) were summoned by notices posted "ad valvas ecclesiarum et limites patriae" to appear before the court. Of course none did so, and all were swiftly indicted. Martinus and Andries Buntgens were likewise cited and indicted. Frans Hendrick was not, as De Jacobi de Cadier continued to maintain that the curate could not be prosecuted for lack of evidence. Still a prisoner in Maastricht's old city hall, Cunegonde had only to be indicted. Since none of these people contested the accusations against them, their cases proceeded quickly, and by mid-November the magistrates had drafted verdicts for all of them, which as required they sent to The Hague for approval.

Once again the government attorneys inspected carefully the work of the Overmaas authorities. They insisted that the magistrates make several changes to the proposed verdicts. They had no substantive criticism of the verdict drafted for the Aachen farmhands. As the magistrates had written, all were to be found guilty of "acts of violence extremely harmful to the Protestant religion . . . and thus injurious and damaging to Their High and Mighty Lordships' sovereignty and territorial jurisdiction." All were to receive the same sentence as Father Bosten. Martinus Buntgens, their "principal flag-bearer, author, instigator, and inciter," was condemned likewise to the same sentence. The government attorneys rejected, however, the charges brought against Andries. In his indictment, De Jacobi de Cadier had called the old man Father Bosten's "advisor and counselor" and accused him of being the "implementer and executor" of the priest's criminal plot. The Vaals magistrates had proposed to find him guilty as charged, but the States General's attorneys instructed them without explanation to find him innocent. Clearly they considered Andries to have committed no crime when he fetched Cunegonde from Würselen. More surprising is that they absolved him also for guiding Cunegonde, on Father Bosten's orders, to the entrance of the Vaals Reformed church.[9]

As for Cunegonde herself, De Jacobi de Cadier had emphasized in his indictment the religious character of Cunegonde's crime: in disrupting the "venerabile sacramentum baptismatis" she had committed sacrilege, an offense that amounted to the crime of "laesae majestatis divinae"—treason against the divine majesty. The government attorneys omitted this charge. In its place they inserted a rehearsal of her misdeeds and a more political evaluation of them: they were "matters of very evil and pernicious consequence, amounting to the disturbance and mocking of the public Reformed religion and administration of the holy sacraments, which cannot be tolerated in a land of justice but ought to be punished rigorously as an example to others."[10] In this way, the attorneys distanced themselves from the lieutenant governor's fervent defense of the faith and cast Cunegonde's deeds as a problem of public order. On the form of punishment she should undergo, however, all the authorities agreed. Given the long imprisonment she had already suffered, as well as other circumstances—an oblique reference to her disability and perhaps also to her acting purportedly on Bosten's order—the authorities felt she should be treated leniently. Accordingly, Cunegonde was not to be whipped and branded, as rumor in Aachen had it. On 9 February 1767, under the guard of six dragoons, Cunegonde was transported back to Vaals to meet her fate.

The next day, in solemn session, the Vaals court pronounced its verdicts. All the men were condemned in absentia to banishment and payment of costs. Theirs was a purely symbolic sentence, as none of them would ever be caught on Dutch soil. Cunegonde, by contrast, was bound to a pillory with twelve rods, symbols of whipping, hung around her neck. In that state she was exposed for one hour to the derision, and perhaps worse, of the Vaals villagers. Then she was banished permanently from the Generality Lands and, like everyone else, required to pay the price of justice.

Early modern justice had a high price tag. Everyone involved was paid for his work, and it was the party who lost a case, not the state, who bore the charges. The magistrates who constituted the court were paid for every hearing they held and every decision they took. When they had to travel on court business, they received a generous per diem. The court secretary profited the most, but then he also did the lion's share of the work. He kept the court's protocols, drafted its sentences and decrees, and wrote its summonses and letters. To meet the needs of the prosecution and defense attorneys, he and his assistant also made copies (by hand) of every document relating to a case. The sheriff charged a fee for every arrest. As keeper of the court's seal, he also charged every time it was used to authenticate a document. The court usher was paid for keeping order when the court heard testimony from witnesses and for delivering the court's missives. Then there were the legal experts whom the court consulted. The prosecuting attorneys demanded payment, of course, for their services. Finally, if defendants were imprisoned, they were expected to pay their jailor not only for the food and drink he provided but also for heating and light.[11]

The indigent Cunegonde could never pay any of these charges, and Dutch authorities knew it. They never expected to receive any compensation from her or her kidnappers, and in any event the court fees for their quick cases were relatively low. Father Bosten was another matter. By the time he was sentenced in September 1766, the investigation and prosecution of his case had taken four and a half years. He and his attorneys had complained bitterly about the inordinate delays, which they accused De Jacobi de Cadier of purposefully causing in order to increase "the manifold costs of the prolonged trial and the ruinous damages and harm . . . done, slanderously and *puro vexandi animo*, to the defendant and his health."[12] Naturally, they had ignored the fact that not all the delays were the prosecution's fault. In any event, their complaints had been to no avail, and the agents of justice had racked up a huge bill. How huge wasn't entirely clear at first, but it was obvious it would exceed Bosten's ability to pay. Providing an inventory of his possessions (which alas has not survived), Bosten offered to sell everything he owned if it would be accepted as full payment for his debt. De Jacobi de Cadier dismissed the offer. He was determined to wring out of Bosten the full sum owed, and if the priest himself couldn't pay, the lieutenant governor apparently expected others to do so for him. To increase the pressure on him, and them, De Jacobi de Cadier had Bosten transferred from the basement of Maastricht's new city hall, where the pastor had been held in conditions that were at least reasonable, to the old city hall, whose cells were distinctly unpleasant. There he was to be held "in stricter confinement" until he paid up. On all these points the States General concurred. They authorized the Vaals magistrates to calculate the full bill and send it to them for inspection.[13]

It had taken Secretary Hasenclever two weeks just to inventory all the documents relating to Bosten's trial; it cost him many more weeks' labor to itemize and tabulate all the charges. When he did so in the spring of 1767, the results were eye watering: the fees demanded by the Vaals court amounted to 3,879 guilders in Brabant/Maastricht coinage, the prosecuting attorneys' fees were 1,898 guilders, and the cost of jail and other out-of-pocket expenses amounted to 3,411 guilders, for a grand total of 9,188 guilders. To grasp what an astronomic sum this was, one might note that when Vaals had a new courthouse built in 1773, constructed of brick with a courtroom, guardroom, lodgings for the court usher, a Mansard roof, and a much-needed jail in the cellar, the total cost amounted to 4,000 guilders. When in May Hasenclever sent Bosten's bill to The Hague for approval, the pastor and his attorneys appealed immediately to the States General. They asked the sovereign to "moderate" the bill, which they claimed was "filled not only with exorbitant charges but with manifold inadmissible ones—voluptuous charges caused by the prosecutor's own fault." The States General and their attorneys agreed, if not in tone, then in substance. In fact, reports of abuses in the judicial system of Overmaas prompted the States General just a few years later to launch a general investigation. It found that courts in Overmaas overcharged on a regular basis, reaping fat profits for their members by setting excessive fees and prolonging cases needlessly.[14] In Bosten's case, the States General handled the issue on an ad hoc basis. They could not alter the expenses already paid out of pocket, but they more than halved the court's fees and reduced by over 40 percent the attorneys' fees. The total bill, excluding miscellaneous items, now stood at 6,321 guilders.[15] Even this sum was beyond the means of a village priest, and as long as Bosten remained imprisoned, it kept rising.

At this juncture, in August 1767, the hierarchy of the Roman Catholic Church mobilized to help its servant. Until then, it had mostly kept quiet. When asked by Bosten's attorneys, the dean of the Aachen Minster had provided a deposition supporting one of Bosten's claims. The chapter itself had once gifted Bosten the sum of 100 florins, perhaps to ease the conditions of his imprisonment.[16] But neither the prince-bishop of Liège nor his other subordinates had intervened on Bosten's behalf. Now, at Bosten's request, the archdeacon of Haspengouw, Frans Karel Count of Velbruck, raised money to get him out of jail. The archdeacon wrote a stirring letter to the priests of his district, which included Vaals and more than three hundred other parishes. In it he told them that Bosten had been convicted of a crime he did not commit, and that because Bosten was unable to pay the charges for his trial, he had been "forced to suffer the squalors of a harsher confinement." This amounted to persecution, wrote the archdeacon, ordering his priests to make a special collection of alms among their parishioners "pro captivi redemptione."[17] Such a collection of funds from Catholic laypeople is perhaps what De Jacobi de Cadier had always intended. The Dutch Republic had a long history of law enforcement officials holding priests for ransom by their fellow Catholics, though in Bosten's case it does not seem—contrary to the priest's accusation—that De Jacobi de Cadier personally profited.

We do not know how much the collection raised, but the sum did not suffice to get Father Bosten released. It was from jail, then, that Bosten turned in December 1767 to the one authority who had the power, not to overturn a conviction ordered by the States General, but to pardon him for it. He appealed for mercy to the stadholder.

Dutch historians tend to be merciless in their judgment of William V, whom they invariably portray as the epitome of a weak character unsuited for rule—a Dutch Louis XVI whose indecisiveness and conservatism helped usher the downfall of the Old Regime.[18] Of course, as stadholder, William was not a sovereign, never mind absolute, ruler, nor did he aspire to become one. To the contrary, he showed great devotion to the traditional constitutional forms of the Republic. By the middle of the eighteenth century, it had become apparent to clear-eyed contemporaries that some of those forms were no longer serving the Republic well and were in need of modernizing, especially if the Republic were to grapple effectively with the economic and social decline of its heartland. Unfortunately, neither William nor his father, from whom he inherited his office, were among the would-be reformers, despite the power and popular applause they might have won had they offered such leadership. William's father had died prematurely in 1751, after which his mother, Anna of Hanover, had functioned as regent. After her death in 1759, the Republic had reverted to a stadholderless system, while the Duke of Brunswick-Wolfenbüttel, a favorite of Anna's, acted as her son's guardian and defended the interests of the House of Orange. The renowned German field marshal was like a father to the young prince. When William V came of age in 1766, he immediately signed an Act of Advisorship that empowered Brunswick to remain, behind the scenes, the man in charge. In the following years, it is said, the prince did nothing, said nothing, wrote nothing without Brunswick's approval. Under the duke's disabling tutelage, the haughty but insecure William never really grew up.[19] He performed with zest the ceremonial duties of his office, riding in parades, exercising his bodyguard, and giving audiences. But he could not bear to shoulder the heavy work of governing, and when paperwork irritated him, he sometimes threw it petulantly into a corner of his study, where piles of it moldered on the floor.

Brunswick was not the only influence on William, though. The duke's chief rival was his one-time friend Willem Bentinck van Rhoon, elder brother of the governor of 's-Hertogenrade. Formerly the principal adviser of William's father, Willem Bentinck was for decades one of the most powerful figures in Dutch politics. A cultivated, highly literate man, he moved in scientific and literary as well as political circles in The Hague, where he belonged to a masonic lodge. It may be due partly to his influence that William V emerged as a patron of culture and science. Bentinck may also have influenced William's religious outlook. In 1762 Bentinck sent as a gift to the fourteen-year-old William a copy of the book *Ceremonies and*

Religious Customs of All the Peoples of the World, first published in seven volumes between 1723 and 1737. This monumental survey, compiled by Jean-Frédéric Bernard and illustrated by Bernard Picart, was one of the most profound contributions of the Enlightenment to a new understanding of religion. By its very design it relativized religion, encouraging its readers to view all faiths as comparable and to view their forms as human contrivances. Whether William ever read the book we do not know, but its message certainly resonated with some members of the Dutch political elite. Bentinck, for one, believed that the book "taught an educated man exactly what he needed to know about religion."[20]

William received Bosten's petition in December 1767. The first thing he did was have the lieutenant governor send him all the documents from Bosten's trial, along with a report on the case. The documents had already made one trip from Vaals to The Hague, for examination by the government attorneys; now they made another. By his own admission, William never read them carefully. As he wrote to the States General, though, a "summary investigation" of the documents sufficed to convince him (and probably Brunswick) that there existed "some grounds . . . that could justify a pardon." In a bow to the States General, the stadholder did not pardon the priest immediately. Instead, he forwarded the documents to Their High and Mighty Lordships, noting their role in the formulation of Bosten's sentence and asking to know their "good opinion and intention" regarding Bosten's petition. T.H.M.L. were "much obliged" to him for doing so. Continuing the deferential dance, they replied that they would have been entirely contented had His Highness pardoned Bosten. Since he had asked, though, they shared with him their view that, given Bosten's long imprisonment and other circumstances, the case did seem to them "pardonable." They would have no objection if His Highness lifted the portion of the sentence condemning the pastor to banishment. However, they set two conditions: first, that Bosten never again exercise any pastoral functions on Dutch territory, and second, that he fulfill the rest of the sentence against him—in other words, that he pay the remainder of his debt. T.H.M.L. "submit these thoughts to His Highness's very enlightened judgement, and leave it to him to decide the matter as His Highness in his great wisdom shall see fit."[21] With that, the States General returned the trial documents to the stadholder, whose privy secretary filed them. The documents never again left The Hague.

That same month, William granted the suppliant "letters of pardon . . . with repeal of banishment," incorporating the conditions set by the States General. Although Bosten would never again be able to serve as priest in the Republic, once he was released from jail he would otherwise be a free man. Before he could be released, though, he still had to pay the remaining fees from his trial. Happily, with this he received help from unexpected quarters. First Levericksvelt, the barrister who had prosecuted Bosten, discounted his fees in order to reduce Bosten's bill. Then Hasenclever did the same. The fees charged by De Jacobi de Cadier's agent in The Hague, an attorney named Kervel, were removed entirely from Bosten's bill. Finally, when about 1,600 guilders remained, Johan Frans à Brassard—the former burgomaster of Vaals, Bosten's second nemesis after the lieutenant governor—paid the final sum out of the local taxes he was in charge of collecting.[22]

What happened to cause these Protestant lawyers and magistrates, formerly responsible for Bosten's prosecution, to assist him? For one thing, the governor of 's-Hertogenrade pressured some of them to do so. Like his brother, Count Charles Bentinck van Nijenhuis was a man of the Enlightenment (fig. 29). In The Hague he counted some of the most radical thinkers of his day as friends and clients. At home on his rural estate in Overijssel, he hosted Jean-Jacques Rousseau, Dénis Diderot, and David Hume. Addison

29. Charles Bentinck, Lord of Nijenhuis (1708–79), governor of the Lands of Dalhem and 's-Hertogenrade. Portrait ascribed to John Zoffany.

and Steele's famous periodicals the *Spectator* and the *Guardian* were among his favorite reading. More than his brother, he had a scholarly bent. His favorite philosopher was the ancient Stoic Epictetus, in whose teachings he sought a remedy for anxiety and depression. In a letter penned in 1763, Charles confided to his brother (in English, the language of their childhood) his deepest beliefs:

> *Whatever is is right;* else it would not be. Then it seems plain to me, by inversion, that *whatever is right is;* otherwise there must be something wanting in the Almighty Allwise & All good Creator; which hindered Him from bringing something that would be right, into being. . . . Whence I have these two excellent conclusions. First, That I have, nor can have no reason to repine against what is. Secondly, That I can have no more reason to wish for whatever is not; for since it is not, it is not right it should be. . . .
>
> To come next to Religion; not sower, ill natured, mischievous bigotry & superstition, but true & genuine Natural & Revealed Religion. Dos [sic] it overturn or invalidate Philosophy? No certainly; it refines it; & in my opinion, they are both good, as long as they go hand in hand. The true knowledge of God cannot but set a thinking man's heart at ease in every circumstance of life, by the certainty of the perpetual presence, & constant & unbounded Benevolence of his Allwise & Allmighty Maker, everlastingly the same, without any shadow of changing. One True Friend every man may have, out of whose reach & hearing he never is.[23]

Like others in his social milieu, Charles found nothing incompatible between such Enlightened beliefs and membership of the Dutch Reformed Church. In the early 1750s he had supported a minister in the city of Zwolle named Antonius van der Os, who championed freethinking within the Reformed Church, arguing that the dogmas of the Church could be interrogated and, if necessary, revised.

Charles had played a central role in trying (without success) to pacify the resulting dispute.[24] His intervention in the case against Father Bosten reveals him doing something similar, using his political influence to resolve religious conflict and promote toleration.

In January 1768, Charles forced his subordinates to loosen their financial grip on Father Bosten. He insisted that the Vaals magistrates, rather than Bosten, pay Kervel's fees, and he demanded that Hasenclever reduce his. Hasenclever's fees were one of the largest items on the pastor's bill, as they covered his services first as solicitor for the prosecution and then as court secretary. But Hasenclever owed Bentinck a favor which the governor now called in. Although court secretaries in Overmaas had to be approved by the States General, they, like lieutenant governors, were appointed in the first instance by the governor. This created a patron-client relationship between the governor and these lesser officials. Normally, governors demanded money in exchange for such preferments, but Bentinck had appointed Hasenclever as court secretary for free. Now he asked his client to return the favor by accepting just 250 guilders for his services as solicitor in the case against Bosten. Hasenclever had initially demanded almost 800 guilders.[25]

Bentinck also took the crucial step of replacing De Jacobi de Cadier. In June 1767 he appointed a former burgomaster of Maastricht to take over as lieutenant governor. Had De Jacobi de Cadier resigned his office voluntarily or been ousted? If ousted, was it because of his conduct in the case against Father Bosten? It is difficult to say. On the one hand, it was unusual for a sitting lieutenant governor not to serve for life, as Abraham van den Heuvel had done. De Jacobi de Cadier had held the post for less than five years; vigorous and enterprising, he was still under the age of forty at the time of his departure. On the other hand, he remained in the equivalent post for the city of Maastricht, so clearly he hadn't been entirely disgraced. Perhaps the difference was that Bentinck had no authority in Maastricht. His new lieutenant governor for 's-Hertogenrade, Willem Brull, served as his faithful agent in wrapping up the case of Father Bosten. It was Brull who informed Hasenclever of the governor's wishes and ordered À Brassard to pay the remaining sum owed by Bosten. He may also have sent William V a report that was favorable to Bosten, in which case he was partly responsible for the stadholder's clemency.

More was going on, though, than an exercise of authority from on high by an absentee governor. Not only did Brull, unlike his predecessor, feel a personal sympathy for the priest; by 1768, his sentiment had come to be widely shared within his circle in Maastricht. "Everyone," he observed, "is moved with compassion for pastor Bosten, and everyone is doing their utmost to show their pity for him, as Attorney Levericksvelt has done in a generous manner."[26] This, the first report of any Protestant sympathy for Bosten, suggests a sea change in attitudes among the Protestant elites of Maastricht and Overmaas. Why had it occurred? Had the campaign for toleration waged by Voltaire and other intellectuals found a receptive audience among those elites? Had the elites reflected on their anti-Catholicism and reassessed their view of Bosten as a fanatical priest? Possibly. Brull spoke of people feeling "compassion" and "pity," emotions that testify to a sense of being bound to the pastor by a common humanity. The words suggest, if nothing else, that the pastor was no longer perceived principally as the agent of a malevolent institution; his dehumanized "otherness" had faded. Perhaps the arguments of Bosten and his attorneys had eventually resonated: they had always emphasized that Bosten belonged to the same class, shared the same common sense, and followed the same gentlemanly code of conduct as his judges. It is conceivable too that Brull's words signal the spread of a new sensibility. Articulated by Rousseau and other authors, this sensibility located the roots of virtue in humanity's instinctive feelings and celebrated the innate moral sentiments that were believed to stir within all people. If this is not reading too much into two words, then a strand of Enlightenment culture had reached Maastricht and influenced the opinion of an elite public regarding Father Bosten.

Our sources attest more amply, though, to another factor shaping attitudes in the regional capital: the deference of eighteenth-century subjects toward their rulers, and the internalization by regional elites of norms set by national ones. What were those norms? On the one hand, the high authorities in The Hague had shown their commitment to defending the Reformed Church and maintaining the Republic's religious hierarchy. They had decreed Father Bosten guilty of attacking the official church and instructed their local agents to convict him. On the other hand, the same authorities had repudiated the excesses of Bosten's relentless adversary, De Jacobi de Cadier. Distancing themselves from the zeal of the former lieutenant governor, they had adopted a more pragmatic, political stance toward the crimes committed by Bosten, Cunegonde, and the other Catholics involved in the events of April 1762. None of the sentences these authorities had decreed were particularly harsh by early modern standards. They had condemned Cunegonde to be whipped symbolically, not physically, and they had merely banished her and the other Catholics, a punishment that didn't amount to much, given that neither she nor they lived on Dutch soil. Subsequently, the stadholder himself had pardoned Bosten, and the governor had intervened to get Bosten out of jail.

In taking pity on Bosten, the Protestant elites in Maastricht were following the cue of their rulers. Like the pardon Bosten received from William V, the financial aid they gave the pastor did not reverse his conviction but only mitigated his punishment. Their aid did not mean that their support for the Reformed Church had diminished or their view on church-state relations changed. Nor did it mean necessarily that they had been converted to believe in Bosten's innocence. They were simply doing what their governor, stadholder, and Their High and Mighty Lordships had done before them: they were exercising a humane compassion and Enlightened moderation toward a man who had already suffered a long incarceration. By 1768, Father Bosten had languished in jail for more than five years. He had not done so as punishment for his crimes; that was just how long the legal procedures in his case, and finding the money to pay for them, had taken. In this respect too, some Protestants felt, the price of justice had been excessive.

CHAPTER NINE

Afterlives

On 13 February 1768, or perhaps the day before, Johannes Wilhelmus Bosten walked out of his cell a free man. Barred from resuming his pastorate in Vaals, he spent the next couple of years residing in Aachen and serving as curate in Burtscheid. His church superiors then found him a better post, appointing him pastor of a village named Sippenaeken, located just south of Vaals in the Habsburg Duchy of Limburg. While his new rectory did not straddle any borders literally, as did his old one, Bosten lived out the rest of his days a stone's throw from the Dutch border. He worked in Sippenaeken for thirteen years, dying in 1783 at the age of seventy-one. His younger brother Frans Hendrick, who had filled in for him during his incarceration, succeeded him as the official pastor of Vaals. Thus in return for their troubles, the Calvinist magistrates of Vaals got a more combative priest, a genuinely nasty man, to deal with as head of the local Catholic parish. Frans Hendrick died in 1780 at the age of sixty-two.[1]

Willem Frederik de Jacobi de Cadier remained an influential figure in Maastricht. Despite his removal from office as lieutenant governor of 's-Hertogenrade, he continued to serve as vice-sheriff of Maastricht, a similar post that put him in charge of law enforcement. An enterprising man, in 1775 he introduced a new industry to Maastricht, building the city's first paper mill. He never married and, despite inheriting a second noble estate, found himself increasingly in debt. In 1781, at the age of fifty-three, he died childless and his estates were auctioned off.[2]

Other than the two young men who had been caught and released in 1762, none of the rioters who had freed Cunegonde were ever captured. Most of them remained safely across the border on Aachen territory. Ironically, their three leaders, Gimmenich, Grommet, and Lotmans, were the only ones free to come and go, because they enjoyed immunity from prosecution. In 1769, the ruffian Gimmenich got into trouble again. Remember the incident in 1766 when his brother-in-law Wilhelm Schmitz was wounded and dragged back to Dutch territory by a group of Protestants from Vaals? Two and a half years later, Gimmenich got even when he caught one of the Protestants, Johannes Gillis Driessen, passing by his farmstead, the Neuenhof. Gimmenich set his dog on Driessen, and then he and a couple of his farmhands beat the young man with a pitchfork and clubs. Gimmenich threatened to do even worse to any of the others involved in the earlier incident, should he ever catch them. As far as we know, he didn't. In 1770, though, one of his farmhands, a relative of the man who had killed Gerhard Ullendahl, attacked a group of Protestants returning from services in Vaals.[3] When exactly such attacks ceased is unclear, but eventually they did. By some time in the 1780s, an anonymous chronicler could report of his fellow Protestants that "the molestation and abuse to which they had previously been exposed have ended; they can travel to church undisturbed."[4] The peace that had prevailed before 1738 was thus finally restored.

Cunegonde, after her punishment and release, seems to have returned in 1767 to live with her father in Würselen. Locked up first in a church tower and then, for over four years, in a squalid cell in Maastricht's old city hall, the poor, disabled young woman had suffered an imprisonment considerably harsher than Bosten's. Perhaps it took a toll on her health. Cunegonde was a very popular name in northwestern Germany, and no fewer than three Cunegonde Mommerses, all first cousins of one another, lived at the time in Würselen. It seems likely, though, that our Cunegonde never married and that she died in 1771 at the age of thirty-one.

Cunegonde's brother Hendrick did not outlive his sister. As early as September 1762, he and his wife, Sara, had fled Vaals, where the anger and upset among Catholics over the baptism of their baby had been so great that Sara could not remain there safely. The couple had moved with their baby boy to the Dutch city of Tilburg in Brabant, where Hendrick probably had relatives. At the time, Tilburg was the second-largest producer of woolen textiles in the Republic, after Leiden. As a cloth shearer, Hendrick must have hoped to find plentiful work there. Sara was immediately accepted in Tilburg as a member of the local Reformed congregation, and the ecclesiastic censure under which she had stood ever since her premarital affair with Hendrick was finally lifted. She expressed her relief with an outpouring of emotion. In November 1764, Hendrick and Sara had another child, a girl named Anna Maria whom they baptized in the Reformed Church. Their joy was tempered by difficulties: the very next month, Sara had to plead with a deacon of her church for alms, telling him that her husband "was now, in the severe winter, without work, and she with her husband and two small children was thus in a destitute condition." Sympathetic, the deacon and his colleagues lent the family support. Just a few months later, though, Sara found herself in more dire straits when some accident or illness felled Hendrick. He was only thirty-seven years old when he died. Piling tragedy on tragedy, little Anna Maria died as well the next year.[5]

Sara remained in Tilburg, suffering poverty with her young son, Mathias Hendrick, for three more years. Then, after some travels, she took the boy in 1770 to Utrecht, where three of her siblings lived. There she settled. Sara had always been made of sterner stuff than Hendrick, and in Utrecht she outlived her son and a second husband as well. Mathias Hendrick, who—despite all efforts to prevent it—had been baptized in the Reformed faith, survived to at least 1781, when at the age of nineteen he made a public profession of faith and was accepted as a full member of the Reformed Church. By 1787, though, he was dead. Now a childless widow, Sara married a childless widower, a fellow Calvinist named Gijsbert Verbrug. When he died just four years later, he left her not rich but wealthy enough to live off the income from his assets. Although she found herself again without husband or children, this time Sara was financially secure and could draw comfort from her siblings and her favorite niece, who was named after her, to whom she bequeathed all her clothes and jewels. Sara lived another twenty-six years, dying only in 1818.[6]

Vaals, in the meantime, was transformed by the Industrial Revolution into a "factory village." Von Clermont's textile business boomed through the 1770s and 1780s, reportedly employing at its peak some 2,300 workers.[7] In 1777 Jacob Kuhnen, a Calvinist from Burtscheid, followed Von Clermont in moving to Vaals and set up a needle factory there. In addition to the grand residences that both men constructed for their families, houses flew up to provide dwellings for their workers and for those of other manufacturers. To promote economic development and benefit his own business, Von Clermont lobbied the Dutch authorities to improve the main road through the village. His appointment as vice-sheriff of Vaals, along with that of his fellow Lutheran Hasenclever as court secretary, illustrates the Republic's evolution in its latter years away from a specifically Reformed religious establishment toward one that was more inclusive and generically Protestant.[8] It still excluded Catholics, though, whose capacity for "moral citizenship" Dutch Protestants continued to question. Catholics in Vaals resented bitterly the contingent of Dutch troops stationed in their village, the last of whom were only withdrawn some months after Father Bosten was released from jail. By then it seemed Vaals was no longer under threat of attack. The troops in Maastricht remained on alert, however, to return to the village at a moment's notice.

Protestants from neighboring lands continued to travel to Vaals to worship for some years. Those from Eupen continued until 1783, when, thanks to a Patent of Toleration issued by their enlightened Habsburg ruler, Emperor Joseph II, they were allowed once again to build a church in their village. This time, unlike at the end of the War of Spanish Succession, they kept their church for good. The Protestants of Aachen and Burtscheid had to wait longer before they could end their travels. They hoped for a change in 1787, when judges from the Chamber Court came to Aachen to settle the disputes that had led the year before to one of the greatest political disturbances in the city's history, the so-called Great Mäkelei. Seeing an opportunity, Aachen's Protestants offered to drop their lawsuit against the city government concerning the road charge if they were allowed to build a church of their own in the city.[9] The government rejected their offer. Change, though, was in the air. In the event, it came five years later at the tip of a revolutionary bayonet. In December 1792, the army of the French Republic marched into Aachen and occupied the city. One of its first acts was to tear down the "column of infamy" that stood on the main market square, planting in its place a liberty tree. The natives did not endorse the sentiment: just a few months later, Aachen's magistrates reerected the column after a military defeat had forced the French army to retreat. French troops tore the column down again in October 1794 when they reoccupied the city, and this time they demolished it. Aachen was incorporated into the French Republic by the Treaty of Lunéville in 1801. The next year, the city's French rulers declared Aachen's Protestants the legal equals of their Catholic neighbors, granted them freedom of worship, and provided for their use one of the city's extant churches. At the same time, Protestants in Burtscheid were granted permission to build a new church. After a century and a half when hundreds of Protestant worshipers had performed a weekly commute to Vaals, sometimes braving great dangers on the journey, the road on Sundays finally grew quiet.[10]

The story of Cunegonde's attempted baby-snatching and her kidnapping in turn by fellow Catholics was known to many contemporaries. The episode was notorious in Aachen and Maastricht and throughout the lands between them. Funds were solicited in more than three hundred Catholic parishes in the region to ransom Father Bosten. The leaders of the Reformed Church in Holland and Gelderland were greatly concerned by the whole course of events and monitored them closely. Political elites in The Hague not only knew about the episode but were deeply involved. A wider Dutch public learned about it primarily from periodicals and books. Every year the resolutions of the States General were published, and they incorporated, often verbatim, documents received by that august body. Among the documents published in this way were the reports of the lieutenant governors, the petitions of Aachen's Protestants, and the verdicts of the government attorneys. These, and the decisions of the States General themselves, became the basis for subsequent accounts of the episode. The annually published *Nederlandsche Jaerboeken* incorporated long extracts from the relevant resolutions. The *Vaderlandsche Historie* (vol. 23, 1789) and *Vaderlandsch Woordenboek* (vol. 29, 1793) cited in turn the *Jaerboeken*. In total, no fewer than seven Protestant accounts of the episode were published in the Netherlands between 1776 and 1806. For

Dutch Protestants, the story of Cunegonde's kidnapping thus came to serve as an exemplar of the benighted fanaticism of unenlightened Catholics. All of these accounts presented the accusations against Father Bosten as certain facts.[11] Two of them illustrated their narratives with lurid etchings showing Catholics beating Protestant families with clubs. One etching depicted a friar—presumably a member of the Aachen clergy—lurking in the shadows behind a tree, pointing a commanding finger as the lay Catholics carry out their assault (fig. 28).

No Catholic works offering a riposte seem to have been published in the eighteenth century. This vacuum reflected the very limited involvement of Catholics, especially Dutch ones, in the public spheres of print and enlightened sociability. In the nineteenth century, Catholic writers came to question the accusations, even as they continued to rely for information on the official documents that condemned Bosten. In 1865, the Catholic theologian M. G. C. Ubaghs exclaimed that Father Bosten had been "atrociously condemned on [the basis of a mere] suspicion." His judgment was echoed in 1875 by the archivist and antiquarian scholar Father Joseph Habets and again in the 1920s by a curate of Vaals, Father Adolph Vaessen. Ubaghs published a transcription of the letter by the archdeacon of Hespengouw (who later became prince-bishop of Liège) appealing for alms to get Father Bosten released from jail. The letter portrayed Bosten as an innocent martyr persecuted for his faith, and so for a long time he continued to be regarded by Catholics. In 1931, the then-minister of the Vaals Reformed congregation, ds. L. Aalders, wrote a short article that was equally clear in its Protestant sympathies. More recently, Catholic scholars Pontianus Polman O.F.M. (1968) and Father Mathieu Franssen (1994) have followed the lead of the Protestant W. P. C. Knuttel (1892) in adopting a neutral stance regarding Bosten's innocence or guilt. The most recent account of the episode, by the Catholic church historian W. A. J. Munier (2000–2001), departs from the old confessional battle lines. It concurs with Protestant versions of the story, accepting the accusation that Bosten ordered Cunegonde to grab Hendrick and Sara's baby. A specialist in the religious history of Limburg, Munier was the first scholar to draw on a large body of manuscript as well as printed sources. Despite combing the Dutch National Archive in The Hague, though, he never found the most crucial and revealing source of all: the massive dossier resulting from Father Bosten's trial, which had been preserved in such an improbable place, the secretariat of the stadholders, and there misfiled.[12]

So, was Father Bosten innocent or guilty, martyr or criminal? Having pored over the dossier and thousands of pages of other documents, I would love to know for sure, but the fact of the matter is that I don't, nor do I believe anyone can. There exists no crystal ball through which we can peer to witness the "actual" course of events in April 1762. During Bosten's trial, both the prosecution and defense attorneys presented copious evidence to support their arguments. Most of the evidence consisted of testimony given by people who themselves had participated in the events. Their testimonies flatly contradicted each other on some points of fact, including the ones most critical for judging Father Bosten. To complicate our predicament further, some participants were inconsistent when giving testimony more than once, and a few, like Martinus Buntgens, contradicted themselves. So how is one to pick and choose among testimonies? Some participants, like Sebastian Gimmenich, might be dismissed as scoundrels. Some testimony, like that given by Martinus Buntgens when he was incarcerated, might be discounted as having probably been coerced, though even here there is no certainty. But none of the people who testified were disinterested observers. As Protestants and Catholics living in or near Vaals, all were party to the bitter religious conflicts that centered on the village.

One useful, though still very fallible, guideline is to privilege earlier over later testimony. There are various reasons for doing so. One is that people's memories may be fresher, and thus possibly more accurate, the sooner they testify after the events related. Another is that with time, people may obtain more information or perceive more clearly their self-interests. Consciously or not, they might then alter their testimony accordingly. A third reason is that we human beings, by a natural process, have a tendency to shape our memories into stories. These stories help us fix the past in our minds. In the process, they filter and order our recollections, leaving us with a more selective memory of them.

The person who testified more often than any other was the young woman at the center of our story, Cunegonde. She presents something of an enigma due to her mental disability, which was so severe that, when asked to sign her testimonies, she wasn't able to draw a neat cross, as did illiterate contemporaries (fig. 30). Based

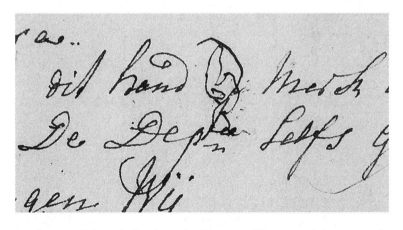

30. Cunegonde's mark. In place of a signature, illiterate people commonly drew a cross. Cunegonde's mark is more chaotic, probably a consequence of her mental disability.

on the diagnosis of the doctors who examined her and the observation of others, it seems she wasn't delusional. Rather, it was her ability to reason and understand that were impaired. How are we then to interpret her testimony? Perhaps just as we would anyone else's. In July 1762, she told the Vaals magistrates that Father Bosten had said to her, "The child is already in the beggars' church to be baptized. Young lady, you must go get it out of there. Then bring it to me, and we'll take it to the Catholic church to baptize it."[13] In all the testimony she subsequently gave, she used variants of the same words in recounting her brief conversation with Bosten. A couple of weeks earlier, though, when she testified before the Aachen magistrates, she hadn't mentioned anyone giving her such a command. Perhaps that was because the Aachen magistrates hadn't asked her the right question, but one finds an even more startling inconsistency when one looks back at the very first testimony Cunegonde gave, on 15 April, the day after her tragic misadventure. On that occasion, she did mention someone who had told her to go grab Hendrick and Sara's baby, but the person wasn't Father Bosten. A certain man, she recounted, whose name she didn't know,

> had come fetch her at her house in the Reich of Aachen at the request of her brother Hen[drick] Mommers . . . saying, "you must come to Vaals, your sister-in-law has given birth and you [are to be] godmother of the child." Whereupon the two of them, after eating something, together went here [to Vaals]. Having come to the Roman [Catholic] rectory, the aforesaid man had gone inside and spoken with the pastor. She the defendant remained standing in the courtyard. Then the aforesaid man went out with her to the front of the churchyard and pointed out to her the door of the Reformed church (since she had never been here) and said to her, "go now to the church

and get the baby out of it. Bring the baby then to me, and we'll take it further."... The aforesaid man had said to her, "she should come and bring the child to the pastor for him to baptize it, for he and the pastor did not wish the child to be baptized in the beggars' church."[14]

Cunegonde's first testimony is not the only evidence pointing toward Andries Buntgens. Two years later, a member of the Burtscheid consistory wrote an account of what had transpired inside the Vaals Reformed church on 14 April 1762. The chronicler, an eyewitness, recounted Cunegonde's actions and words after her second attempt to grab the baby had failed: "Then she began to cry and explained that she was a sister of Hendrick Mommers from Würselen. When questioned, she answered that she had been summoned by an unknown man to be godmother of her brother's child. This man had also shown her this church and ordered her to get the child out of it."[15] Did the sexton's father merely repeat a command which the pastor had already given Cunegonde, or was he the one to first give it? Over the entire course of Bosten's trial, neither the prosecution nor the defense ever suggested that perhaps Andries Buntgens, not Father Bosten, had ordered Cunegonde to snatch the baby. It would be ironic if it were true, for of all the people prosecuted for their roles in the episode, only Andries was found innocent.

Not a single Dutch authority seems to have considered the possibility that Andries, the sexton's elderly father, might have been responsible for the command that sent Cunegonde on her futile mission. Why? Did they know something we don't, something that doesn't appear in the surviving sources? Possibly, but the "moral certainty" of De Jacobi de Cadier suggests a different answer: that finding Father Bosten guilty fit powerful preconceptions held by the Dutch authorities. One preconception was based on social prejudice.

Andries Buntgens may have been a man rather than a woman; he may have worn a powdered wig and, as courier, been entrusted with important documents. Nevertheless, from the authorities' perspective, Andries belonged just as much as Cunegonde to the "common folk," a broad stratum from whom the elites of early modern Europe expected little initiative. Early modern elites conceived of common folk as essentially passive participants in the great affairs of state and society. They tended to consider them incapable of leadership, and so when a riot, for example, occurred, elites were inclined to think that someone higher up the social scale must have orchestrated it. According to this preconception, Andries wasn't the sort of person who issued commands. Nor was his son Martinus the sort to organize and dispatch, on his own authority and initiative, an armed band to rescue Cunegonde. Father Bosten, on the other hand, was. As village priest, he may not have stood high in the hierarchy of the Catholic Church, but neither did he belong to the common folk. A man of some education and social stature, he filled a role of acknowledged authority and leadership in his community.

Bosten wasn't just any member of the rural elite, moreover: he was a priest. The preconceptions about Catholic clergy held by Dutch authorities had deep roots in Protestant religious culture. One preconception was that priests were fanatics intent upon expanding their church by any means. Another was that priests exercised an almost preternatural power over the minds of their lay followers. For almost two hundred years, regents and officials of the Dutch Republic had been holding priests responsible for the religious offenses of Catholic laypeople. Time and again they had accused priests of exploiting their gullible followers to achieve their own nefarious goals. Blaming Father Bosten for using the hapless Cunegonde to get hold of Hendrick and Sara's baby fit the authorities' preconceptions about how Catholic clergy behaved. So did blaming him for the raid to free her. After all, the States General themselves once commented that the violent acts perpetrated by Aachen's Catholics all "have their origin in the incitement of the Roman clergy there." As an appointee of Aachen's canons, with a parish and rectory that straddled the border, Bosten was one of those clergy. Blaming him was the kneejerk reaction of a Dutch political establishment that remained in the 1760s distinctly anti-Catholic.

None of which means that Father Bosten was innocent of the crimes for which he was prosecuted. It is only to say that, whether he was innocent or guilty, his conviction was almost inevitable. The Enlightened sensibility that led subsequently to Bosten's pardon and release only mitigated the consequences of these enduring social and religious prejudices. Indeed, in some ways Enlightenment thought even reinforced those prejudices.

Conclusion

What lessons, then, should we draw from the story of "Cunegonde's Kidnapping"? How might this microhistory inform our understanding of wider histories—of the Dutch Republic and eighteenth-century Europe, of interfaith marriage and religious toleration?

Every genre of historical writing has its limitations, and microhistory is no exception. It focuses on things that are small in scale: a local community, a brief series of events, an individual or a small group. This raises the problem of generalization: How indicative are microhistories of larger patterns in the societies they study? Microhistories tell obscure stories about obscure people. How relevant are they, then, to the main threads of history—the grand narratives by which historians explain how human beings got from where they once were to where they are today? Microhistories rely on exceptional documentary sources to reveal what other sources do not. They thus invite us to accept as true things that cannot be corroborated. Historians have wrestled with these methodological issues ever since microhistory was invented in the 1970s. In writing this book, I have tried to compensate somewhat for the genre's limitations by drawing on a large quantity of source materials in addition to the dossier of documents from Father Bosten's trial. These materials include the resolutions of governing bodies, both secular and ecclesiastic, at all levels, from the local to the national; dossiers from other court cases; packets of correspondence; birth, marriage, and death registers; chronicles by Catholic and Protestant contemporaries; and more. These sources have enabled me to place events in Vaals in the 1760s in a much longer, and somewhat wider, context. Increasing the scale of analysis, they have provided a basis for discerning patterns and distinguishing norms from exceptions.[1]

Even when restricted, though, to the most "micro" of scales, microhistory has a proven ability to make three distinctive contributions to historical understanding. First, it can call our attention to things that "shouldn't be"—phenomena whose very existence, even in a singular case, defies accepted generalizations. In this way, microhistory can challenge our paradigms of the past. Although it cannot, to my mind, prove the validity of an alternative paradigm, microhistory can suggest its contours. Second, when its findings do fit accepted generalizations, microhistory can offer fuller, deeper understandings of them. It can show how abstract entities and processes manifested themselves concretely, and how real people experienced them. It can also reveal aspects of the phenomena that had gone unnoticed. Finally, microhistory can reveal the agency exercised by people whose actions are not recorded or acknowledged in other sorts of historical writing. It should not—must not—deny the larger forces and constraints that shaped the lives of ordinary people. But by telling the stories of obscure individuals—farmhands and journeymen, housewives and midwives, sextons and couriers, village magistrates and parish priests—it allows us to see how they too made meaningful choices in their lives and took actions that helped fashion the world around them. We can draw conclusions from Cunegonde's kidnapping in all three ways.

One firm conclusion was drawn almost half a century ago by the Catholic cleric and historian Pontianus Polman: "How relative," he remarked, "is the custom of labeling the eighteenth century the age of Enlightenment and tolerance."[2] Polman's use of the word *relative* is perhaps unfortunate, as it suggests that one can measure amounts of enlightenment and toleration, like quantities of liquid in a cup, and compare them. But his observation is surely correct in pointing out an inconsistency between the story of Cunegonde's kidnapping and the dominant image of the eighteenth century as a period when Europeans, under the influence of the Enlightenment, ceased to engage in religious conflict. Of course, the Enlightenment has always been understood as a movement and a process rather than a state of affairs that was ever fully achieved. But intellectual historians in particular have usually represented the history of toleration in the eighteenth century as a story of inexorable rise. The modern "principle" of toleration, they claim, was "firmly established" as early as the 1680s by the incontrovertible arguments of John Locke and other philosophical giants. Over the following century, as those arguments were popularized and disseminated, the principle came to be accepted ever more widely. As often through silence as through explicit claims, historians give the impression that the behavior of Europeans evolved over the same period to conform to the principle.[3] Such is the power of this historical schema that it has shaped historians' research agendas: how people of different faiths actually related and behaved toward one another in the eighteenth century has been little studied. Whatever religious conflicts they acknowledge did occur in that century historians have usually dismissed as aberrations from the norm, relics of an earlier, more "primitive" phase in the development of European civilization.[4]

Taken by itself, Cunegonde's kidnapping cannot disprove the truth of this schema.[5] What it can do is tell a story that is patently at odds with the latter. The story takes place in a region that was largely rural but included a major German city, where commercial agriculture was flourishing and the textile industry rapidly modernizing; a region in whose affairs the regents of the Dutch Republic were intimately involved. What our microhistory shows is that in 1762, a seemingly trivial dispute over the baptism of a baby triggered a kind of religious war. It did so because Catholics and Protestants in the region were already locked together in conflict. The antagonisms that divided the two groups went back to the late sixteenth and early seventeenth centuries and remained powerful in the eighteenth century. Contrary to our image of evolutionary progress, economic and religious developments in the 1730s seem to have increased the power of those antagonisms, causing religious violence to begin again after a period of quiescence. The violence continued sporadically for several decades, until the events of 1762 brought it to a notably late climax. This violence was unlike its counterpart in the preceding century, when religious minorities suffered persecution by officials and attacks by military forces; since then, religious strife in the region had been at least partly demilitarized and depoliticized. The violence of the eighteenth century had a more popular character; it was perpetrated mostly by Catholic burghers and peasants from the middling and lower social strata of Aachen and its rural territory. These groups were vehemently anti-Protestant. They nurtured vivid memories of the tumults of previous centuries, which they and their rulers frequently invoked. They bitterly resented the Protestant worship that took place in Vaals, which they experienced as an alien intrusion into Catholic lands. If in the eighteenth century they took direct, violent action against

Protestants and their worship, it was partly because their rulers had ceased to do so. Protestants in the region rarely reciprocated, partly because they could count on the forces of the Dutch state to do it for them.

Our microhistory reveals several sharp limits to Enlightenment influence. First, it seems clear that Enlightenment culture never developed as strongly in the region of Vaals as in Holland or some other parts of Europe. Second, it arrived there late. In fact, the first local periodical that championed the new ideas, *Der Menschenfreund*, began to be published only in 1772 and was suppressed three years later; a successor did not appear until 1790.[6] Third, Enlightenment culture seems not to have penetrated socially much beyond elite circles, and even there it met resistance among the "Old Party" that dominated the Aachen city government. Despite the ideas promulgated by intellectuals, most people saw in earthquakes and plagues the punishing hand of a wrathful God, and they took part by the thousands in processions and other rituals of atonement. In a telling manner, Aachen's clergy were split. While the powerful and wealthy canons of the minster pooh-poohed claims of present-day miracles, mendicant preachers whipped up crowds into antimasonic furies. Attacks on fellow Catholics who dared to read the Bible critically, as well as on Freemasons, were manifestations of a popular backlash against the new ideas.

As elsewhere in Europe, so in our region Enlightenment influence was more prevalent among Protestants than Catholics. Such influence mixed in complicated ways, though, with Protestant religious culture, and a new benevolence toward people of other faiths did not simply supplant an older anti-Catholicism. That the two were in some respects compatible is made clear by the letters of Charles Bentinck, the figure in our story most deeply imbued with Enlightenment values. He expressed revulsion at "bigotry and superstition," in which category he included the piety of most

Catholics. On Protestants such as Bentinck Enlightenment influence seems to have had contradictory effects. On the one hand, it made intolerance toward Catholics less acceptable. On the other, it reinforced older perceptions of Catholicism as a fanatical, superstitious, and tyrannical religion. In general, it seems, the Protestants in our microhistory coped with the contradiction by behaving tolerantly toward Catholic individuals while deploring the influence of the Catholic Church.

Until a French revolutionary army marched into Aachen and swept away the Old Regime, Protestant worship remained illegal there. So too, until the fall of the Dutch Republic, the structures of Dutch religious life went for the most part unchanged. Some Dutch Protestants groped in the eighteenth century toward a rapprochement between their various churches. Dutch government eventually opened up a crack to Lutherans and other Protestant dissenters. But the Dutch Reformed Church always retained its status as the Republic's official, uniquely privileged church, and Catholics remained at the bottom of its religious hierarchy. Even if the placards against them were not actively enforced, the mass and other Catholic services were still illegal throughout most of the Republic and tightly restricted. To be sure, Catholics in the Lands of Overmaas seem to have become less shy in the eighteenth century about asserting their presence in the public sphere and performing religious rituals there. Clearly they felt secure and self-confident enough to do so. This feeling was encouraged by a 1730 resolution of the States General that recognized, backhandedly, their right to worship publicly. But their assertive behavior contributed to a rise in Protestant-Catholic tensions within local communities. In this fashion, what one might consider an increase in toleration on the official level led to a decrease on the popular level, fueling an upsurge of violence. This dynamic had parallels in other parts of the Republic, where in the 1730s there were official moves to recognize (and regulate) Catholic institutions and a wave of popular anti-Catholicism partly in reaction. Whether or not Dutch Catholics actually began at this time to behave more aggressively, many Protestants certainly perceived them as doing so. Invariably, they accused Catholic priests of being behind the aggression. From the level of village gossip to the highest echelons of government, they automatically accused priests such as Father Rademacker and Father Bosten of instigating whatever malfeasance Catholic laypeople perpetrated. Dutch authorities spoke of the Aachen clergy as a unified, malevolent force.

Such dehumanizing discourse did not cease, but with regard to Father Bosten it seems that some Protestants in Maastricht changed their attitude in 1767 or early 1768. Did they do so under the influence of books and periodicals championing tolerance, such as those recently published by Voltaire and Rousseau? Possibly: the elites of the city read French and could have obtained such books, including one by Voltaire's friend Jean-François Marmontel entitled *Bélisaire*, which would provoke enormous controversy in the Netherlands just a few years later.[7] What is certain is that a feeling of sympathy for the long-suffering priest was propagated from The Hague by members of the national political elite. William V and Charles Bentinck not only put direct pressure on their subordinates in Maastricht to exercise moderation and compassion. Their interventions in the case of Father Bosten also inspired imitation, prompting people like Brull and Levericksvelt to aid the same man on whose prosecution they or their predecessors had been intent just a few years earlier. In this way, an "Enlightened judgment" of the case spread, apparently rather suddenly, within the regional elite that governed Overmaas.

Enlightenment influence thus played a key role in effecting, at the end of our story, Bosten's release from jail. In this respect, one can perhaps see the story as manifesting a rise of toleration in the 1760s. If so, it was a rise that left the attitudes and behavior of the majority of the population unchanged. The anti-Catholic senti-ments of the Dutch ruling elite were confirmed even as they were moderated. And existing laws and institutions remained until they were swept away by a revolution several decades later. This is not the "rise of toleration" portrayed or suggested by most histories.

If our microhistory does not fit the dominant image of the eigh-teenth century, it fits no better the image of the Dutch Republic. Descriptions of the Republic invariably cast it as a highly urbanized, highly literate, orderly place where power was decentralized and people of different faiths tolerated one another. These descriptions are not wrong, just crude. They project onto the entire Republic the image of Holland, the most powerful, most populous, and in some ways most remarkable of Dutch provinces. Recent scholarship has corrected the resulting distortion somewhat. Yet students of history still often fail to appreciate how varied, despite its small size, the Republic was. Certainly Dutch Overmaas and its modern-day coun-terpart, the Dutch province of Limburg, defy many persistent ste-reotypes of what was, and is, "typically Dutch." Even physically, with their hills and woods, they seem scarcely to belong to the same country as the water-soaked flatlands for which the Netherlands have always been famous.

Dutch Overmaas owed many of its characteristics to its status as a borderland, and some of the characteristics that distinguished it most sharply within the Republic it shared with the borderlands of other countries. It has been noted, for example, that in many borderlands local government is weak. Overmaas likewise enjoyed none of the autonomy of the seven Dutch provinces. It fell under the direct sway of the national authorities who closely supervised its political, economic, and religious affairs. Military forces often have a powerful presence in borderlands. Maastricht likewise was a for-tress town, and when Dutch sovereignty over Vaals was challenged, the village got an oversized garrison of its own. Again like some other borderlands, Overmaas was notorious for lawlessness, never more so than in the mid-eighteenth century, when it was afflicted by organized brigandage as well as religious strife. The fragmentation of Overmaas into parcels of territory, which multiplied its borders, increased greatly the difficulty authorities had maintaining order there. The taxpayers of a little district like Vaals could ill afford to erect a proper jail; only the traumatic events of 1762 convinced them of the necessity. In the meantime, prisoners sent away for safekeeping had to be escorted by soldiers lest they be liberated while crossing foreign soil. Like other border communities, Vaals was vulnerable to incursions by foreign forces, and lawbreakers could escape with laughable ease the jurisdiction of its magistrates.

Dutch Overmaas did not constitute a borderland by itself, though. Our microhistory reveals Vaals as the center point of a region that included the Habsburg Lands of Overmaas, adjacent parts of Liège and Limburg, Aachen and its rural Reich, and parts of Jülich as well. This region constituted a distinct area not despite but because of the political borders that crisscrossed it. The coherence of this borderland was manifested in the relations between its parts. Networks of people and flows of activity not only spanned the borders between states but were configured by those borders in ways that created new links and interdependencies between communities that the borders ostensibly separated. Textile production, for example, flourished in the region partly because the political borders produced a form of deregulation, preventing authorities in any one land from controlling the industry.[8] The result was a distribution across borders of interconnected manufacturing and commercial activities. Families, too, came to be distributed across borders as they followed economic opportunities and took advantage of legal differences, as did Hendrick and Sara in order to marry.

Our microhistory thus confirms some of the generalizations scholars have made about the political, economic, and social characteristics of borderlands. It also reveals a characteristic that previous studies have failed to note: a religious deregulation that operated in parallel with the economic. The borders that crisscrossed the region enabled Protestant dissenters to live in states where their worship was forbidden and ensured that Catholics in Dutch Overmaas would enjoy rights and resources that their counterparts elsewhere in the Republic could only envy. The borders set people on the move, prompting hundreds to take to the region's roads every Sunday. They also fostered relationships between the communities they divided—relationships that could be called symbiotic in a religious as well as an economic sense. Aachen, Burtscheid, and Eupen all depended on Vaals to provide religious services to members of their own communities. In a sense, they were excused from the need to tolerate Protestant worship thanks to the proximity of Vaals. To put it another way, they could have their cake and eat it too, maintaining the religious purity of their communities while profiting from the dissenters in their midst. Conversely, Dutch authorities could close Catholic churches secure in the knowledge that local Catholics would neither rebel nor break the law, since they could easily worship elsewhere. Dutch authorities accepted that local Catholics depended on foreign prelates to provide pastoral care and material support. Above all, the Dutch state depended on Calvinist minorities in neighboring states to bolster Calvinist congregations in Dutch Overmaas. Thanks to those minorities, Vaals could serve as a symbolic affirmation and regional bulwark of the Republic's official faith.

Our microhistory thus reveals the contradictory, double dynamic of religious politics in a borderland. On the one hand, the confrontation of states with different official religions turned the region of Vaals into a cauldron of religious tensions. Back in the 1630s, Dutch authorities may have hoped to use Overmaas as a showcase for their religious toleration—an example that would encourage Catholics in the Habsburg Netherlands to unite politically with the Republic. But when they found their hopes dashed, they quickly turned to using Overmaas, and Vaals in particular, as a vehicle to support their coreligionists in the region and promote the Reformed faith. That is what they continued to do for the next century and a half. They used the borders between states to create safe havens for their fellow Protestants, in the process validating the importance of the borders. At the same time, they connived at the violation and blurring of the borders by projecting their influence beyond them, taking Protestant minorities in neighboring states under their protective wing. Understandably, Catholics in the region viewed the Dutch as interlopers, resented their intrusion into the region's religious affairs, and bitterly opposed the Dutch policy. Nowhere did these feelings run higher than in Aachen. Vaals thus found itself right on the most sensitive border in the region, between the champion of Protestantism and the most volatile, violence-prone, militantly Catholic community. It thus became a focal point for religious strife.

In essence, the strife pitted segments of Aachen's Catholic populace against the Dutch state. These were the two strong actors in the conflict who, despite the obvious asymmetry between them, assumed the role of champion of their respective faiths. Aachen's magistrates, by contrast, were wary of clashing directly with the Republic, the political and military superpower of the region. They resorted instead to one of the principal weapons of the weak, duplicity. While publicly condemning the violence of their subjects, they tacitly tolerated and perhaps even encouraged it. Likewise, the Protestant inhabitants of Aachen and Burtscheid found themselves in a weak position. Vastly outnumbered by their Catholic neighbors, they sensed all too keenly their vulnerability. When the Dutch state took aggressive action, they usually paid the price. It comes therefore as no surprise that they didn't always support the action.

On the one hand, then, the borderland was a place where religious foes clashed. The proximity of states with different official faiths made religious opponents all the more sensitive to perceived attacks and all the more eager to assert their faiths. This exacerbated religious tensions and turned political borders—above all, the one between Aachen and Vaals—into fronts in an undeclared religious war. On the other hand, the same proximity also made it inevitable that people of different faiths—people like Hendrick and Sara—would encounter and interact with one another. It created venues for people of different faiths to discover mutual interests, share strands of culture, and forge relationships. This would have been the case even if each of the states in question had been religiously homogeneous and all their inhabitants had belonged to their official churches. In fact, the proximity of religious borders made it well-nigh impossible for authorities to suppress dissent within their states. Aachen's magistrates may have appreciated the economic benefits of tolerating Protestant manufacturers, but there can be little question that the sizable Protestant communities in Aachen owed their survival mostly to two things: the Peace of Westphalia, which guaranteed them the right to perform Auslaufen, and the patronage of Dutch authorities. Neither would have been of great consequence had the trip from Aachen to the Dutch border taken a day instead of an hour. In fact, the relatively small number of Protestants who made the trip from Eupen, in the Duchy of Limburg, reveals where the outer limit of the religious borderland lay: at a distance of about four hours' travel from the Dutch border. Within that limit, the borderland provided religious dissenters with safe havens, resources, and patronage close at hand. It promoted religious mixing not only across borders but behind them as well.

Not that the borders in question should be conceived in purely spatial terms. To be sure, the geographic position of Vaals is of enormous importance to the story of Cunegonde's kidnapping. But even the comparatively well defined border between Vaals and the Reich of Aachen had its ambiguities. As we have seen, the scope of a state was defined in the eighteenth century in two ways, by territory and by jurisdiction. It was plotted on maps, but more often, especially for legal purposes, it was defined by listing the names of communities. This inconsistency in no way prevented early modern borders from defining the outer limits of states or from structuring and regulating relations between the populations they divided. Far from having a purely enclosing and restricting effect, though, the borders between states of different faiths offered protections and forms of religious freedom that for some would not have existed otherwise.

Our microhistory has highlighted the religious strife that was once endemic in the region of Vaals. Tracing the roots of the strife back to the sixteenth and early seventeenth centuries, it has revealed the persistence of religious enmities and their reactivation in the mid-eighteenth century. It has shown how, even in that supposedly enlightened age, seemingly minor incidents could trigger major clashes, and examined how one such clash spiraled tragically out of control, growing through cycles of reprisals and counterreprisals. It has recounted acts of hideous violence.

Yet the story of Cunegonde's kidnapping is not one only of intolerance. Remember the midwife Anna Olivier? This devout Catholic brought children for baptism to different churches depending on the faith of their parents. Though illiterate, she understood that her church recognized Calvinist and Lutheran baptisms as valid and was bold enough to declare that she enjoyed hearing the rite performed in a language she understood. She was hardly the only person in Vaals who dealt with people of other faiths in the course of her work and social life, and usually got along with them. Until their falling-out, Father Bosten and Burgomaster À Brassard had for many years been friends as well as next-door neighbors. À Brassard's own sister was married to a Catholic. Stephen Schmalhausen, a deacon of his Reformed congregation, acted as solicitor for Father Bosten. Doctors of different faiths examined Cunegonde together and reached a unanimous judgment regarding her disability. An unnamed Catholic man, probably a family servant, protected two little Protestant boys when they were attacked by his coreligionists. Protestant soldiers traveled to Aachen to buy goods from shopkeepers who, by law, had to be Catholic. Above all, we must not forget how Hendrick Mommers and Sara Erffens defied the leaders of both their churches, bucking enormous pressure in order to marry. These examples of good relations between Protestants and Catholics vary from the coolly economic to the passionately intimate. We know of them because an extraordinary series of events produced an extraordinary dossier. Ordinarily, though, when Catholics and Protestants got along with one another, it left no documentary trace. The problem is a general one for historical inquiry: while conflict echoes loudly in the historical record, peace does not.

Obviously, relations between Protestants and Catholics in the region of Vaals were highly fraught. Historical memories, imbalances in numbers and power, economic resentments, the porousness of political borders, and mutually rejecting religious cultures all combined to set the two groups against each other. It did not take a great deal in the mid-eighteenth century to trigger a showdown: the repair of an old crucifix, a bit of mischievous marksmanship, or the disruption of a baptism sufficed. If our microhistory shows anything, it is the factors that made peaceful coexistence in the region such a tenuous, fragile thing; the immediate causes of its breakdown; and the dynamics by which conflict escalated.

We must be careful, though, not to commit one of the errors to which microhistory is prone: the fallacy of mistaking the exceptional for the normal. Here a wider focus is invaluable, for if the record of peace is quiet, it is not mute. When a Protestant chronicler in Aachen details only two episodes of religious violence in the eighteenth century (in 1738 and 1762–64), it does not mean that no other incidents occurred—in fact, we know they did. One can safely infer, though, that none of the other incidents matched the scale or impact of those two. Likewise, it seems almost certain that Hendrick and Sara's baby was the only child born to a mixed couple in Vaals in the eighteenth century to be the target of a kidnapping attempt. Too many authorities would have reacted to other attempts for it not to be significant that, in all their records, they mention none. By placing the dossier from Father Bosten's trial alongside other sources, we have established that in some respects the religious violence of 1762–64 fit a well-established pattern. By their very silences, however, those other sources also suggest that the vast majority of interactions between Protestants and Catholics were peaceful. Our microhistory in no way invalidates this generalization. To the contrary, the story that it tells, predominantly of conflict, presupposes that Catholics and Protestants lived alongside one another, having a wide range of interactions in the normal course of daily life.

Properly conceived, conflict and toleration are not mutually exclusive. To the contrary, conflict cannot occur if parties are not engaged with one another. The only pure form of intolerance, arguably, is when one group of people refuses to concede the very existence of another group and seeks to end it—in other words, genocide. Thankfully, such pure intolerance is a rare phenomenon compared to the many other forms that conflict takes, ranging from the most benign to the most destructive. Inversely, one might ask whether any relationships between groups of people do not entail elements of conflict. To this question social scientists answer no. Groups define their identities partly by differentiating themselves from one another. They are distinct from one another socially by virtue of processes of inclusion and exclusion, acceptance and rejection. These dynamics are in themselves forms of conflict, and to this extent at least, the very coexistence of different groups presupposes some conflict between them. Rather than conceiving of religious conflict and toleration as opposites, then, we might do better to think of them both as necessary elements in the interaction of faith groups. The challenge is to understand the forms these elements take, and their interplay.

Ultimately, groups do not interact unless individuals act. Conflict and toleration must be seen not just as aggregate patterns but as elements in a dynamic process by which people who belong to different groups engage in the construction of relationships. This is a point easily lost by historians—including myself—who have been trying in recent years to write a new, social (as opposed to intellectual or political) history of religious toleration. Precisely because it tells a story in narrative form, microhistory offers an opportunity to reconnect this new social history, with its aggregate and static qualities, with history as action and event, the product of human choices. Interfaith marriage is an example of a pattern that belongs to the social history of toleration. One can usefully calculate how often such marriages took place, how often spouses converted to their partner's faith, and how many children of such couples were raised in one faith or the other. But those individuals, like Hendrick and Sara, who entered into mixed marriages faced the challenge of negotiating—at key junctures, like the birth of a child, or in the most vexed cases even day by day—the terms of their coexistence. At stake at each turn were the religious identities of their families and their selves. In mixed marriages, as in the wider society, toleration only existed by virtue of a set of practices that individuals had to enact and reenact: sufferance, accommodation, cooperation, mutual support. Our microhistory shows individual Catholics and Protestants engaged in these actions, and in conflict with one another. It shows how a bunch of very distinct characters made choices that did not simply reflect their membership in a religious or social group. As Anna Olivier reminds us, some uneducated members of the lower classes were no less tolerant than their rulers, some Catholics no less so than Protestants. Some powerful Protestants, like De Jacobi de Cadier, defended the Protestant supremacy in the Dutch Republic with what their peers regarded as an excessive zeal. And some Catholic youths, like Sebastian Gimmenich, didn't just loathe Protestantism: they were coarse, unscrupulous troublemakers. Living in a borderland between Protestant and Catholic states, they all had to grapple, not just as members of groups but as individuals, with the thorny issues posed by religious coexistence.

NOTES

Abbreviations

BDA   Bischöfliches Diözesanarchiv Aachen
BHIC   Brabants Historisch Informatie Centrum, Den Bosch
Dossier   NA, Archief van de Stadhouderlijke Secretarie (1.01.50) 348–49: "Stuk-
           ken betreffende het proces van de hoogdrossaard van 's-Hertogenbosch
           [sic] tegen Johannes Willem Bosten, pastoor te Vaals, voor schepenen
           van Baals [sic] wegens het aanzetten tot de ontvoering van een kind van
           Hendrik Mokmers [sic] uit de gereformeerde kerk om het te laten
           dopen in de katholieke kerk, 1762–1765"
DTB   Doop-, Trouw- en Begraafregisters
EvKgA   Archiv der Evangelischen Kirchengemeinde Aachen
GAV   Gemeentearchief Vaals
GPB   Cornelis Cau et al., eds., *Groot placaet-boeck, Inhoudende de placaten ende
           ordonnantiën ende edicten van de Doorluchtige Hooghmogende Heeren Staten
           Generael der Vereenighde Nederlanden, ende vande Edele Groot Mogende
           Heeren Staten van Hollandt ende West-Vrieslandt, mitsgaders van de Edel
           Mogende Heeren Staten van Zeelandt*, 9 vols. (The Hague, 1658–1797)
LKAD   Landeskirchliches Archiv Düsseldorf
LvO   Landen van Overmaas
NA   Nationaal Archief, The Hague
Resolutiën Staten-Generaal, *Resolutiën, 1721–1792*, 72 vols. (The Hague, 1780–
           92?)

RHCL   Regionaal Historisch Centrum Limburg, Maastricht
StAA   Stadtarchiv Aachen
StG   Archief van de Staten-Generaal, 1576–1796
UA   Het Utrechts Archief
ZAGV   *Zeitschrift des Aachener Geschichtsvereins*

Note on Sources

References for quotations and specific facts are provided in the chapter notes below. *Dossier* provides the crucial core of source material upon which our story is based. Other manuscript sources produced by the trials of Father Bosten, Cunegonde, and her would-be liberators are contained in RHCL, LvO (01.075) 9420 and 9429; and LKAD, EvKgA (004) 18. The resolutions of the States General (*Resolutiën*) constitute the most important printed source. They need to be supplemented by the letters and reports sent to the States General, collected in NA, StG (1.01.02) 5857-1, 5865, and 5866. Fundamental also are the records of the Calvinist congregations of Aachen, Burtscheid, and Vaals (those of Eupen have not survived), above all the protocols of their consistories: LKAD, EvKgA (004) A1/7, A5/2, and A5/3; and RHCL, Hervormde Gemeente Vaals (14.E006) 7. For a contemporary description of the Lands of Overmaas and their institutions, see Rinse van Noordt and M. Tyderman, *Tegenwoordige staat der Vereenigde Nederlanden. dl. 2. Vervattende eene beschryving der Generaliteits Landen, Staats Brabant, Staats Land van Overmaaze, Staats Vlaanderen en Staats Opper-Gelderland met den staat der bezetting in de barriere-plaatsen enz. Met nauwkeurige landkaarten en printverbeeldingen versierd* (Amsterdam, 1751) (1st ed., 1740), ch. 14.

Genealogical and biographical information on the figures in this book, including members of the Erffens, Mommers, Bosten, Buntgens, Van den Heuvel, and De Jacobi de Cadier families, has been pieced together from a great number of sources, including the DTB registers at StAA, RHCL, and UA; the online Genealogische Databank Limburg (http://www.allelimburgers.nl/); the online Familienbuch Euregio (http://www.familienbuch-euregio.de/); the genealogical dossiers held by the Centraal Bureau voor Genealogie in The Hague; Pierre J. H. Ubachs and Ingrid M. H. Evers, eds., *Historische encyclopedie Maastricht* (Zutphen, 2005); Jos. M. H. Eversen, "Alphabetische lijst der Magistraatsleden van Maastricht (1660–1809)" (typescript available at RHCL); and Regionaal Archief Tilburg, Genealogische Database (http://www.regionaalarchieftilburg.nl/zoeken-in-databases/genealogie).

Several eighteenth-century chronicles offer rich accounts of events in Vaals, Aachen, and Burtscheid between the 1730s and 1760s: on the Catholic side, Johannes Janssen, "Die historischen Notizen des Bürgermeisterei-Dieners Johannes Janssen," in *Beiträge und Material zur Geschichte der Aachener Patrizier-Familien*, ed. Hermann Ariovist von Fürth, 3 vols. (Aachen, 1882–90), 3:3–390; on the Protestant side, BDA, Manuscripts HS 57. Eyewitness accounts of Cunegonde's attempted kidnapping of Hendrick and Sara's baby appear in LKAD, EvKgA A5/3, account following the acta for 4 Oct. 1764; RHCL, LvO 9420, letter written by Pferdmenges dd. 23 Dec. 1762; and *Dossier,* 100/C. A long-term perspective on the history of the Protestant congregations is offered by LKAD, EvKgA (004) 27, "Pro Memoria die protestanten in Achen betreffend."

On the Protestant Reformation and Catholic/Counter-Reformation in Aachen in the sixteenth and seventeenth centuries, see Hansgeorg Molitor, "Reformation und Gegenreformation in der Reichsstadt Aachen," *ZAGV* 98/99 (1992/93): 185–204; Walter Schmitz, *Verfassung und Bekenntnis. Die Aachener Wirren im Spiegel der kaiserlichen Politik (1550–1616)* (Frankfurt, 1983); Hugo Altmann, "Die konfessionspolitischen Auseinandersetzungen in der Reichsstadt Aachen in den Jahren 1612–1617 im Lichte neuer Quellen," *ZAGV* 88/89 (1981/1982): 153–82; Heinz Schilling, "Bürgerkämpfe in Aachen zu Beginn des 17. Jahrhunderts. Konflikte im Rahmen der alteuropäischen Stadtgesellschaft oder im Umkreis der frühbürgerlichen Revolution?" *Zeitschrift für Historische Forschung* 1 (1975): 175–231; Heinz Schilling, *Niederländische Exulanten im 16. Jahrhundert. Ihre Stellung im Sozialgefüge und im religiösen Leben deutscher und englischer Städte* (Gütersloh, 1972); August Brecher, *Die kirchliche Reform in Stadt und Reich Aachen von der Mitte des 16. bis zum Anfang des 18. Jahrhunderts* (Münster, 1957); C. F. M. Deeleman, "De hervorming te Aken (1524–1820)," *Jaarboekje der Limburgsche Protestanten Vereeniging* 10 (1923): 13–48; Mathias Classen, "Die konfessionelle und politische Bewegung in der Reichsstadt Aachen zum Anfang des 17. Jahrhunderts," *ZAGV* 28 (1906): 286–442; H. F. Macco, *Die reformatorische Bewegungen während des 16. Jahrhunderts in der Reichsstadt Aachen* (Leipzig, 1900); and Johann Arnold von Recklinghausen, *Reformations-Geschichte der Länder Jülich, Berg, Cleve, Meurs, Mark, Westfalen und der Städte Cöln und Dortmund,* 3 vols. (Elberfeld/Solingen und Gummersbach, 1818–37), 1:255–88. Thomas Richter, of RWTH Aachen University, is currently writing a doctoral thesis on the Protestant congregations in Aachen, Burtscheid, and Vaals in the seventeenth century. Fundamental among the sources for this topic are, of course, the protocols of the Reformed consistories: LKAD, EvKgA (004) A1/3, A1/4, A1/6, and A5/1; and RHCL, Hervormde Gemeente Vaals (14.E006) 1 and 2.

The two court cases initiated by Protestants against the Aachen city government in the *Reichskammergericht* produced documents that survive in three dossiers: StAA, Reichskammergericht A134 and A168; and LKAD, EvKgA 18.

On the Lands of Overmaas, the relevant secondary sources include Frank Hovens et al., eds., *De geschiedenis van Limburg* (Zwolle, 2010); P. J. H. Ubachs, *Handboek voor de geschiedenis van Limburg* (Hilversum, 2000); W. A. J. Munier, *Het simultaneum in de landen van Overmaas. Een uniek instituut in de Nederlandse kerkgeschiedenis (1632–1878)* (Leeuwarden, 1998); Anton Blok, *De Bokkerijders. Roverbenden en geheime genootschappen in de Landen van Overmaas (1730–1774)* (Amsterdam, 1995); J. A. K. Haas, *De verdeling van de Landen van Overmaas, 1644–1662. Territoriale desintegratie van een betwist grensgebied* (Assen, 1978); and W. Jappe Alberts, *Geschiedenis van de beide Limburgen. Beknopte geschiedenis van het gebied omvattende de tegenwoordige Nederlandse en Belgische provincies Limburg, sedert de vroegste tijden,* 2 vols. (Assen, 1972–74). On Aachen, see Michael Rowe, *From Reich to State: The Rhineland in the Revolutionary Age, 1780–1830* (Cambridge, 2003), ch. 1; Thomas R. Kraus, *Auf dem Weg in die Moderne. Aachen in französischer Zeit 1792/93, 1794–1814* (Aachen, 1994); Herbert Kolewa, *Reichsstadt und Territorium. Studien zum Verhältnis zwischen der Reichsstadt Aachen und dem Herzogtum Jülich, 1769–1777* (Frankfurt, 1993); Klaus Müller, "Die Reichsstadt Aachen im 18. Jahrhundert," *ZAGV* 98/99 (1992/93): 205–30; Horst Carl, "Die Aachener Mäkelei, 1786–93. Konfliktmechanismen in der Endphase des Alten Reiches," *ZAGV* 92 (1985): 103–87; J. Liese, *Das klassische Aachen—1. Johann Arnold von Clermont, sein Geschlecht und sein Schaffen im Vaalser Paradies,* 2 vols. (Aachen, 1936–39); and Albert Huyskens, *Aachener Leben im Zeitalter des Barock und Rokoko* (Bonn, 1929). Many other valuable articles on Aachen have likewise been published in the local periodical *Zeitschrift des Aachener Geschichtsvereins (ZAGV).*

Local histories of Vaals, most of them focusing on religious worship there, include the invaluable W. A. J. Munier, "Kerken en kerkgangers in Vaals van de Staatse tijd tot op heden," *Jaarboek van het Limburgs Geschied-en Oudheidkundig Genootschap* 136–37 (2000–2001): 85–262; Protestantse Kerkgemeenschap Gulpen-Vaals, J. Vermeijden, et al., eds., *350 jaar Hervormde Gemeente Vaals, 1649–1999: jubileumuitgave van de "Bergketen"* (Vaals, 1999); Mathieu Franssen, *Acht eeuwen St. Pauluskerk Vaals* (Vaals, 1994); J. Th. H. de Win, *De Geschiedenis van Vaals* (Vaals, 1941); L. Aalders, "De jaren 1762 en 1785 in de geschiedenis van het protestantisme te Aken-Vaals," *Nederlands archief voor kerkgeschiedenis* 24, no. 1 (1931): 69–80; L. Aalders, "L'Église éteinte, dite l'église wallonne réformée de Vaals," *Bulletin de la Commission de l'Histoire des Eglises wallonnes des Pays-Bas,* 4e ser., no. 3 (1930): 6–12; L. Aalders, "Verhinderde kerkgangen," *Jaarboekje der Limburgsche Protestanten Vereeniging* 15 (1928): 112–16; L. Aalders, "De drie kerken der Reformatie in Vaals," *Jaarboekje der Limburgsche Protestanten Vereeniging* 13 (1926): 152–68; and Adolph Vaessen, "Die Geschichte von Vaals" (1923–1925), at http://www.obib.de/ Geschichte/Vaals.html. On the architectural history of the Vaals churches, see Sabine Broekhoven et al., *Monumenten in Nederland. Limburg* (Zwolle, 2003); and J. F. van Agt, *Vaals, Wittem en Slenaken* (The Hague, 1983).

On the economic history of the region, see C. Wijnen, "De lakennijverheid in de Staatse landen van Overmaas aan het einde van de achttiende eeuw," *Textielhistorische bijdragen* 35 (1995): 44–61; Herbert Kisch, *From Domestic Manufacture to Industrial Revolution: The Case of the Rhineland Textile Districts* (Oxford, 1989); Joachim Kermann, *Die Manufakturen im Rheinland, 1750–1833* (1972), 118–60; Herbert Kisch, "Growth Deterrents of a Medieval Heritage: The Aachen-area Woolen Trades before 1790," *Journal of Economic History* 24, no. 4 (1964): 517–37; W. F.

Schweizer, "Vaals, eens een textielcentrum van Europese betekenis," *Textielhistorische bijdragen* 4 (1963): 52–66; Herbert von Asten, "Die religiöse Spaltung in der Reichsstadt Aachen und ihr Einfluss auf die industrielle Entwicklung in der Umgebung," *ZAGV* 68 (1956): 77–190; Heribert Kley, *Geschichte und Verfassung des Aachener Wollenambachts wie überhaupt der Tuchindustrie der Reichsstadt Aachen* (Siegburg, 1916); and Heinrich Schnock, "Über gewerbliche Verhältnisse in der ehemaligen 'Herrlichkeit Burtscheid,' " *Aus Aachens Vorzeit* 18 (1905): 34–60. Much of the industrial unrest of the 1740s–60s is documented in Janssen's chronicle, cited above. Aachen's guilds and industrial policies were severely criticized by contemporaries, particularly Protestants: Johann Arnold von Clermont (attrib.), *Freymüthige Betrachtungen eines Weltbürgers zum Wohl von Aachen* (Frankfurt am Main/Leipzig, 1788); Johann Georg Adam Forster, *Ansichten vom Niederrhein, von Brabant, Flandern, Holland, England und Frankreich, im April, Mai und Junius 1790*, 3 vols. (1791), 1:251–325.

The history of Dutch Catholicism in the eighteenth century was classically treated by P. A. J. M. Polman, *Katholiek Nederland in de achttiende eeuw*, 3 vols. (Hilversum, 1968); and W. P. C. Knuttel, *De toestand der Nederlandsche katholieken ten tijde der Republiek*, 2 vols. (The Hague, 1892), vol. 2. More recent works, several of them focusing on anti-Catholic sentiment among Dutch Protestants, include Edwina Hagen, "Een zaal van staatsmannen, niet van godgeleerden. Godsdienstige sentimenten in de Nationale Vergadering," in *Het Bataafse experiment. Politiek en cultuur rond 1800*, ed. Frans Grijzenhout, Niek van Sas, and Wyger Velema (Nijmegen, 2013), 125–53; Edwina Hagen, *"Een meer of min doodlyken haat." Antipapisme en cultureel natiebesef in Nederland rond 1800* (Nijmegen, 2008); Th. Clemens, "De ingehouden verlichting onder de Nederlandse katholieken," in *Een veelzijdige verstandhouding. Religie en Verlichting in Nederland, 1650–1850*, ed. Ernestine van der Wall and Leo Wessels (Nijmegen, 2007), 239–76, and other essays in the same volume; Willem Frijhoff, *Embodied Belief: Ten Essays on Religious Culture in Dutch History* (Hilversum, 2002); Th. Clemens, "IJkpunt 1750—op zoek naar nieuwe grenzen in het politiek-religieuze landschap van de Republiek," in *Vervreemding en verzoening: de relatie tussen katholieken en protestanten in Nederlanden, 1550–2000*, ed. C. Augustijn and E. M. V. M. Honée (Nijmegen, 1998), 69–101; Th. Clemens, "De terugdringing van de rooms-katholieken uit de verlicht-protestantse natie," *Bijdragen en mededelingen betreffende de geschiedenis der nederlanden* 110 (1995): 27–39; and Anton van de Sande, "Roomse buitenbeentjes in een protestantse natie? Tolerantie en antipapisme in Nederland in de zeventiende, achttiende en negentiende eeuw," in Marijke Gijswijt-Hofstra, ed., *Een schijn van verdraagzaamheid. Afwijking en tolerantie in Nederland van de zestiende eeuw tot heden* (Hilversum, 1989), 85–106. On the state of Catholicism in Aachen and elsewhere in the German Rhineland, see the works cited in chapter 5.

For eighteenth-century debates in the Netherlands about toleration, see esp. Joost Kloek and Wijnand Mijnhardt, *1800: Blueprints for a National Community* (Assen, 2004), 167–89; Joris van Eijnatten, *Liberty and Concord in the United Provinces:*

Religious Toleration and the Public in the Eighteenth-Century Netherlands (Leiden, 2003); Ernestine G. E. van der Wall, *Socrates in de hemel? Een achttiende-eeuwse polemiek over deugd, verdraagzaamheid en de vaderlandse kerk* (Hilversum, 2000); Joris van Eijnatten, *Mutua Christianorum Tolerantia: Irenicism and Toleration in the Netherlands; The Stinstra Affair, 1740–1745* (Florence, 1998); and Ernestine G. E. van der Wall, "Toleration and Enlightenment in the Dutch Republic," in *Toleration in Enlightenment Europe,* ed. O. P. Grell and R. Porter (Cambridge, 2000), 114–32. Peter van Rooden, *Religieuze regimes. Over godsdienst en maatschappij in Nederland, 1570–1990* (Amsterdam, 1990), is an influential study of the changing place of religion in Dutch society.

Introduction

1. The one medieval precedent was the marriage of western Christians, in eastern Europe, to eastern Orthodox ones, which was generally illegal as well.

2. Wiebe Bergsma, *Tussen Gideonsbende en publieke kerk: een studie over het gereformeerd protestantisme in Friesland, 1580–1650* (Hilversum, 1999), 96 n. 1.

3. *Dossier.*

4. On the Drielandenpunt and Vaals in the modern era, see Roger Janssen, *Vaals en het drielandenpunt* (Zaltbommel, 2007).

5. Voltaire, *Treatise on Tolerance and Other Writings,* ed. Simon Harvey (Cambridge, 2000), 49.

6. For claims about unitary entities, see, e.g., Paul Hazard, *La Crise de la conscience européene, 1680–1715* (Paris, 1935); Norman Hampson, *The Enlightenment* (Harmondsworth, UK, 1968), which uses terms such as "homo Europeensis" (27); and Perez Zagorin, *How the Idea of Religious Toleration Came to the West* (Princeton, NJ, 2003), who speaks still of "Western consciousness" (299). For qualified claims, see, e.g., Isser Woloch, *Eighteenth-Century Europe: Tradition and Progress, 1715–1789* (New York, 1982), 231; Donald Kagan, Steven Ozment, and Frank M. Turner, *The Western Heritage,* 7th ed. (Upper Saddle River, NJ, 2001), 589; and Roy Porter, *The Creation of the Modern World: The Untold Story of the British Enlightenment* (New York, 2000), 224.

7. Joost Kloek and Wijnand Mijnhardt, *1800: Blueprints for a National Community* (Assen, 2004), 119.

8. On "enlightened" attitudes toward plebeians, see, among others, W. Th. M. Frijhoff, "The Dutch Enlightenment and the Creation of Popular Culture," in *The Dutch Republic in the Eighteenth Century: Decline, Enlightenment, and Revolution,* ed. Margaret C. Jacob and Wijnand W. Mijnhard (Ithaca, NY, 1992), 292–307; Roger Chartier, *Cultural History: Between Practices and Representations,* trans. Lydia G. Cochrane (Ithaca, NY, 1988), 151–71; and Porter, *The Creation of the Modern World,* 364–82.

9. The preeminent exponent of this interpretation currently is Jonathan I. Israel; see his *Radical Enlightenment: Philosophy and the Making of Modernity, 1650–1750*

(Oxford, 2001), and other works. See also Porter, *The Creation of the Modern World*, esp. 98 and 205.

10. Benjamin J. Kaplan, *Divided by Faith: Religious Conflict and the Practice of Toleration in Early Modern Europe* (Cambridge, MA, 2007).
11. See esp. David D. Bien, *The Calas Affair: Persecution, Toleration, and Heresy in Eighteenth-Century Toulouse* (Westport, CT, 1979).
12. When two accounts of a scene or conversation agree completely but offer different details, I have felt free to merge them. I have not merged quotations from different documents, though, but left them in separate sets of quotation marks.

ONE

Between Them Sleeps the Devil

1. The following dialogue is from *Dossier,* 76 and 85/16.
2. Church of Rome, *Declaratio SSmi D. N. Benedicti PP. XIV. super matrimoniis Hollandiae et Foederati Belgii. Et Acta in Sacra Congregatione . . . Cardinalium Sacri Concilii Tridentini Interpretum, coram SS. D.N. 13. Maii 1741. exhibita.* (Louvain, 1742), 7. On the history of mixed marriage in the early modern Netherlands, see Benjamin J. Kaplan, "Intimate Negotiations: Husbands and Wives of Opposing Faiths in Eighteenth-Century Holland," in *Living with Religious Diversity in Early-Modern Europe*, ed. C. Scott Dixon, Dagmar Freist, and Mark Greengrass (Farnham, UK, 2009), 225–48; Benjamin Kaplan, "Integration vs. Segregation: Religiously Mixed Marriage and the 'Verzuiling' Model of Dutch Society," in *Catholic Communities in Protestant States: Britain and the Netherlands, 1580–1720*, ed. Benjamin Kaplan et al. (Manchester, UK, 2009), 48–66; Benjamin J. Kaplan, " 'For They Will Turn Away Thy Sons': The Practice and Perils of Mixed Marriage in the Dutch Golden Age," in *Family and Piety in Early Modern Europe: Essays in Honour of Steven Ozment*, ed. Benjamin J. Kaplan and Marc R. Forster (Aldershot, UK, 2005), 115–33; H. F. W. D. Fischer, "De gemengde huwelijken tussen katholieken en protestanten in de Nederlanden van de XVIe tot de XVIIIe eeuw," *Tijdschrift voor Rechtsgeschiedenis* 31 (1963): 463–85.
3. C. Molina [Christianus Vermeulen], *Den Oprechten Schriftuerlijcken Roomsch-Catholycken Mondt-Stopper,* 15th ed. (Antwerpen, 1745), 180.
4. Augustinus de Roskovány, *De matrimoniis mixtis inter Catholicos et Protestantes,* 2 vols. (Quinque-Ecclesiis, 1842), quotation from 2:674–75. See also Karl-Theodor Gehringer, "Die Konfessionsbestimmung bei Kindern aus gemischten Ehen in der Zeit zwischen dem Konzil von Trient und dem Ende der Glaubenskriege," in *Fides et ius: Festschrift für Georg May zum 65. Geburtstag,* ed. Winfried Aymans et al. (Regensburg, 1991), 303–16; Karl-Theodor Gehringer, "Die Konfessionsbestimmung bei Kindern aus gemischten Ehen in der Zeit seit

dem Ende der Glaubenskriege (1648) bis Benedikt XIV. (1758)," in *Scientia Canonum. Festgabe für Franz Pototschnig zum 65. Geburtstag*, ed. Hans Paarhammer and Alfred Rinnerthaler (Munich, 1991), 27–54; Karl-Theodor Gehringer, "Die Konfessionsbestimmung bei Kindern aus gemischten Ehen. Gesetzgebung und Praxis in der Zeit zwischen Clemens XIII. bis Leo XII. (1758–1829)," in *Theologia et Jus Canonicum. Festgabe für Heribert Heinemann zur Vollendung seines 70. Lebensjahres*, ed. Heinrich J. F. Reinhardt (Essen, 1995), 533–47.

5. Joannes Mauricius, *Gewigtige redenen, Om sig niet te begeven in den Huwelyken Staat met de gene, die Roomsgesind sijn. Voorgesteld tot een Christelyke Onderrichtinge voor alle Protestanten, Voornamentlyk Gereformeerden, Luterschen, en Mennonisten* (Amsterdam, 1708), 237.

6. Drenthe constituted an eighth province but remained disenfranchised, without a vote in the States General. For recent general histories of the Dutch Republic, see Jonathan I. Israel, *The Dutch Republic: Its Rise, Greatness, and Fall, 1477–1806* (Oxford, 1995); Maarten R. Prak, *The Dutch Republic in the Seventeenth Century: The Golden Age*, trans. Diane Webb (Cambridge, 2005); and Arie Th. van Deursen, *De last van veel geluk. De geschiedenis van Nederland, 1555–1702* (Amsterdam, 2005). On the political institutions of the Republic, see also Robert Fruin, *Geschiedenis der staatsinstellingen in Nederland tot den val der Republiek* (The Hague, 1980).

7. The relevant ordinances appear in *GPB*, 6:228, 238–39, 527, 2429–48, 7:813–15, 8:543–44. See also W. A. J. Munier, "De toepassing van het Echtreglement in de Landen van Overmaas en de neerslag ervan in de trouwregisters, 1656–1683," *Publications de la Société Historique et Archéologique dans le Limbourg* 121 (1985): 69–103. Quotation from BHIC, Raad van Brabant 1586–1811 (19) 433.

8. The following narrative is based chiefly on a great number of documents in *Dossier*, esp. 68/A, 79/8, and 84/1 and 2.

9. According to one source (UA, Index op de 1813 volkstelling), Sara would have been around twenty-three when she met Hendrick; according to another source (UA 481, inv. nr. 432, Burgerlijke stand—Overlijden, aktenr. 167), she would have been about eighteen. But the former seems more likely, given contemporary norms regarding age of marriage and age of obtaining membership in the Reformed Church, and given that no source mentions a notable disparity in age between the two spouses.

10. *Dossier*, 79/8.

11. *Dossier*, 79/9. The provenance of this document is given here as recounted by Hendrick and Sara. The content of the document allows us to date it with confidence to the summer of 1761, even though the only surviving copy of it, written in 1764, is labeled 23 August 1762. The wording of the document makes sense only if, at the time of its writing, Hendrick and Sara did not yet have any children, at least living ones, and they were living in an officially Catholic territory. Neither was the case in August 1762, or indeed any other time after March

of that year. Moreover, the document makes direct reference to the trick Father Finck had played on them.

12. *Dossier,* 68/A.

13. Joannes Henricus Manigart, *Praxis pastoralis seu manipulus theologiæ moralis. De VII. Ecclesiæ sacramentis, . . . ac de aliis multis: opusculum aureum,* 3 vols. (Liège, 1754), 2:215–16, 3:258, 270; J. F. Schannat et al., eds., *Concilia Germaniae,* 11 vols. (Cologne, 1759), 9:298; A. M. P. P. Janssen, "Conversie in Sittard en omgeving in de zeventiende en achttiende eeuw," in *Religie aan de grens. Aspecten van de Limburgse kerkgeschiedenis,* ed. R. M. de La Haye et al. (Delft, 1997), 54–55, 60–61.

14. *Dossier,* 79/8.

15. *Dossier,* 84/3.

16. *Dossier,* 84/3.

17. The following dialogue is from *Dossier,* 85/16, 68/B, 90/23.

TWO

Baptism Is Baptism

1. Council of Ferrara-Florence, bull of union with the Armenians, 22 Nov. 1439, at http://www.ewtn.com/library/councils/florence.htm (accessed 29 July 2013); J. F. Schannat et al., eds., *Concilia Germaniae, quae . . . J. F. Schannat . . . magna ex parte primum collegit . . . ,* 11 vols. (Cologne, 1759), 5:618 (first quotation); Joannes Henricus Manigart, *Praxis pastoralis seu manipulus theologiæ moralis. De VII. Ecclesiæ sacramentis, . . . ac de aliis multis: opusculum aureum,* 3 vols. (Liège, 1754), 1:33 (second quotation); P. van Leeuwen, "Voorwaardelijke doop sedert Trente," *Oecumene* 4 (1965): 181–244; A. M. P. P. Janssen, "Conversie in Sittard en omgeving in de zeventiende en achttiende eeuw," in *Religie aan de grens. Aspecten van de Limburgse kerkgeschiedenis,* ed. R. M. de La Haye et al. (Delft, 1997), 51–68.

2. Étienne François, *Die unsichtbare Grenze: Protestanten und Katholiken in Augsburg, 1648–1806* (Sigmaringen, 1991), 180–81.

3. LKAD, EvKgA (004) 43, 1752 case; RHCL, Classes van Maastricht en de Provinciale Kerkbesturen van Limburg (14.E001) 2–7, inv. nr. 6, 1752 May art. 19, July art. 39, October art. 7, 1753 May art. 8, 1757 May art. 1.

4. See the Note on Sources above for references to the sources of genealogical and biographical information on which the following account draws.

5. According to the Mechelen burial register, Wilhelmus Bosten died in 1732 "morte in partheij exstinctus." One of his brothers, Joannes Bosten, made in 1734 a "titre d'ordination au profit de son neveu Johannes Wilhelmus Bosten"—the latter being his godson as well as nephew. I'm indebted to Monsieur Christian Dury, Archiviste diocésain de Liège, for this information. On

the Vaals benefice, see Joseph Habets, *Geschiedenis van het tegenwoordig Bisdom Roermond en van de Bisdommen, die het in deze gewesten zijn voorafgegaan*, 3 vols. (Roermond, 1875), 1:442–43.

6. Mathieu Franssen, *Acht eeuwen St. Pauluskerk Vaals* (Vaals, 1994), 23–26.

7. The following series of dialogues is from *Dossier*, 34 (testimony by Anna Olivier), 4 (Hendrick Mommers), 11 (Martinus Buntgens), 32/2 (J. W. Bosten), 85/16 (Agnes Korr), and 68/B and 90/24 (Hendrick Mommers according to Norbertus Wirtz).

8. The following dialogue is from *Dossier*, 33 and 58.

9. *Dossier*, 85/16.

10. The following dialogue is from *Dossier*, 76, 85/16, 34, and 68/C.

11. The following dialogue is from *Dossier*, 34 and 76.

12. The following dialogue is from *Dossier*, 33 (Andries Buntgens) and 100/D (Cunigunda Mommers).

13. The following dialogue is from *Dossier*, 68/C, 86/18, 39, 58, and 32/2.

14. RHCL, LvO (01.075) 9420, letter dd. 23 Dec. 1762 by J. Pferdmenges.

15. *Dossier*, 68/B.

16. *Dossier*, 33, 32/2, 87/19, 39, 100/D, and 55.

17. The events inside the church are recounted in many documents. The most detailed and reliable accounts were both written by participants: LKAD, EvKgA (004) A5/3, account following acta for 4 Oct. 1764; and RHCL, LvO 9420, letter written by Pferdmenges dd. 23 Dec. 1762. These are the sources of all the dialogue.

THREE
On This Soil

1. *GPB*, 1:261–2 (placard dd. 14 Apr 1649). On the privileged position of the Reformed Church as "public" church of the Dutch Republic, see W. Nijenhuis, "De publieke kerk veelkleurig en verdeeld, bevoorrecht en onvrij," in *Algemene Geschiedenis der Nederlanden*, new ed., 15 vols. (Bussum, 1977–83), 6:325–43; and J. J. Woltjer, "De plaats van de calvinisten in de Nederlandse samenleving," *De zeventiende eeuw* 10 (1994): 3–23. In Vaals, uniquely, Dutch Lutherans got the right in 1759 to be married by a legally binding ceremony in the local Lutheran church. LKAD, EvKgA (004) 41, "Pro Memoria"; W. A. J. Munier, "Kerken en kerkgangers in Vaals van de Staatse tijd tot op heden," *Jaarboek van het Limburgs Geschied-en Oudheidkundig Genootschap* 136–37 (2000–2001): 156–58.

2. On the concept of borderlands, see esp. Jeremy Adelman and Stephen Aron, "From Borderlands to Borders: Empires, Nation-States, and the Peoples in Between in North American History," *American Historical Review* 104 (1999):

814–41; David Newman, "Boundaries," in John A. Agnew, Katharyne Mitchell, and Gearoid O Tuathail, eds., *A Companion to Political Geography* (Oxford, 2003), 123–37; and David H. Kaplan and Jouni Hakli, eds., *Boundaries and Place: European Borderlands in Geographical Perspective* (Oxford, 2002).

3. Albert Huyskens, "Stadtbefestigung, Landgraben und Warten der ehemaligen Reichsstadt Aachen," *ZAGV* 61 (1940): 167–200; Joseph Nellessen, "Zur Geschichte des Aachener Landgrabens," *ZAGV* 33 (1911): 290–91.

4. StAA, RA II Allgemeine Akten 929; NA, StG (1.01.02) 8977.

5. Roger Janssen, *Vaals en het drielandenpunt* (Zaltbommel, 2007). The old Dutch and Belgian marker stones date from the nineteenth century; Aachen's marker stone appears on the so-called Copso-Karte of 1772.

6. J. A. K. Haas, *De verdeling van de Landen van Overmaas, 1644–1662. Territoriale desintegratie van een betwist grensgebied* (Assen, 1978), 239, quoting L. J. Rogier.

7. Haas, *Verdeling.*

8. From 1614 the dukes of Jülich-Berg were members of the Wittelsbach family who ruled Palatinate-Neuburg and, from 1742, also the Electoral Palatinate. At the time of our story, they were thus among the leading princes of the Holy Roman Empire, ruling Jülich from afar via an administration based in Düsseldorf.

9. Anton Blok, *De Bokkerijders. Roversbenden en geheime genootschappen in de Landen van Overmaas (1730–1774)* (Amsterdam, 1995); J. H. M. M. van Hall, "Een onderzoek naar de rechtspraak in de Staatse landen van Overmaze door de advocaat-fiscaal J. F. van Steelant in 1772," in *Ten werentliken rechte. Opstellen over Limburgse rechtsgeschiedenis*, ed. A. M. J. A. Berkvens et al. (Maastricht, 1990), 59–86.

10. GAV, Gemeente Vaals 1.

11. The claim that guild restrictions harmed Aachen's economy severely has been qualified recently, but there is no doubt that they helped push some manufactures out of the city's territory. The claim goes back to the eighteenth century: see Johann Arnold von Clermont (attrib.), *Freymüthige Betrachtungen eines Weltbürgers zum Wohl von Aachen* (Frankfurt/Leipzig, 1788), esp. 10–14; and Johann Georg Adam Forster, *Ansichten vom Niederrhein, von Brabant, Flandern, Holland, England und Frankreich, im April, Mai und Junius 1790*, 3 vols. (1791), esp. 1:259–73.

12. Benjamin J. Kaplan, "Fictions of Privacy: House Chapels and the Spatial Accommodation of Religious Dissent in Early Modern Europe," *American Historical Review* 107 (2002): 1031–64.

13. The religious history of Dutch Overmaas in the seventeenth century, and the practice there of Simultaneum, is examined in detail in W. A. J. Munier, *Het simultaneum in de landen van Overmaas. Een uniek instituut in de Nederlandse kerkgeschiedenis (1632–1878)* (Leeuwarden, 1998). In 1730 the States General finally conceded that the Lands of Overmaas fell under the terms of the 1632 Capitulation of Maastricht; this meant that Catholicism had official permission to be practiced publicly in Overmaas as it was in Maastricht. *Resolutiën*, 19 July 1730.

14. Evidence as to whether there were any Calvinists at all in the village is contradictory. Protestantse kerkgemeenschap Gulpen-Vaals, J. Vermeijden et al., eds., *350 jaar Hervormde Gemeente Vaals, 1649–1999: jubileumuitgave van de "Bergketen"* (Vaals, 1999), 31, lists three Calvinists living in Vaals as of December 1649 who received aid from the deacons. Munier, "Kerken en kerkgangers," says there were "hooguit enkelingen of passanten" (95). This is contradicted by the 1658 Catholic visitation entry quoted earlier: Joseph Habets, *Geschiedenis van het tegenwoordig Bisdom Roermond en van de Bisdommen, die het in deze gewesten zijn voorafgegaan*, 3 vols. (Roermond, 1875), 1:442. It is contradicted also by LKAD, EvKgA (004) 27, p. 16, which says there were no Calvinists in the village, but this source is a self-interested claim on the part of the Aachen Protestants.

15. LKAD, EvKgA (004) 17a, printed "Requeste," undated [1719]. Officials found 207 Calvinists, constituting 8 percent of the local population, when in 1809 they conducted the first Dutch census: J. A. de Kok, *Nederland op de breuklijn Rome-Reformatie. Numerieke aspecten van protestantisering en katholieke herleving in de noordelijke Nederlanden, 1580–1880* (Assen, 1964), 460.

16. On Auslaufen in general, see Benjamin J. Kaplan, *Divided by Faith: Religious Conflict and the Practice of Toleration in Early Modern Europe* (Cambridge, MA, 2007), ch. 6.

17. Munier, *Simultaneum*, esp. 101–17; René Leboutte, "Le mariage à Olne et à Dalhem," in *Protestantisme aux frontières. La Réforme dans le duché de Limbourg et dans la principauté de Liege (XVIe—XIXe siècles)*, ed. Philippe Denis (Aubel, 1985), 235–65.

18. The following section is based primarily on the protocols of the Vaals, Aachen, and Burtscheid Reformed congregations: LKAD, EvKgA (004) A5/2 and A5/3; LKAD, EvKgA (004) A1/3, A1/4, A1/6, and A1/7; RHCL, Hervormde Gemeente Vaals (14.E006) 1, 2, and 7. See also Munier, "Kerken en kerkgangers"; Herbert von Asten, "Die religiöse Spaltung in der Reichsstadt Aachen und ihr Einfluss auf die industrielle Entwicklung in der Umgebung," *ZAGV* 68 (1956): 77–190; and Johann Arnold von Recklinghausen, *Reformations-Geschichte der Länder Jülich, Berg, Cleve, Meurs, Mark, Westfalen und der Städte Cöln und Dortmund*, 3 vols. (Elberfeld/Solingen und Gummersbach, 1818–37), 1:255–88.

19. "Die Westphälischen Friedensverträge vom 24. Oktober 1648: Instrumentum Pacis Osnabrugensis," http://www.pax-westphalica.de/ipmipo/index.html (accessed 7 Jan. 2014), article V, esp. paragraph 31.

20. Although Walloons were Calvinists too in theology and practice, for ease of identification I will henceforth use "Calvinists" to refer (unless otherwise specified) to people who attended the services of the main, German-Dutch congregation.

21. A genealogy of the family appears in W. F. Schweizer, "Vaals, eens een textielcentrum van Europese betekenis," *Textielhistorische bijdragen* 4 (1963): 52–66, 65.

22. Vaals had a few Jewish inhabitants, and it is said in 1790 that there existed in the village a place of worship for them as well. Forster, *Ansichten*, 296.

23. The argument that the political fragmentation of the region encouraged economic liberalism and industrial development is made in Michael Rowe, *From Reich to State: The Rhineland in the Revolutionary Age, 1780–1830* (Cambridge, 2003), 13–47.

FOUR
Flouting Authority

1. LKAD, EvKgA (004) A5/3, entry after 4 Oct. 1764, "Eine kurze und zuverlässige Nachricht."

2. *Dossier*, 1, 4 Apr. 1762; *Resolutiën*, 4 June 1762.

3. LKAD, EvKgA (004) A5/3, entry after 4 Oct. 1764, "Eine kurze und zuverlässige Nachricht."

4. LKAD, EvKgA A5/3, entry after 4 Oct. 1764, "Eine kurze und zuverlässige Nachricht."

5. The following dialogue is drawn from *Dossier*, 5/2, 11, 32/2, and 32/3.

6. The word I have translated as "scum," used here by Bosten and by others subsequently, was French: "Canaille," meaning scum(bag), trash, rubbish, low-life, rascal, blackguard, or scoundrel, and in the plural meaning rabble or riff-raff. It suggested both that the person or persons were of low social class and that they were disreputable and without honor.

7. *Dossier*, 5/2.

8. *Dossier*, 41.

9. *Dossier*, 11.

10. *Dossier*, 46.

11. The following dialogue is drawn from *Dossier*, 83/12, 68/D, and 45; and RHCL, LvO (01.075) 9420, Annex bij clacht en conclusie tegen coster J. M. Buntgens dd. 13 Sept. 1766.

12. The following dialogue is drawn from *Dossier*, 84/13, 84/14, and 39.

13. The following dialogue is from *Dossier*, 10 and 12.

14. J. H. M. M. van Hall, "Een onderzoek naar de rechtspraak in de Staatse landen van Overmaze door de advocaat-fiscaal J. F. van Steelant in 1772," in *Ten werentliken rechte. Opstellen over Limburgse rechtsgeschiedenis*, ed. A. M. J. A. Berkvens et al. (Maastricht, 1990), 74 ("slaat hem op de kop, dan hinkt hij niet").

15. The following dialogue is drawn from *Dossier*, 11, 45, 46, and 41.

16. The following dialogue is drawn from *Dossier*, 9, 10, and 7.

17. *Dossier*, 100/D.

18. The following dialogue is drawn from *Dossier*, 45 and 41.

19. *Dossier*, 7, 9, 10, 29/W3.

20. *Dossier,* 1, 23 June 1762, letter to Aachen magistrates signed by Fellinger.
21. A. J. C. M. Gabriëls, *De heren als dienaren en de dienaar als heer. Het stadhouderlijk stelsel in de tweede helft van de achttiende eeuw* (The Hague, 1990), 236–41, 378–79.
22. NA, StG (1.01.02) 5864, letter from Abraham van den Heuvel to HHM, 2 June 1762.
23. *Resolutiën,* 11 June 1762.
24. *Dossier,* 18 and 32/3. The events of 24 June and the days surrounding it are reported in NA, StG 5864, letters from Abraham van den Heuvel dd. 25–28 June 1762.
25. NA, StG 5864, letter from Abraham van den Heuvel dd. 2 July 1762 and accompanying documents; LKAD, EvKgA A5/3, entry after 4 Oct. 1764, "Eine kurze und zuverlässige Nachricht" (quotation).
26. *Dossier,* 1, 20 July 1762.
27. *Dossier,* 36.
28. The following account of Pieter Koetgens's prosecution and release is based on *Dossier,* 1, 19 July through 5 Aug. 1762; *Dossier* 19, 20, 21, 23/1, 23/2, 23/3, 24, 25, 26, 29/W3, 30, and 31.
29. *Dossier,* 19.
30. Quotation from *Dossier,* 1, 21 July 1762.
31. Simon van Leeuwen, *Manier van procederen in civile en criminele saaken, etc.* (Leiden, 1666), 181–83, 332–34; Pieter Bort, *Alle de Wercken van Mr. Pieter Bort . . . begrepen in ses tractaten . . .*, ed. Johan van Alphen (1702), 336; M. van de Vrugt, *De criminele ordonnantiën van 1570* (Zutphen, 1978), 140–48; Anton Blok, *De Bokkerijders. Roversbenden en geheime genootschappen in de Landen van Overmaas (1730–1774)* (Amsterdam, 1995), 339–85. See John H. Langbein, *Torture and the Law of Proof* (Chicago, 2006).
32. The building referred to in the sources as Maastricht's old city hall was also known as the Dinghuis. After the construction of the new city hall (1659–84), it served a variety of functions, including as a jail. Pierre J. H. Ubachs and Ingrid M. H. Evers, eds., *Historische encyclopedie Maastricht* (Zutphen, 2005), 414.

FIVE

Beggar Dogs

1. For the history of the Protestant Reformation and Counter-Reformation in Aachen in the sixteenth and early seventeenth centuries, see the works cited above in the Note on Sources. Modern accounts tend to echo the Catholic version of events even in their label—"Aachener Wirren" or "Aachener Religionsunruhen."
2. On these occasions the city magistrates assembled in the minster to attend a high mass in Charlemagne's honor, at which a special hymn was sung that

captured the city's self-image: "Urbs Aquensis, Urbs Regalis / Regni sedes Principalis / Prima Regum Curia. / Regi Regum pange laudes / Quae de Magni Regis gaudes / Caroli praesentia. . . ." Johann Noppius, *Aacher Chronick, das ist, eine kurtze historische Beschreibung aller gedenckwürdigen Antiquitäten und Geschichten, samt zugefügten Privilegien und Statuten dess Königlichen Stuls und H. Römischen Reichs Statt Aach . . . biss an das Jahr . . . 1630* (1643), 12.

3. Noppius, *Aacher Chronick*, quotation from Dedication.

4. Johannes Janssen, "Die historischen Notizen des Bürgermeisterei-Dieners Johannes Janssen," in *Beiträge und Material zur Geschichte der Aachener Patrizier-Familien*, ed. Hermann Ariovist von Fürth, 3 vols. (Aachen, 1882–90), 3:76.

5. LKAD, EvKgA (004) 18, "Vorläuffige Unterthänigste Exceptiones cum Petitione et Reservatione."

6. LKAD, EvKgA 18, "Unterthänigste Replicae mit bitt." Aachen's Protestants claimed, under the 1624 *Normaljahre* clause of the Peace, the right to worship privately, hold citizenship, and belong to a craft guild. The electors of Brandenburg and Cologne were charged by a conference with mediating the dispute and overseeing casu quo the restitution of their rights, but a document dating from around 1660 reveals that Aachen's Protestants decided for tactical reasons not to press their case, as long as they were allowed freedom of conscience and permitted to perform Auslaufen to Vaals. The Protestants did not, however, give up their claims entirely, but intended to submit them again to peace conferences in 1677 and 1748. See LKAD, EvKgA (004) 13, "Kurtzer bericht"; Johann Gottfried von Meiern, *Acta pacis executionis publica. Oder Nürnbergische Friedens-Executions-Handlungen und Geschichte . . .*, 2 vols. (Tübingen, 1736); regular entries for 1649–60 in LKAD, EvKgA (004) A1/3; and LKAD, EvKgA (004) A1/4.

7. W. A. J. Munier, *Het simultaneum in de landen van Overmaas. Een uniek instituut in de Nederlandse kerkgeschiedenis (1632–1878)* (Leeuwarden, 1998), 84–85; W. A. J. Munier, "Kerken en kerkgangers in Vaals van de Staatse tijd tot op heden," *Jaarboek van het Limburgs Geschied-en Oudheidkundig Genootschap* 136–37 (2000–2001): 98.

8. Historian W. A. J. Munier mentions a couple of specific incidents in which Catholic peasants may have been involved, but his repeated suggestion that peasants as well as soldiers regularly attacked Protestants performing Auslaufen to Vaals in the seventeenth century is not supported by the sources he cites or other primary sources. Munier, "Kerken en kerkgangers" (139, incident in 1674); Munier, *Simultaneum* (270–71, incident in 1681).

9. Thus was it represented in a 1763 petition to the *Reichskammergericht* and in two late-eighteenth-century Calvinist chronicles: LKAD, EvKgA (004) 18, "Unterthänig-höchst nothdringliche vorstellung, & supplication und bitt pro clem'mo mandato"; LKAD, EvKgA (004) 27, "Pro Memoria die protestanten in Achen betreffend"; and BDA, Manuscripts HS 57.

10. The following account of the episode is based on LKAD, EvKgA (004) A1/6, 24 June–29 Dec. 1738; LKAD, EvKgA (004) A5/2, 25 June–15 Dec. 1738; NA, StG (1.01.02) 5857-1, 12 Aug.–8 Sept. 1738; RHCL, LvO (01.075) 9418, "Hoog Drossard v. Petrus Raedermaecker," StAA, RA II Allgemeine Akten 929, ff. 138r–164v; *Resolutiën*, 18–29 Aug. 1738. Cf. Mathieu Franssen, *Acht eeuwen St. Pauluskerk Vaals* (Vaals, 1994), 90–91.

11. Calvinists claimed in 1660 that local Catholics had only recently placed it there, as if in a purposeful provocation vis-à-vis a church building whose use the two groups were sharing at the time: "hebben nog onlangs een groot crucifix met een aanhangede [sic] beeld genomen uijt 't veldt, ende in den inganck van de kerck gestelt." Munier, "Kerken en kerkgangers," 110, 155; cf. Munier, *Simultaneum*, 106.

12. LKAD, EvKgA A5/2, Lit. J (letter from ds. Farjon dd. 2 Sept. 1738).

13. RHCL, LvO 9418, "Hoog drossard contra Petrus Raedermaecker" and letter from Father Rademacker dd. 8 Feb. 1738.

14. RHCL, LvO 9418, "Aen d'Edele Erentfeste Heeren Schouth en Schepenen," by Abraham van den Heuvel (n.d.).

15. StAA, Akten 929, f. 138r.

16. RHCL, LvO 9418, letter by Father Rademacker dd. 8 Feb. 1738.

17. LKAD, EvKgA A5/2, 10 Nov. 1738, Lit. F.

18. StAA, Akten 929, 150r; NA, StG 5857-1, report by Abraham van den Heuvel dd. 25 Aug. 1738.

19. LKAD, EvKgA A5/2, 10 Nov. 1738, Lit. F.; StAA, Akten 929, 158r.

20. RHCL, LvO 9418, letter by regents of Vaals to delegates of Council of State dd. 31 Aug. 1739.

21. LKAD, EvKgA 18, "Unterthänig-höchst nothdringliche vorstellung, & supplication und bitt pro clem'mo mandato"; LKAD, EvKgA 27, "Pro Memoria die protestanten in Achen betreffend"; and BDA, Manuscripts HS 57.

22. BHIC, Classis Den Bosch (254) 55, Acta Synode Gelderland 1756 art. 22; LKAD, EvKgA (004) A1/7, 11, 16, and 17 Jan. 1756.

23. BHIC, 1586–1811 Raad van Brabant (19) 466.315; RHCL, LvO (01.075) 9419, "Hoog Drossard c'a H. Alleleen et al. wegens . . . doodslag van Jac. Hulsen, 1750–1757." RHCL, LvO 9419, "Hoog Drossard contra . . . wegens het afschieten van een vleugel," 1757.

24. RHCL, LvO (01.075) 9638.

25. For works on the economic history of the city and region, see the Note on Sources, above.

26. Reversing the position taken in 1678, the resolution attributed this right to the terms of the 1632 capitulation of Maastricht, which it said applied also to the Lands of Overmaas. *Resolutiën*, 19 July 1730.

27. BHIC, Classis Den Bosch 254, 1744 art. 18.

28. On Protestant-Catholic tensions in Overmaas in the 1730s, see Munier, *Simultaneum*, 342–44, 355–60. On such tensions elsewhere in the Republic, see Edwina Hagen, "*Een meer of min doodlyken haat.*" *Antipapisme en cultureel natiebesef in Nederland rond 1800* (Nijmegen, 2008), 29–39; Joris van Eijnatten, *Liberty and Concord in the United Provinces: Religious Toleration and the Public in the Eighteenth-Century Netherlands* (Leiden, 2003), 191–93; Th. Clemens, "IJkpunt 1750—op zoek naar nieuwe grenzen in het politiek-religieuze landschap van de Republiek," in *Vervreemding en verzoening: de relatie tussen katholieken en protestanten in Nederlanden, 1550–2000*, ed. C. Augustijn and E. M. V. M. Honée (Nijmegen, 1998), 69–101; W. Th. M. Frijhoff, "De paniek van juni 1734," *Archief voor de Geschiedenis van de Katholieke Kerk in Nederland* 19 (1977): 170–233; P. Polman, "De aprilstorm van 1732 tegen toelating van een apostolisch vicaris in de Hollandse Zending," *Mededelingen van het Nederlands Historisch Instituut te Rome*, 3rd ser., 10 (1959): 242–66.

29. Michael Rowe, *From Reich to State: The Rhineland in the Revolutionary Age, 1780–1830* (Cambridge, 2003), 21–22; Michael Printy, "Catholic Enlightenment and Reform Catholicism in the Holy Roman Empire," in *A Companion to the Catholic Enlightenment in Europe*, ed. Ulrich L. Lehner and Michael Printy (Leiden, 2010), 165–213; Michael O'Neill Printy, *Enlightenment and the Creation of German Catholicism* (Cambridge, 2009); Joachim Whaley, *Germany and the Holy Roman Empire*, 2 vols. (Oxford, 2012), 2:477–79; Marc R. Forster, *Catholic Germany from the Reformation to the Enlightenment* (Basingstoke, UK, 2007), 144–87; Rudolf Schlögl, *Glaube und Religion in der Säkularisierung: Die katholische Stadt— Köln, Aachen, Münster—1700–1840* (Munich, 1995), esp. 237–39; Albert Huyskens, *Aachener Leben im Zeitalter des Barock und Rokoko* (Bonn, 1929), ch. 7; Alfons Fritz, "Geschichte des Kaiser-Karls-Gymnasium in Aachen. I. Das Aachener Jesuiten-Gymnasium," *ZAGV* 28 (1906): 68–70.

30. Janssen, "Notizen," 3:311, 313.

31. Janssen, "Notizen," 3:226–28.

32. Noted by Frijhoff for the Netherlands and Rowe for Aachen, the widening of this gap in the eighteenth century was a more general European phenomenon. W. Th. M. Frijhoff, "The Dutch Enlightenment and the Creation of Popular Culture," in *The Dutch Republic in the Eighteenth Century: Decline, Enlightenment, and Revolution*, ed. Margaret C. Jacob and Wijnand W. Mijnhard (Ithaca, NY, 1992), 292–307; Rowe, *From Reich to State*, 29–30; James Van Horn Melton, *The Rise of the Public in Enlightenment Europe* (Cambridge, 2001), 12, 38, 86, 113–17, 237–38, 259–62; Dorinda Outram, *The Enlightenment* (Cambridge, 1995), 28–29; Roger Chartier, *Cultural History: Between Practices and Representations*, trans. Lydia G. Cochrane (Ithaca, NY, 1988), 151–71.

33. Printy, *Enlightenment and the Creation of German Catholicism*, 9; Whaley, *Germany and the Holy Roman Empire*, 2:479; Schlögl, *Glaube und Religion*, 239 (though Schlogl does not attribute the change to the influence of the

Enlightenment, which he dates as arriving later, but rather to a process of secularization that preceded it); Rowe, *From Reich to State*, 29; Janssen, "Notizen," 3:292.

34. August Pauls, *Geschichte der Aachener Freimaurerei. Bd. 1: Die Aachener Freimaurerei in der reichsstädtischen Zeit (bis Ende September 1794)* (Clausthal-Zellerfeld, 1928), 128–407.

35. Natalie Zemon Davis, "The Rites of Violence," in *Society and Culture in Early Modern France*, ed. Natalie Zemon Davis (Stanford, CA, 1975), 152–87.

36. Munier, *Simultaneum*, 58, 145–47, 279.

37. On Van den Honert, see Joris van Eijnatten, *Mutua Christianorum Tolerantia: Irenicism and Toleration in the Netherlands; The Stinstra Affair, 1740–1745* (Florence, 1998).

38. This combination—devotion to the principle of tolerance and anti-Catholicism—was characteristic of Enlightenment culture in the Netherlands, whose participants were almost exclusively Protestant. Indeed, Edwina Hagen argues that anti-Catholicism (which she prefers to call "anti-popery") was even implicit in the principle of tolerance as it was conceived in the Dutch Enlightenment. She also argues, though, that new concepts of national community and moral citizenship gave the anti-Catholicism of the late eighteenth century a new and different basis from traditional anti-Catholicism. Like Mijnhardt and Kloek, however, I would emphasize rather the continuities between the two and the way they reinforced each other. Hagen, *"Een meer of min doodlyken haat";* Joost Kloek and Wijnand Mijnhardt, *1800: Blueprints for a National Community* (Assen, 2004), 171.

39. *Dossier*, 57.

SIX

Reprisals

1. *Dossier*, 1, 20–27 July 1762, and 19.

2. *Dossier*, 14 and 100/B.

3. NA, StG (1.01.02), 4 June 1762; NA, StG (1.01.02) 5864, letter from Abraham van den Heuvel dd. 6 July 1762.

4. NA, StG (1.01.02) 5865, letter from De Jacobi de Cadier dd. 24 Feb. 1766.

5. *Dossier*, 104 "Deductie."

6. Georges Pariset, *L'État et les églises en Prusse sous Frédéric-Guillaume 1er (1713–1740)* (Paris, 1897), esp. 774–76; Mack Walker, *The Salzburg Transaction: Expulsion and Redemption in Eighteenth-Century Germany* (Ithaca, NY, 1992), 128.

7. W. A. J. Munier, *Het simultaneum in de landen van Overmaas. Een uniek instituut in de Nederlandse kerkgeschiedenis (1632–1878)* (Leeuwarden, 1998), 63, 93, 139; RHCL, LvO (01.075) 9655.

8. LKAD, EvKgA (004) A5/3, after entry for 4 Oct. 1764, "Eine kurze und zuverlässige Nachricht."

9. LKAD, EvKgA A5/3, after entry for 4 Oct. 1764, "Eine kurze und zuverlässige Nachricht"; another account of the day's events appears in BDA, Manuscripts HS 57; and many details are also mentioned in the documents included in LKAD, EvKgA (004) 18.

10. LKAD, EvKgA A5/3, after entry for 4 Oct. 1764, "Eine kurze und zuverlässige Nachricht."

11. LKAD, EvKgA A5/3, after entry for 4 Oct. 1764, "Eine kurze und zuverlässige Nachricht"—Decretum dd. 25 Feb. 1763.

12. LKAD, EvKgA A5/3, after entry for 4 Oct. 1764, "Eine kurze und zuverlässige Nachricht."

13. StAA, Reichskammergericht A134.

14. Resolutiën, 18 May and 19 Oct. 1763. In July 1763 an incident also occurred in Aachen during which a Catholic crowd tried to take a Protestant theology student, who the crowd thought was a minister, captive in order to use him as a hostage, to exchange him for the release of Father Bosten. BDA, Manuscripts HS 57, f. 6.

15. LKAD, EvKgA (004) 18, "Unterthänigste Duplica und Bitte"—"Beijlage sub Lit: A."

16. Resolutiën, 10 Feb. 1764.

17. Resolutiën, 24 Apr. 1764 "Memorie" and 8 Oct. 1764.

18. NA, StG 5864, letter from Heiden Hompes and Alstorpius dd. 13 Aug. 1764.

19. BDA, Manuscripts HS 57, f. 10.

20. Dossier, 105; Resolutiën, 14 Mar. 1765.

21. LKAD, EvKgA 18, Unterthänig-höchst nothdringliche vorstellung, & supplication und bitt," also found in the protocols of both the Aachen and Burtscheid Reformed consistories.

22. RHCL, LvO (01.075) 9421, "Hoog Drossard contra Wilh Smeets en P. Bisschop."

23. Heinrich Schnock, "Über gewerbliche Verhältnisse in der ehemaligen 'Herrlichkeit Burtscheid,'" Aus Aachens Vorzeit 18 (1905): 38–39.

24. Johannes Janssen, "Die historischen Notizen des Bürgermeisterei-Dieners Johannes Janssen," in Beiträge und Material zur Geschichte der Aachener Patrizier-Familien, ed. Hermann Ariovist von Fürth, 3 vols. (Aachen, 1882–90), 3:259; BDA, Manuscripts HS 57.

25. Janssen, "Notizen," 3:249.

26. LKAD, EvKgA 18, "Vorläuffige Unterthänigste Exceptiones cum Petitione et Reservatione."

27. Most of the records of the Weg-gelt suit are to be found (many in duplicate) in StAA, Reichskammergericht A168 and LKAD, EvKgA 18.

28. LKAD, EvKgA 18, "Unterthanigster Gegenbericht."

SEVEN
A Moral Certainty?

1. *Resolutiën*, 5 July and 30 June 1762.
2. *Resolutiën*, 17 Nov. and 3 Dec. 1762.
3. Law books spoke of the need for a "halve preuve, ofte groot ende vehemente suspitie." See, e.g., Simon van Leeuwen, *Manier van procederen in civile en criminele saaken, etc.* (Leiden, 1666), 181; Pieter Bort, *Alle de Wercken van Mr. Pieter Bort . . . begrepen in ses tractaten . . .*, ed. Johan van Alphen (1702), 366.
4. Anton Blok, *De Bokkerijders. Roversbenden en geheime genootschappen in de Landen van Overmaas (1730–1774)* (Amsterdam, 1995).
5. *Dossier*, 41.
6. *Dossier*, 44.
7. RHCL, LvO (01.075) 9420, "Notulen gehouden in judicio extraord'o."
8. The following dialogue is drawn from *Dossier*, 76/81, 78 "Notariaele Declaratie," and 85/16.
9. The following dialogue is drawn from RHCL, LvO 9420, "Notulen gehouden in judicio extraord'o"; NA, StG (1.01.02) 5865, letter from De Jacobi de Cadier dd. 24 Feb. 1766; and *Dossier*, 45.
10. The following dialogue is drawn from *Dossier*, 78/61.
11. *Dossier*, 46. According to the lieutenant governor, Buntgens had written his statement during the previous night: NA, StG 5865, letter from De Jacobi de Cadier dd. 24 Feb. 1766.
12. The following dialogue is drawn from RHCL, LvO 9420, "Notulen gehouden in judicio extraord'o."
13. The following dialogue is drawn from *Dossier*, 85/16, 78 "Notariaele Declaratie," 78/61, and 68/D.
14. *Dossier*, 68/D.
15. *Dossier*, 74, 23 Feb. 1764, 81/58–60, and 82.
16. On Levericksvelt see Ferd. Sassen, *De illustre school te Maastricht en haar hoogleraren (1683–1794)* (Amsterdam, 1972), 34.
17. Following ordinary court procedure, as laid down for criminal cases in Dutch Overmaas, both the prosecution and the defense provided the court with lists of witnesses and questions to be put to them. When testimony was required of witnesses who lived outside the court's jurisdiction, the court issued "requisition letters" asking the governing authorities of the places where the witnesses lived (such as Aachen) to question them on the court's behalf. First the prosecution's witnesses were questioned, then the witnesses for the defense. No attorneys were present at the questioning, so obviously there was no cross-examination. Neither side knew what any of the witnesses, including their own, had said until all their testimony was gathered. Then the "demonstration" was "opened" and

both prosecution and defense received transcripts of all the testimony. *GPB,* 2:3109–32.

18. *Dossier,* 86/18, 100/D, and 55.

19. *Dossier,* 103, 105, 68.

20. *Dossier,* 68; cf. 87/19.

21. *Dossier,* 97.

22. RHCL, LvO 9420, "Staat van honoris et salaris."

23. The following is drawn from *Dossier,* 99/72.

24. The legal implications of the doctors' diagnosis were sufficiently ambiguous that De Jacobi de Cadier had them write a second statement clarifying their first one. The new statement, however, did not resolve the issue. *Dossier,* 100/A.

25. *Dossier,* 68.

26. *Dossier,* 102 "Reprochen," 70, and 104 "Deductie."

27. *Dossier,* 105 and 69.

EIGHT

Their High and Mighty Lordships

1. On the political institutions of the Republic, see Robert Fruin, *Geschiedenis der staatsinstellingen in Nederland tot den val der Republiek* (The Hague, 1980); and Jonathan I. Israel, *The Dutch Republic: Its Rise, Greatness, and Fall, 1477–1806* (Oxford, 1995). For developments in the latter half of the eighteenth century, see A. J. C. M. Gabriëls, *De heren als dienaren en de dienaar als heer. Het stadhouderlijk stelsel in de tweede helft van de achttiende eeuw* (The Hague, 1990).

2. *Resolutiën,* 30 Sept. 1765.

3. Little has been written about the role of the States General as final arbiters in judicial cases from the Generality Lands, and even less on the government attorneys of the eighteenth century and their work for the States General. The handling of Father Bosten's case was not an isolated occurrence, though: see A. M. J. A. Berkvens, "Een aanzet tot hervorming van het strafprocesrecht in Staats opper-Gelder in 1762?" *Pro Memorie* 4 (2002): 347–61.

4. *Resolutiën,* 11 June 1762.

5. RHCL, LvO (01.075) 9420, letter dd. 20 Jan. 1766 from HHM to vice-schout and schepenen.

6. The documents produced by the inquiry, all dated January–February 1766, are found in RHCL, LvO 9420 and NA, StG (1.01.02) 5865. The lieutenant governor's report to the States General appears in the latter, letter dd. 24 Feb. 1766 from De Jacobi de Cadier to HHM.

7. *Resolutiën,* 1 Sept. 1766.

8. BDA, Manuscripts HS 57, f. 12.

9. RHCL, LvO 9420, "Clacht en conclusie voor Hoog Drossard tegen Johannes Klauw . . ." and "Clacht en conclusie voor Hoog Drossard tegen Andreas Buntgens en . . . Martinus Buntgens."

10. RHCL, LvO 9420, "Clacht en conclusie voor Hoog Drossard tegen Cunigunda Mommers" and "Vonnis tegen Cunigunda Mommers."

11. The financial records documenting the costs of Father Bosten's trial have survived in RHCL, LvO 9420 and RHCL, LvO (01.075) 9429.

12. *Dossier,* 68.

13. *Resolutiën,* 21 Nov. 1766, 26 Jan., 23 and 27 Feb., and 27 Mar. 1767; RHCL, LvO 9420, "Staet van kosten" dd. 6 May 1767.

14. J. H. M. M. van Hall, "Een onderzoek naar de rechtspraak in de Staatse landen van Overmaze door de advocaat-fiscaal J.F. van Steelant in 1772," in *Ten werentliken rechte. Opstellen over Limburgse rechtsgeschiedenis,* ed. A. M. J. A. Berkvens et al. (Maastricht, 1990), 66, 75. Cf. the complaint made to the States General, *Resolutiën,* 2 June 1767.

15. RHCL, LvO 9420, "Generaele specificatie" and "Verbaelen en decreten" for 13 Nov. 1766; NA, StG 5865, letter dd. 29 Apr. 1767; *Resolutiën,* 24 Aug. 1767. The costs of building the courthouse are documented in GAV, Gemeente Vaals 1, 1771.

16. Landesarchiv NRW, Abteilung Rheinland, Aachen Marienstift (120.13.1–2) 11 bb, 29 Nov. 1765.

17. M. G. C. Ubaghs, "Geschiedkundig overzigt van Gulpen en deszelfs onderhoorige plaatsen," *Publications de la Société d'Archéologie dans le Duché de Limbourg* 2 (1865): 340–42.

18. The comparison is made by Simon Schama, *Patriots and Liberators: Revolution in the Netherlands, 1780–1813* (London, 1977), 56.

19. Gabriëls, *De heren als dienaren,* 107–10.

20. Lynn Hunt, Margaret C. Jacob, and W. W. Mijnhardt, *The Book That Changed Europe: Picart and Bernard's Religious Ceremonies of the World* (Cambridge, MA, 2010), 304.

21. *Resolutiën,* 1 Nov. 1768.

22. All in RHCL, LvO 9429.

23. British Library, Egerton Manuscripts 1730, ff. 401r–v. On the engagement of Charles Bentinck and his brother with Enlightenment culture, see Margaret C. Jacob, *The Radical Enlightenment: Pantheists, Freemasons and Republicans* (London, 1981), 182, 198–201.

24. R. A. Bosch, *Het conflict rond Antonius van der Os, predikant te Zwolle, 1748–1755* (Kampen, 1988), 46, 49–53, 58–61, 66, 79–84, 147.

25. RHCL, LvO 9429, letters from Brull to Hasenclever dd. 8 and 14 Feb. 1768.

26. RHCL, LvO 9429, letter dd. 8 Feb. 1768.

NINE

Afterlives

1. For the biographical sources on which this section is based, see the Note on Sources above.
2. See in addition J. Belonje, "Enige bezitters van Groot-Blankenberg," in *Huldeblijk: bundel opstellen aangeboden aan de genealoog Jan J. M. H. Verzijl bij gelegenheid van zijn zeventigste verjaardag op 25 maart 1967* (Roermond, 1967), 14–25; J. G. J. Koreman, "Het zg. Pesthuis te Maastricht," *De Maasgouw* 77 (1958): 111–22.
3. RHCL, LvO (01.075) 9421, "1769 Interrogatorien betr. het mishandeling van Joh. G. Driessen"; StAA, RA II Allgemeine Akten 929, pp. 202–9. In the second instance, the attacker, Paulus Hahnbucken, was (surely by no coincidence) a native of the village of Gimmenich, in the Habsburg Duchy of Limburg, to which he was suspected of fleeing in order to escape justice.
4. LKAD, EvKgA (004) 27, "Pro Memoria die protestanten in Achen betreffend."
5. Regionaal Archief Tilburg, Archief van de Hervormde Gemeente Tilburg, 1651–1990 (304) 4, pp. 58 and (quotation) 77 (19 Dec. 1764); Regionaal Archief Tilburg, Archief van de Diaconie van de Hervormde Gemeente Tilburg, 1651–1989 (180) 45, accounts for 1764–70.
6. See at UA the entries under the surname Erffens (and variants) in the DTB registers; NHK Utrecht Lidmatenregisters; Alfabetische Lijst der Utrechtse Nieuweburgers, 1701–1828; Momboirkamer; Manual 100e penning 1793; Transporten Oude Eigenaars and Nieuwe Eigenaars; Octrooien om te testeren; Index op de 1813 Volkstellingregisters; and Notariële Akten.
7. According to J. Th. H. de Win, *De geschiedenis van Vaals* (Vaals, 1941), 72.
8. In this connection should be seen the 1759 decision of the States General allowing Dutch Lutherans in Vaals to be married legally in their own church, and their 1751 decision to allow a Lutheran minister to run a school in Vaals (for Lutheran children only). W. A. J. Munier, "Kerken en kerkgangers in Vaals van de Staatse tijd tot op heden," *Jaarboek van het Limburgs Geschied-en Oudheidkundig Genootschap* 136–37 (2000–2001): 156–58.
9. StAA, Reichskammergericht A168, extract from letter by Drs. Carlier and Zwierlein dd. 31 Jan. 1788. On the events of 1786–91, see Horst Carl, "Die Aachener Mäkelei, 1786–93. Konfliktmechanismen in der Endphase des Alten Reiches," *ZAGV* 92 (1985): 103–87.
10. See esp. Thomas R. Kraus, *Auf dem Weg in die Moderne. Aachen in französischer Zeit 1792/93, 1794–1814* (Aachen, 1994); Michael Rowe, *From Reich to State: The Rhineland in the Revolutionary Age, 1780–1830* (Cambridge, 2003), 31; Munier, "Kerken en kerkgangers," 205–11.
11. The seven works were: *Nederlandsche jaerboeken*, vol. 17, part 2 (Amsterdam, 1763), 778–804; *Beknopte historie van 't Vaderland, van de vroegste tyden af tot aan*

het jaar 1767, vol. 4 (Harlingen, 1776), 102–3; J. F. Martinet, *Historie der waereld*, vol. 5 (Amsterdam, 1784), 130–31; Petrus Loosjes, *Vaderlandsche historie*, vol. 23 (Amsterdam, 1789), 328–33; Jacobus Kok and Jan Fokke, *Geschiedenissen der Vereenigde Nederlanden. Voor de vaderlandsche jeugd*, vol. 12 (Amsterdam, 1789), 138–39; Jacobus Kok et al., *Vaderlandsch woordenboek*, vol. 29 (Amsterdam, 1793), 71–73; and Jan Fokke, *Geschiedenis van de Agttiende eeuw*, vol. 6 (Haarlem, 1796), 182–83. An additional four works described in more general terms the attacks by Catholics on Protestants who worshiped in Vaals: *Nieuwe Algemeene Vaderlandsche Letter-Oefeningen*, vol. 4, part 1 (Amsterdam, 1789), 592; J. F. Martinet, *Kort begrip der Waereld-historie* (Amsterdam, 1789), 307; Jan Wagenaar, *Vaderlandsche historie . . . verkort*, vol. 2 (Amsterdam 1800), 115; and W. A. Bachiene, *Vaderlandsche geographie*, vol. 5 (Amsterdam, 1791), 1079–80, a summary of whose account appeared subsequently in English in John Erskine, *Sketches and Hints of Church History*, vol. 2 (Edinburgh, 1797), 310.

12. M. G. C. Ubaghs, "Geschiedkundig overzigt van Gulpen en deszelfs onderhoorige plaatsen," *Publications de la Société d'Archéologie dans le Duché de Limbourg* 2 (1865): 308; Joseph Habets, *Geschiedenis van het tegenwoordig Bisdom Roermond en van de Bisdommen, die het in deze gewesten zijn voorafgegaan*, 3 vols. (Roermond, 1875), 2:306–14; Adolph Vaessen, "Die Geschichte von Vaals," 1923–25, http://www.obib.de/Geschichte/Vaals.html (accessed 7 Jan. 2014); L. Aalders, "De jaren 1762 en 1785 in de geschiedenis van het protestantisme te Aken-Vaals," *Nederlands archief voor kerkgeschiedenis* 24 (1931): 69–80; P. A. J. M. Polman, *Katholiek Nederland in de achttiende eeuw*, 3 vols. (Hilversum, 1968), 3:202–3; Mathieu Franssen, *Acht eeuwen St. Pauluskerk Vaals* (Vaals, 1994), 91–100; W. P. C. Knuttel, *De toestand der Nederlandsche katholieken ten tijde der Republiek*, 2 vols. (The Hague, 1892), 2:232–34; Munier, "Kerken en kerkgangers," 178–89. Another modern work to mention the incident is the unscholarly Jef Leunissen, *Minnerij, misdaad en magie: merkwaardige zaken uit Maastricht's onbekend verleden* (Maasbree, 1979), 94–96, which offers few details and gets some of them wrong.

13. *Dossier*, 100/D.

14. *Dossier*, 100/C.

15. LKAD, EvKgA (004) A5/3, entry after 4 Oct. 1764.

Conclusion

1. Microhistorians such as Carlo Ginzburg, Edoardo Grendi, and Giovanni Levi have used concepts such as the "exceptional normal" to make bold claims about the significance of microhistorical findings for our understanding of large-scale phenomena. I agree with them that microhistories are not simply "case studies" of such phenomena; their approach is not to analyze important examples or variations of the latter. Rather, microhistories focus purposefully on seemingly

incidental or peripheral objects of inquiry; they treat such objects as "clues" that reveal something about a wider totality that would otherwise be missed. To my mind, however, this worthy ambition does not resolve the question of generalization. More often than not, microhistorians leave their claims about the representative character of their findings unsubstantiated. See, among others, Francesca Trivellato, "Is There a Future for Italian Microhistory in the Age of Global History?" http://escholarship.org/uc/item/0z94n9hq (accessed 7 Jan. 2014); Matti Peltonen, "Clues, Margins and Monads: The Micro-Macro Link in Historical Research," *History and Theory* 40 (2001): 347–59; Giovanni Levi, "On Microhistory," in *New Perspectives on Historical Writing*, ed. Peter Burke (University Park, PA, 1992), 93–113; Edward Muir, "Introduction: Observing Trifles," in *Microhistory and the Lost Peoples of Europe*, ed. Edward Muir and Guido Ruggiero (Baltimore, 1991), vii–xxviii; and Carlo Ginzburg, *Clues, Myths, and the Historical Method*, trans. John and Anne C. Tedeschi (Baltimore, 1989), esp. 96–125.

2. P. A. J. M. Polman, *Katholiek Nederland in de achttiende eeuw*, 3 vols. (Hilversum, 1968), 3:203.

3. Quotation from J. W. Gough, "The Development of John Locke's Belief in Toleration," in *John Locke: A Letter Concerning Toleration in Focus*, ed. John Horton and Susan Mendus (London, 1991), 74. See likewise Jonathan I. Israel, *Radical Enlightenment: Philosophy and the Making of Modernity, 1650–1750* (Oxford, 2001). W. K. Jordan saw the arguments as fully developed as early as 1660: Wilbur Kitchener Jordan, *The Development of Religious Toleration in England*, 4 vols. (Cambridge, MA, 1932). Henry Kamen concurs: Henry Kamen, *The Rise of Toleration* (New York, 1967), esp. 216–17, 240. Jonathan Israel is explicit in claiming that the "decisive advance of practical toleration" occurred in the late seventeenth and early eighteenth centuries: Jonathan I. Israel, *Locke, Spinoza and the Philosophical Debate Concerning Toleration in the Early Enlightenment (c. 1670–1750)* (Amsterdam, 1999), 5–6.

4. See, e.g., David D. Bien, *The Calas Affair: Persecution, Toleration, and Heresy in Eighteenth-Century Toulouse* (Westport, CT, 1979), 3, 178; S. J. Connolly, *Religion, Law, and Power: The Making of Protestant Ireland, 1660–1760* (Oxford, 1992), 302–3; and Andreas Lindt, "Zum Verhältnis der Konfessionen in der Schweiz im 18. Jahrhundert," in *Zwischen Polemik und Irenik. Untersuchungen zum Verhältnis der Konfessionen im späten 18. und frühen 19. Jahrhundert*, ed. Georg Schwaiger (Göttingen, 1977), 58–59.

5. No microhistory can. Indeed, the problem goes even deeper, in that the schema is a self-confirming belief system that does not admit of any empirical disproof.

6. Thomas R. Kraus, *Auf dem Weg in die Moderne. Aachen in französischer Zeit 1792/93, 1794–1814* (Aachen, 1994), 401–7; Martina Kurzweg, *Presse zwischen Staat und Gesellschaft: die Zeitungslandschaft in Rheinland-Westfalen (1770–1819)* (Paderborn, 1999), esp. 281ff.

7. Ernestine G. E. van der Wall, *Socrates in de hemel? Een achttiende-eeuwse polemiek over deugd, verdraagzaamheid en de vaderlandse kerk* (Hilversum, 2000).

8. Michael Rowe, *From Reich to State: The Rhineland in the Revolutionary Age, 1780–1830* (Cambridge, 2003), 20–21.

Index

Page numbers in italics indicate illustrations.